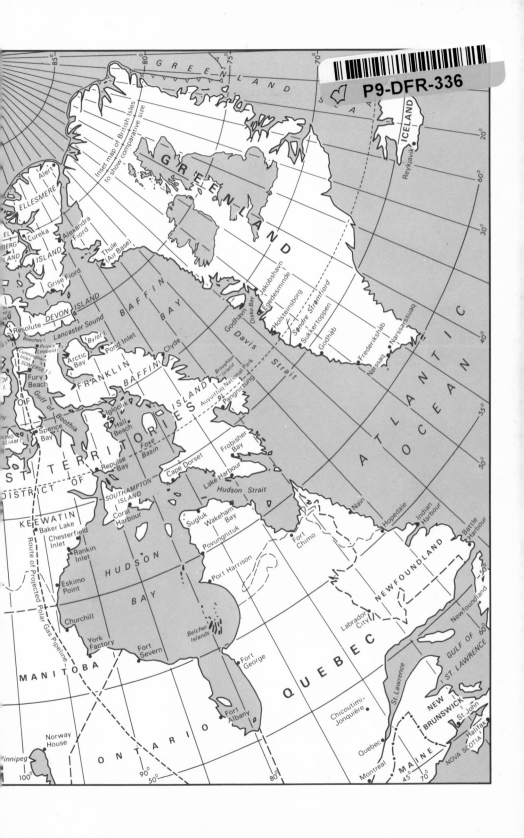

919.8 Dyso
Dyson, John.
The hot Arctic.

MAR. 21. 1984 **DATE DUE**		
JUN. -8. 1984	DEC 5	1993
JAN 3 1986	JAN 1 8 1996	
MAR 3 0 1996	APR 2 5 2001	
	AUG 0 6 2004	
APR 2 8 1996	JAN 1 9 2008	
NOV 0 5 1997		
MAY 1 3 1989		
JAN 2 5 1990		
OCT 0 7 1998		

1-607-754-4243   MAR 2 1 1980

THE HOT ARCTIC

THE HOT ARCTIC

JOHN DYSON

LITTLE, BROWN AND COMPANY
BOSTON   TORONTO

LIBRARY OF CONGRESS CATALOG CARD NO. 79-92364

FIRST AMERICAN EDITION

MV

*Published simultaneously in Canada
by Little, Brown & Company (Canada) Limited*

PRINTED IN THE UNITED STATES OF AMERICA

Contents

PART II · SCORCHING THE ICE

PART III · SPACE-AGE ESKIMO

Preface

Why the *hot* Arctic?

The Arctic is a weird and eccentric part of the world that scatters most preconceptions to the winds.

It is hot in the sense that Eskimos are physiologically adapted to heat rather than cold, and it is sweat that kills. Dehydration is a greater risk for humans in the polar wilderness than in the world's hottest deserts.

Warmth, not cold, threatens Arctic animals because warmer conditions bring more snow that buries their meagre forage, or melts the snow which freezes and seals it in a porcelain-hard glaze of ice. Heat exhaustion often results in death for animals alarmed by Man's activities.

Oddly, in winter, the icy lid on the frozen sea is generally warmer than the land.

The Arctic *feels* hot because its cold burns like a blowtorch, and living there *is* hot because people turn up their furnaces to stifling levels. Travelling thousands of miles by aeroplane, I spent more time during the Arctic winter in shirt-sleeves than I normally would at home in London, and wished that more modern polar adventurers packed roll-on deodorant in their survival kits.

Most of all, the true Arctic region of the western hemisphere – the bare, treeless lands of Alaska, Canada and Greenland – is "hot" because it is contentious and is in the focus of several different kinds of economic and political spotlight. For the Eskimo people, the heat of their rapid modernisation is now bringing things to the boil. As industry puts heat into developing the cold, pitting the white heat of technology against Nature's frozen deserts, it is the people of the Arctic and the animals on which they subsist that are most likely to get burned. New polar technology, such as the generation of super-icebreakers now on the drawing boards, is likely to cause a dramatic shift in the pivot of world power.

All these points, with something of my own reactions to this strangely fascinating and little-known part of the world forming the fragile roof of the glass-house we all live in, are explained and elaborated in the chapters that follow.

It is necessary to apologise in advance for two sweeping liberties. The polar Eskimos, just finding their feet in the modern world, are rightly conscious of their cultural identity and deplore the all-embracing term "Eskimo" which some regard as derogatory. To use any other term in a book of this kind, however, is technically burden-some.

North Slope Eskimos like to be known as *Inupiat*, Canadian Eskimos as *Inuit* (those in the western Canadian Arctic preferring to be distinguished as *Inuvialuit*), and Greenlanders as *Kalâtdlit*; all these terms, with subtle differences in emphasis, mean "the people". In the interests of simplicity and clarity, and at the risk of offending purists, I have used the term which is universally known.

The second problem, almost one of tit for tat, has been finding a succinct definition of the great mass of people inhabiting USA, Canada and Europe. To refer to them as "southerners" is confusing. Rightly or wrongly, I settled on the term "White". In every context within this book it is intended to embrace all those whose way of life is that of the "cash and carry", suburbanised Western culture, whatever their skin colour may be; the term is used only in contra-distinction to that of Eskimo, to distinguish clearly between those up there on the roof of the world, and the rest of us down here.

Values expressed in dollars have not been converted to pounds sterling, or vice versa. At the time, exchange rates fluctuated greatly but Canadian and US dollars were only a few cents apart. In round figures, one pound sterling was two dollars or ten Danish Kroner.

A research enterprise on this scale could not have been completed without a great deal of help from an enormous number of people, some in company head offices and universities, others whom I met on the trail. During my research I took notes from conversations with four hundred and sixty-six people, and met many more. Each one of these people gave me the benefit of his or her time, and very often hospitality also. In addition to those mentioned in the book, I would especially like to acknowledge my debt to the following individuals and organisations:

CANADA: Panarctic Oil; Imperial Oil; Canmar; *Oilweek*; the Federal Government of Canada, especially the Department of

Indian Affairs and Northern Development, Department of External Affairs, Canadian Wildlife Service, Atmospheric Environment Service; Royal Canadian Mounted Police; Arctic Institute of North America; 405 Squadron and Northern Region Headquarters, Canadian Forces; Mr S. G. Hodgson, Commissioner of the Northwest Territories, and Ross Harvey; Dr George Hobson and Fred Alt, Polar Continental Shelf Project; Ed Spracklin and Keewatin region store managers, Hudson's Bay Company; Dr S. D. MacDonald, National Museum of Natural Sciences; Dr Al Milne, Beaufort Sea Project; Professor L. C. Bliss, University of Alberta; Joan and Bob Hornal; Sheila and Dr J. Wm Kerr; Allison and Roland de Caen; Grace and Stewart Shackell; Captain Tom Pullen; Helge Tomter; Dr Peter Schledermann; Ward Elcock; Joy and Erik Watt; Jim Robertson, mayor of Inuvik; Metro Solomon. ALASKA: United States Air Force; United States Coast Guard; Naval Arctic Research Laboratory; North Slope Borough; British Petroleum; Ruth and Dr Terry McFadden; University of Alaska; Institute of Social, Economic and Government Research; Carla Hefferich and Lee Leonard, *The Northern Engineer*; Friends of the Earth; Pat and Herb Bartel. GREENLAND: Mr Hans Lassen, Governor of Greenland; Royal Greenland Trade Department; Ministry for Greenland; Andreas Jorgensen; Sigfred Mathiesen; Maria and Henning Meyer; Mirjam and Henning Brøndstedt. GREAT BRITAIN: the Rt Hon Viscount Amory, KG, PC, GCMG; Basil Greenhill, director, National Maritime Museum; Geoffrey Larminie; Royal Geographical Society; Scott Polar Research Institute.

John Dyson
London
July, 1978

For Kate,
Jemima, Jenny and Jack,
who shivered back home
while I sweltered

Part I

AMONG THE
SNOW-GO PEOPLE

1

LOW FLYING

*How the vast scale of blank spaces at
the top of the map numbs your senses
– the look of the Arctic*

The snow-covered mountain ridge loomed nearer and steeper, like a
wave peaking as it rushes into shallow water. Sitting in the transparent nose-bubble and swigging ginger ale to moisten a suddenly
dry mouthful of chicken leg, I was relieved to hear the captain
remind his co-pilot at the controls that he didn't want to leave any
grease marks.

"Whaddaya say, up two hundred?"

"Firm on that."

"Give me climbing torque, engineer."

"Roj – coming up!"

The mountain crest seemed to accelerate as it approached, fling-
ing itself beneath us as the big Argus maritime reconnaissance
aircraft of the Canadian Forces skimmed over it. My headset filled
with whistles as the crew glimpsed the sea-fjord that whipped into
view beyond, an immense curving canyon filled with dense shade
like a purple mist, hardly a blemish marring the smooth layers of
snow on its steep walls and ice-covered floor. Despite the ear-
splitting roar of the plane's four eighteen-pot Pratt & Whitneys you
could almost hear the aching silence of the place, and sense its dread
stillness.

The plane dived to show the flag over one of the world's most
northerly habitations, a collection of huts, fuel tanks, an airstrip and

a garbage dump that comprised the weather station on the shore of Eureka Sound, on Ellesmere Island in the Canadian Arctic archipelago. As we beat the place up with a series of thunderous low passes some of the eleven meteorologists came out in the −33 °F (−36 °C) cold to wave. "I hope you got my best side," their radio operator said, when he learned we had been taking photographs.

"Sure we did – how's the golf?"

"We had a lot of storms and lost the last of our red balls."

"That's too bad. Any wildlife around?"

"We're pretty lonely right now. Expecting the musk ox and wolves back any day. The wolves are real friendly and eat right out of our hands..."

Minutes later, circling to photograph a level plateau that might serve as an emergency military landing strip, there was a shout in the intercom when an observer in the tail sighted the black dots of a herd of musk ox running to form a defensive circle as the silence of their High Arctic valley was shattered by engine roar. An engineer muttered that it looked like Mounties doing a musical ride. Then two other musk ox were seen away from the herd, one on its knees, the other standing guard and desperately horning at wolves as they attacked. The pack had the beasts surrounded and as one wolf feinted from the front others tore at ribbons of flesh hanging from the wounded musk ox's hind-quarters.

The mountains tilted sharply as the pilot lurched into a tight turn. "Christ, you'd never see anything like this on TV!" The big aircraft made a series of low passes on probably its most bizarre mission. At each dummy strafe the wolves glanced up, danced away a few paces, then ripped into the long-haired, goat-like musk ox. Finally we had to climb away. "Make a note for the report," Captain Brian Maclean said drily, "that we also observed the wolves looked tame enough to eat out of our hands..."

Next "tasking" on this seventeen-hour northern surveillance patrol was to photograph a target at Cape Isachsen on Ellef Ringnes Island. While the 405 Squadron ("Probe deeper, live longer") crew opened cans of crab, lobster and clams for a big brew of what was called shit-bag soup, the monotonous, featureless wastes unfolding below paralysed the mind. The low-lying islands along the ragged northwest perimeter of the archipelago lay beneath an even blanket of snow and ice that reached in all directions to the curve of the earth.

Even the professionals were confused by the frozen sameness. The target was supposed to be another landing ground. Although we were still in Canada, we were as far from Toronto as Venezuela is, though it might as well have been the moon. The navigation computer confirmed we had flown to the right coordinates of lat. and long., but which way should the observer point the camera? Then the captain hit on the answer. "I reckon a C130 could land anywhere here," he said. "The whole bloody place is a runway – look at it!"

Sir James Ross, one of the British polar explorers who had put the "loathsome shores" of these Arctic Islands on the map during last century, wrote of them as "lands of uniformity, silence and death". It was easy to see why. Scorched by cold, scoured by wind, the winter Arctic seems totally barren and featureless. To anyone conditioned to lusher, busier environments, the yearning for the rustle of a leaf, the lap of a wave, becomes obsessive. It is a landscape that seems to have been concreted over. There is nothing to walk up to, nothing to put your back to in order to get a different perspective. The ground lacks contour, colour or texture. The world is stiff, silent and bloodless, as if it has been frightened to death.

In summer, I was to discover the melting of the snow reveals the Arctic terrain for it is – a true desert. The archipelago is one of the driest regions of the world because the cold air can carry so little moisture. Yet it is a *wet* desert because the top few inches of frozen soil thaws and water, unable to drain away, collects in extensive bogs and ponds. Total precipitation averages less than five inches a year in many areas, and seldom exceeds ten inches. The Fosheim Peninsula on Ellesmere Island, where we had dummy-strafed wolves attacking musk ox, averages less than 2·5 inches a year. And much of it *looks* like a desert, as brown as Arabia with nothing growing due to a combination of factors such as the shortness of the growing season, lack of nutrients in the soil, and cold temperatures. North of the Northwest Passage thirty per cent of the island land area is totally bare, with not even microbal activity worth mentioning. A fifth of this area is covered perpetually in ice, which reduces Nature's life force to a frozen zero, and a quarter of it is categorised "polar semi-desert" with mostly lichens and mosses finding places to grow between large areas wasting away from sheet or gully erosion – a "hell with the fires out" badlands on a gigantic, slow motion scale. Scattered through these deserts – where, from the cabin comfort of low-flying aircraft, one expects to see camels rather than polar bears – are scattered oases of low sedge meadows and comparatively lush tussock. Such areas occupy less than five per cent of the total area and are havens for wildlife: flying over one is sensational. After long periods of staring down at bare rock and gluey soil where the largest living thing is a purple stain of algae, suddenly you encounter a marshland humming with waterfowl, musk ox, snowy owls and caribou – a polar paradise.

Scorched by cold, scoured by wind, the winter Arctic (as seen here through the nose bubble of a Canadian Forces surveillance aircraft) seems totally barren and featureless – what the 19th century British explorer Sir James Ross described as "loathsome shores ... lands of uniformity, silence and death."

It comes as a shock to realise that, in the context of a temperate landscape, even these excitingly alive and vividly contrasting scenes – oases in the polar desert – are actually as desolate as boggy Yorkshire moors. The idea of having to live in such barren lands by hunting, constantly on the move to follow seasonal migrations of game, appalls the imagination. Yet the lands and frozen seas of the Arctic are by no means a frontier in human terms. The polar Eskimos have occupied more territory, and for longer, than any other racial and linguistic group in the world. Migrating from central Siberia in successive waves over a period of at least thirty thousand years, bringing their own language and ranging as far eastwards as Greenland, they were so isolated from the rest of the world that up to the 1920s some bands thought they were the only people in existence. The modernisation of the polar Eskimos has been so swift (see Part III) that even now, in the Canadian Arctic and Greenland, there are few over the age of twenty who were not born in a skin tent, sod hut, or igloo. Now their hunting lands – vast in area because the animals that roam them require square miles rather than acres on which to survive – are under siege by technology (see Part II). Flying for so many hours over such featureless ground it is hard to credit that a handful of indigenous people and a handful of modern engineers fight for space to develop industry or hunt.

To feel crushed to the point of listlessness by the sheer immensity of geographic scale was the last thing I expected of the Arctic. As if suffering from different kinds of jet lag, I found the senses become disoriented. Body rhythms get out of step due to the unaccustomed rearrangement of hours between long daylight or darkness. Clothes are bulkier and boots heavier, so doing anything requires more effort. The air tastes different: toothpaste fresh, and your mouth salivates because the air is so dry. Visual perception is distorted by disconcerting clarity, like the first few days of wearing new spectacles when vision seems almost too perfect. Sunglasses are essential, but unless you are accustomed to tinted lenses this adds to the sense of detachment from real life. Like a clever advertising photographer, God seems to have changed your colour film and fitted different filters, so no image seems quite right.

With time and experience your mental screen becomes adjusted, but it is not until you get into a low-flying aeroplane adding the dimension of speed to those of overwhelming length and breadth, that you come to terms with the Arctic's great scale.

For a long time the sheer size and featurelessness of the place reduced me to such a low pitch of feebleness that I felt quite deserted by any sense of adventure. It is not only small-country people like myself who experience this kind of depression on coming to the Arctic, for even North Americans accustomed to the deserts and prairies of lower latitudes admit to a strange feeling of disembodiment due to the lack of any kind of rural furniture such as trees by which to measure scale and distance. Walking there one has the same sense of detachment as looking out of a plane window at high altitude. You walk and walk, but because you pass nothing, you seem to remain discouragingly in exactly the same place.

The puzzle is partly solved when you realise there are two scales of distance in the Arctic, each exaggerated as if by a wide-angle lens – the small and the great, the near and the very far. The fragile beauty of the Arctic must be discovered on your hands and knees, in specks of brilliantly coloured lichens, tiny poppies that track the sun like miniature dish aerials, jagged tips of melting ice catching the sun like clear diamonds, the golden glitter of ice crystals floating like fairy dust in a cold sky, spearheads of snow ridges jutting above the flesh of the land like flexed tendons. The middle distance is lost. Most of the year it is merely a cold-wrought blur of textureless white, one flatness falling into another to a far horizon where there is a quite different kind of fascination in the outline of massive geographic features: sheer cliffs, rolling hills, mountain peaks, headlands and sea channels in a setting where distance is a visible quality to wonder at.

On a later flight, in summer, in a big Lockheed Electra tearing through low cloud at one hundred and eighty knots, I had a revelation that transformed my awareness of the Arctic landscape.

Attached to the ceiling of the plane, behind the pilots, was a special chair in which you could sit to look out through a Perspex blister like a fighter canopy. It was an eerie sensation, as if the whole aircraft was something you put on, like a helmet. The tail fin stuck up behind like a slender quill and the wings jutted out as if attached to my ears. In front, the white-painted alloy of the fuselage sloped down to meet the eyebrows of the cockpit windows. Specks of rain smacked into the dome like gravel hitting plate glass and were brushed away by the slipstream. The altimeter at throat level in front of me registered fifteen hundred feet. Beside it, three overflowing ashtrays suggested that ice reconnaissance was a nervy business, and pencilled on the metal frame was: PLEASE ENSURE ALL FOUR ENGINES ARE RUNNING BEFORE FEELING SAFE.

Staring out into a grey void I heard the pilot say on the intercom that we would come down another five hundred feet. A hand tapped my knee, holding up a paper cup of coffee, and I signalled my thanks. In the body of the plane the ice observers were preparing instruments that automatically profiled and measured the extent, height and temperature of the ice we would be flying over in the sea passages of the Arctic archipelago, and checked out the micro-wave oven that would cook pizzas for lunch. The nine-hour flight would cover roughly the same ground that the polar explorer Vilhjalmur Stefansson had covered in five years by dog team and schooner half a century before.

Suddenly the grey curtain whipped away and the Electra broke out of cloud into a scene of breathtaking desolation. The grey waters of Peel Sound below were scattered with small iceflows as whitely sterile as polystyrene chips on a greasy tarmac. The profile of land reaching out to meet us, black behind a film of grey drizzle, had the eyeless and skin-stretched look of a carcass in a desert. As it slid beneath the wing I could see nothing that relieved its starkness. No driftwood on its shingle shoreline, no trees or grasslands, just levels of bare gravel desert patterned with frost cracks, and steep clay slopes slumping with the spent air of a sandcastle abandoned to a summer downpour.

Then the picture of wall-to-wall cheerlessness became instantly electric. As the sun stabbed through the overcast it was evident the landscape was far from dead but – like the world on its fifth day – merely awaited its finishing touches. As the zinc-plated sea was galvanised by sharp flickers of sunlight it seemed all the arc-welders of Creation were back on the job. The dull and splintered ice floes flashed with sizzling light. But the most striking thing was the way our speeding in and out of the sagging clouds consumed distance and reduced the scale of the land's size and bleakness: when conquered by speed, the immensity of the Arctic kindles the spirit rather than deadens it.

That flight covered two thousand miles and the procession of bays, headlands and coastlines of varying shapes and sizes, on each side of the aircraft, was almost continuous. But our only sight of human activity was the red-hulled icebreaker which we circled in the wind-whipped mist of the Queen Maud Gulf while relaying radio facsimiles of the ice charts our observers had drawn during the trip.

First inklings of the giant geographic scale of the Arctic come when you fly north from a "southern" city like Edmonton, Alberta. After USSR and China, Canada is the third largest country in the world but only a small percentage of her twenty-three million people live further than one hundred miles from the US border. You do not realise what a narrow belt of this huge country is settled until you head north. City suburbs fall away before the No Smoking sign in the jet's passenger cabin goes off. Lines of trees planted as windbreaks catch the low sun and draw long shadows on the squared paper of snowy fields, making graphs like those drawn by oil companies to illustrate the energy crisis. You are still climbing steeply when this neat, T-squared prairie geography gives way to the chaotic hodge-podge of dark trees, scrubby heaths under layers of soft snow, and thousands of lakes, which comprise the continent's great boreal green-belt.

Like a green wave running up a beach, the tide of wooded country peters out along a well-defined line that crosses the breadth of North America, forming a distinct boundary between the sub-Arctic and the true Arctic. The tree-line separates forest from tundra, Indian from Eskimo, a relatively lushly endowed ecology from one of precariously unstable simplicity.

Jetting north at about six hundred miles an hour, the settled and tamed part of Canada – scathingly known among old Arctic hands as the banana belt – is left behind in ten minutes, while the sub-Arctic forested wilds stretch ahead for as much as three hours before you begin to see changes. The trees become sparser and more stunted until, over quite a short distance, they disappear completely and it is hard to be certain whether you are looking down upon a vista of snow or a layer of congealed cloud. But you do know you have entered the air-space of that most forbidding of natural environments – the Arctic.

The Arctic is many things to many people. It is the last frontier of North America, the new frontier of super technology trying to discover whether the Arctic is a storehouse of energy, a homeland for eighty thousand Eskimos, a place of hope for Whites living in the South who see it as a kind of social laboratory where they have a chance to do everything "right". Physically, it is easier to define.

At the top of the world there is more than one "pole". The North Pole has almost no significance except on maps, for it marks the point where the meridians of longitude converge. In reality it is a featureless portion of the polar pack ice circulating clockwise around the Arctic Ocean. The centre of this drifting ice, displaced four hundred miles towards eastern Siberia, is the "pole of inaccessibility". The magnetic north pole, invisible focus of all the world's compasses and the one place on the planet where a freely suspended compass needle points straight downwards, tracks northeastwards across the Arctic at a rate of about six miles a year and is currently at Bathurst Island. There are "poles of cold" where deep chill occurs, but these are in the still air of sub-Arctic forested regions such as Verkhoyansk, in northern Siberia, where temperatures drop to $-91\,°F$ ($-68\,°C$). But thermometers do not measure the severity of cold. It is when cold is combined with wind that the harshest conditions are felt, and it is north of the tree-line in the true Arctic, where there is nothing to break the force of pitiless winds, that these occur. The Arctic does not experience extremely low temperatures but it *feels* colder than anywhere else and the cold persists for two-thirds of the year, reducing the average annual temperature to the point that trees cannot survive and the ground remains permanently frozen.

This persistent rather than deep cold characteristic of the Arctic is ameliorated in northern Scandinavia and European Russia by the warming effects of the Gulf Stream thrusting into the Barents Sea, in summer pushing the edge of the sea ice back for hundreds of miles. Like the north-flowing Mackenzie River system, which allows sub-Arctic forests to creep north of the Arctic Circle in western Canada, extensive river systems on an even greater scale in Siberia raise the annual average temperature and blunt the severity and persistence of the climate. As a result much of Siberia is a marshy forest known as taiga which reaches almost to the north coast leaving only a narrow perimeter of tundra that can be called true Arctic. This means that the true Arctic does not centre on the North Pole, as you might expect, but is offset towards the western hemisphere, at Hudson Bay coming to within about 750 miles of the US border and reaching a latitude almost as far south as Scotland.

In Alaska the tree-line marking the Arctic boundary cuts across the south-facing slopes of the Brooks Range that spans the State like a powerful set of shoulders. Eight thousand feet high, lying just north of the Arctic Circle, the mountains are a formidable challenge to engineering operations like the construction of the Alyeska oil pipeline. South of the range, interior Alaska is a bowl of deep cold and lush vegetation. In autumn, its dark green spruce mingled with swirls of flame-yellow aspen, and the greeny-gold of fading cotton-woods and birch amid a myriad of brilliant lakes, is a sight to remember. Curving through them, brown as a granite highway, sweeps the mighty Yukon River. On the north side of the Brooks Range, a plain of rock and tussock frozen hard in winter and swampy in summer, is America's true Arctic and her treasure-house of oil – the North Slope.

At the Canadian border the tree-line dips briefly southwards as it crosses the Richardson Mountains in the top corner of the Yukon Territory, then trends north and almost meets the edge of the Beaufort Sea in the region of the vast low-lying Mackenzie Delta. In winter a sheet of ice, in summer it becomes a shattered mirror of lakes and waterways heliographing separate messages to passing aircraft as they catch the sun.

Wending across the "barrens" of the Canadian Shield, a region of long fingers of gravel, swamp-filled hollows, thickets of tangled scrub, and weathered rocks, the tree-line dips a long way south of the Arctic Circle to cross the coastline of Hudson Bay just north of Churchill. The boundless wastes of the barrens are the refrigerator of the North because they are so far from the warming effects of the ocean, and Hudson Bay has little effect because it is land-locked and for most of the year is frozen over. On the eastern side of Hudson Bay all but the tip of Quebec and Newfoundland are forested, because of the proximity of the open ocean.

North of the Canadian mainland, which roughly follows the seventieth parallel, the Arctic archipelago is a huge chunk of geography that covers an area greater than all Europe, or all of the US east of the Mississippi and Chicago. It is the largest island group in the world, its total coastline exceeding the circumference of the earth. Baffin, first part of the Arctic to be discovered and last to be mapped, is fifth largest island in the world (after Greenland, Borneo, New Guinea and Madagascar), and is bigger than any European country except France.

If the northwestern islands of the archipelago paralyse the mind with their spell of deathless uniformity, the eastern rim of the wedge of islands is forbidding for quite the opposite reason. Here is a spectacular frontier of glaciated mountains, few of them climbed or named, and deep fjords. From the tip of Ellesmere Island, which is only 475 miles from the North Pole, extending along the entire length of Baffin Island, the rugged coastline crowned with giant domes of solid ice compares in size and beauty with that of Norway, or British Columbia and the Alaska pan-handle. Its mountains end so abruptly, bastions of icy rock rising five thousand feet sheer from the ice-covered sea, that it seems the islands must have been torn apart from their neighbour across Baffin Bay and Davis Strait – Greenland. In fact, this is just what happened. Greenland is geologically part of North America, but aeons ago the tectonic influences that forced the continents apart also drove a wedge between Greenland and North America. As if made by an axe driven into a log, the "split" ran off in different directions to open out what is now the Northwest Passage; another, branching weakly to the south, opened a little crack that became the Mackenzie Valley. As the lands drifted apart their edges fell inwards, further widening the gap.

Despite the great size of Greenland only a tiny proportion is not covered by ice and most of this area is so vertical that no community has an airstrip long enough to take even a short take-off Twin Otter: Egedesminde houses and apartments are crowded to the very edge of the rocky shoreline protected from winter storms by outlying islands.

The Hot Arctic

Greenland is a unique land because of its massive dome of ice, 1,500 by 600 miles at its maximum, and up to two miles thick, contained within a circle of granite mountains. The ice cap comprises nearly a million cubic miles of ice, reckoned to be enough to supply every man, woman and child in the world with two hundred million gallons of water. The ice is formed by snow that falls on the ice cap and is buried and compressed by still more snow. As it sinks lower the ice flows outwards and the tiny air bubbles in it are compressed. Ultimately it is squeezed outwards through the rim of mountains and reaches the sea as an iceberg, and when you capture a piece of it to put in your drink the bubbles explode with a soft fizzing noise releasing pure and uncontaminated air more than two hundred thousand years old.

The ice cap is the only truly lifeless desert in the world, not counting the radar operators watching their scopes for Russian bombers and missiles in insulated cabins pegged into the ice on legs, like drilling rigs in the sea. Most of Greenland's fifty thousand people live in small communities in the fjords along the west coast, a habitable area as large as Norway with a similar mountainous character (but only 1·4 per cent of Norway's population). The warm currents which keep the major ports south of the Arctic Circle free of ice make the inhabited fringes of this great island technically sub-Arctic in character, but trees do not grow in Greenland because there is so little soil that even the graves have to be chiselled out of granite with pneumatic hammers, and Greenland's way of life is decidedly Arctic.

The pinched-in nature of the geography at the top of the world holds many surprises. Every map is triangular, like a slice of pie, because lines of longitude converge so sharply. On a Mercator projection Arctic territories seem to lie on opposite sides of the world when in fact they are near neighbours, and the Arctic is seldom seen as a place where the continents of Europe, Asia, and North America are closest. For example, Thule, the USAF base in northern Greenland, is closer to Seattle than to New York and, significantly, is closer still to the great Soviet military bases on the Kola Peninsula near Murmansk. The Prudhoe Bay oil-field is nearer to Britain than the Persian Gulf is, and when icebreaking supertankers manage to smash through the polar ice pack BP could tap the field for its domestic market with a direct and greatly reduced shipping route. Point Barrow, the most northerly point of the USA, is as close to Britain as to Washington DC, and is as near to Leningrad as to Los Angeles. Fairbanks, in central Alaska just south of the tree-line, is two hours' flying time nearer to Frankfurt than to Florida. Green-

Iceland ponies graze on the iceberg-littered shoreline of Narssaq in southern Greenland; the island is nine-tenths solid ice but the North Atlantic has a warming influence and early this century sheep farming was revived on the sites of the old Norse settlements established a thousand years ago by Erik the Red.

land is only sixteen miles from Canada, which at its broadest is 3,500 miles wide, but across the top of the world Alaska and Greenland are only 1,400 miles apart.

The relative and somehow unexpected nearness of nations in the Arctic is little help when travelling, for nearly all channels of communication run north–south. Most frustrating of all is to be in Frobisher, on Baffin Island, with business to do in Godthåb, capital of Greenland. They lie only an hour's jet time apart, but to make the 500-mile hop across Davis Strait you must travel through Montreal, Copenhagen and Søndre Strømfiord, changing planes four times, and spending at least twenty hours in the air (plus at least two overnight stops), all for a cost rather greater than that of a flight around the world. Yet transatlantic jets over-fly the two places.

Concepts of place and distance are jolted in all sorts of unexpected ways. In Chesterfield Inlet I spent an evening drinking rye and ginger with Jon and Judy Gurr, a Toronto couple who had come north to work as schoolteachers to save money for a house. With its curtains drawn, their sitting room could have been anywhere in suburban North America rather than drifted up with snow on the western shore of Hudson Bay. The trouble with living in the Arctic, Judy complained – facetiously, I thought at first (like the Danish official who told me the trouble with Godthåb was that it was too far from the zoo) – was getting books out of the library. Her books, selected by catalogue, were posted in a special despatch box from Hay River, by way of Edmonton and Winnipeg. Twenty years ago mail came to Chesterfield Inlet only twice a year, by dog team. Now schoolteachers complained when library books were slow to arrive! Judy might as well have lived in London and had her books sent from Warsaw by way of Athens and Barcelona, or lived in Boston, Mass., and had her books sent from Omaha through Dallas and Savannah. This settlement was not especially remote. Had she lived in Pond Inlet, on Baffin, her books would come a distance equal to that between New York and Naples, or London and Nepal.

Until the early 1950s the Arctic was as little known and mysterious as darkest Africa a century before. The polar Eskimos who inhabited these lands and frozen seas for thousands of years were jerked from Stone Age to Space Age in the course of two decades, while the land itself has been woken from a long-lingering dreamtime to a blitz of white-hot technology. None of the usual intermediate stages of development have occurred in the Arctic, such as the horse and cart, railways, or highways. Oil men commute to drilling rigs in the High Arctic every three weeks with the casualness of weekend cottage owners driving out of town. Eskimos born and brought up in snow houses and skin tents charter planes to go hunting or to bring in cargoes of liquor. Tourists make day trips to see the midnight sun.

In the entire Western hemisphere of the Arctic zone, an area as big as the whole of Canada, there are fewer people about than you would find in a middle-sized English county town such as Exeter or Lincoln. Until 1978 the only vehicle access to the Arctic was by way of the (then) private haul road alongside the Alyeska pipeline to Prudhoe Bay. The total mileage of public roads in this huge geographic area barely exceeds that of a county parish. Yet Arctic settlements do have an equivalent of the village cross-roads – in their airstrips.

Aeroplanes have been the instruments of change in the Arctic – its taxis, school-buses, rental cars, pick-ups, ambulances, Mack trucks, patrol cars, work-horses and mail vans. During my own seven months in the Arctic I made eighty-six different flights and spent a total of twelve days and nights in the air, encountering aircraft that ranged from tiny single-seaters to big C130 (Hercules) "thunder-belly" transporters. They carried everything: drilling rigs, tanks of fuel, dead bodies, Carnation milk, caribou carcasses, aerial cameras, badminton teams, sacks of rocks, politicians, garbage, and barrels of frozen dishwater. But it is the only means of travel, and the serious Arctic hitch-hiker finds out where the pilots are filling up with coffee, and by happening to say the right things and helping them load up he can go anywhere.

Sudden and localised summer fog, and winter breezes that churn up the dry, powdery snow thus reducing forward visibility to nearly zero, make the Arctic what pilots call a "hurry up and wait" sort of place. It leads to remarks that make one's blood run cold. Waiting at Inuvik airport with sixty oil men to be flown to the Canmar offshore drilling operations in the Beaufort Sea I overheard despatcher Al Plume report to his base: "The weather's supposed to be out but it can't be, we've got too many men to shift." As Vilhjalmur Stefansson wrote half a century before, to travel in a spirit of optimism is the only way – "Too many Arctic travellers suffer real agonies because they are haunted by the spectre of their own death: if you are not worried about it, it won't haunt you."

In the "early" days (in Arctic terms, the mid-1950s) aircraft came north with the geese in May and went away with them in September. At that time they were little Piper Cubs which carried either one passenger behind the pilot, or a drum of fuel that gave a range of nine hours. It was a three-day hop, step and jump to Resolute from Montreal or Edmonton, and if you ran into dirty weather you landed, put up a tent, and sat it out.

Canada's pioneer High Arctic "bush" pilot was Weldy Phipps (known by his initials as Whisky Papa) who was first to fit his tiny wood-and-fabric planes with large, soft-tyred wheels made for DC3's. With their slow stalling speed of only forty knots this enabled them to land on almost any soft or rough terrain. As planes got bigger flying seasons grew longer and landing speeds increased, as did costs.

Today the ubiquitous Twin Otter, carrying twenty passengers and freight, makes remarkable off-strip landings on terrain so rough you would hesitate to drive a Land Rover on it, let alone a car. Tough as a jeep, the de Havilland Twin Otter is in its element on the level, tree less wastes and has done more to modernise the Arctic than any

other invention. And you learn not to be alarmed when, after take-off with a load of empty drums, the air inside them expands from heat in the cabin and the plane is filled with loud bangs like rifle shots.

On the face of it, the Arctic has no secrets.

Landing on the gravel at Beechey Island to look at the graves of members of the ill-fated historic Franklin Expedition, I walked along the foreshore behind two archaeologists who found stone circles that showed where prehistoric Eskimo hunters had pitched tents – "Look, these stones are pink because they must have been oxidised by heat from cooking fires." A few feet away the two pilots made a different deduction as they stared at faint wheeltracks showing where a plane had landed badly – "Look, he must have bounced all the way to that rock, then touched one wheel..."

The Arctic landscape has always been dotted with caches. For aeons Eskimos hid supplies of seal or caribou meat from polar bears under cairns of rock. In the nineteenth century caches also were comprised of the boats, equipment, and barrelled provisions left by explorers whose names (Parry, Franklin, Ross, McClure, McClintock) and those of their ships (*Hecla, Griper, Fury, Erebus, Terror, Investigator*) adorn the maps unfolded on pilots' knees. Now more essential than ever in off-the-track Arctic travel, caches consist of drums of fuel for helicopters and Twin Otters which land alongside and refuel by hand pump.

As caches have been transformed from blubber to Av-gas, so has the character of camps dotted about with the randomness of cities of Western Europe, and separated by comparable distances. The sight of the silhouette of a Twin Otter dropping out of the clouds, spiralling down tightly so as not to alarm wildlife if it is a biologists' camp, is a welcome one. Not only is it the link with the outside world, but it is the means by which they can travel to almost anywhere they need to go.

On the face of it, the Arctic has no secrets. Archaeologists inspect stones used to weigh down the edges of Eskimo hunting tents in primitive times. In the background: the Twin Otter which has landed them at this majestically desolate spot near the headstones marking graves of members of the Franklin Expedition on Beechy Island in the High Arctic.

One day, ferrying scientists and equipment around remote areas, our Twin Otter made nine off-strip landings, covered 1,200 miles, and spent ten hours in the air. On the way home we thumped down on a patch of sand in a distant valley and taxied to the edge of an emerald lake where Pat, the pilot, leapt out with his fishing rod. Hardly had we landed than another Twin Otter flew in, and in the space of two minutes this remote valley miles from the nearest habitation was crawling with more than thirty off-duty oil men, scientists and pilots hooking big Arctic char, some of them as vividly coloured as the aircrafts' rescue-orange tail fins.

For pilots – still known as "bush" pilots although they are many miles north of anything that grows as tall as a bush – the Arctic is still a go-anywhere place with few regulations and few things to worry about. "That's what it's like up here," one pilot told me, "long periods of boredom punctuated by moments of sheer terror." One of these occurred when crossing Viscount Melville Sound by helicopter in thick fog. Batting along at about one hundred knots only a few feet up, orienting himself by the pancakes of sea ice streaking towards us out of the grey void, the pilot had just remarked that at least we didn't have to worry about hitting powerlines out here when out of the murk flicked two tall alloy masts. The pilot leap-frogged over the yacht's limp burgee and we circled round to look at *Williwaw*, on her way to being the first yacht (and possibly only the second vessel ever) to circumnavigate the Americas.

Worse than fog is the Arctic whiteout. Feared by pilots, it is not the obliteration of visibility by driving snow, as the name implies, but a condition of light when clouds are thick enough to diffuse the sun's rays and there is snow on the ground. The clouds turn as white as the snow and shadows disappear so there is total lack of contrast and you are trapped in a white void, as if suspended in a bottle of milk. Visibility may be great, because the air is so clear, but lacking surface texture the foreground cannot be separated from background and depth perception is lost. The white blur in front of you might be a hillside three miles away, or a snowdrift three feet away. Dog-team drivers had to walk ahead, tossing an object in front of them to provide a datum point. Helicopter pilots have the same trouble knowing where the ground is and drop things out to see how far they fall. Fixed-wing pilots just hope they don't get caught.

Accidents do happen, some of them weird. Ice-observer Ken Peister flew into a cloud in a Twin Otter, secure in the knowledge that their altitude of five thousand feet comfortably cleared any high points along their route. Without warning the plane suddenly lurched and stopped dead. The pilot had to check his air-speed indicator to confirm that the incredible had happened. He throttled back and looked out. Ken opened his side door: there was no slip-stream. Below and all around them there was only a blurred white-ness, like cloud, but looking back he saw a disembodied wheel lying on its side. The plane's gyrocompass had been defective and they had landed in two feet of soft snow on top of the Devon Island ice cap which is almost exactly five thousand feet high. Without realising it they had flown out of cloud into a whiteout over ice, and as the dome of ice rose gently up to meet their wheels they had made a remarkable hands-off landing. Half an hour later the sky cleared, they called for help, put the kettle on, and were rescued before the coffee was made.

If low flying restores the feelings of excitement and enchantment which desert you at first sight of these bizarre and little-known territories at the top of the map, the sense of being humbled by distance and vastness is never really shaken off. Always at least part of your mind is on the ground, simultaneously grateful for the fact that there is so much runway space for use in emergency while dreading the possibility of having to fight for survival in the wilder-ness.

But flying is to the Arctic what driving is to the suburbs of any town: it is part of the fabric of life, and emergencies or delays are accepted phlegmatically. Returning to Frobisher from our seventeen-hour patrol of the Arctic Islands in the Canadian Forces Argus, the crew had in mind another Argus which, only a week before, had crashed on landing and killed several of its crew. Tension increased as we approached the paved runway. Our wheels touched and we bounced, flying for endless seconds until the wheels touched and the big plane bounced yet again. When at last it settled and was braked sharply at the limit of the runway the crew cheered and whistled. "I think I just completed three night landings," said the shaken pilot.

"This is the tower," drawled the voice of the air controller on the radio. "I have timed you in at two twenty-one, two twenty-two and two twenty-three..."

2

FREEZING IN THE DARK
BUILDS CHARACTER

*You are only as cold as you feel but
when you stop feeling you're frozen —
the* feel *of the Arctic*

Winjer was a black and white cat living at latitude 74° 41'N in
Resolute Bay, on the northern coastline of the Northwest Passage.
Her home was with Katie and Maurice Cloughley. Maurice, a New
Zealander, was headmaster of the little school and Katie, a
Londoner, secretary in the government office. Their cat was nothing
special, though she meowed a lot and this explains the origin of her
name, from Down-under slang for one who complains. On a diet of
seal meat and fish she was sleek and fat, and like any other cat knew
her place – inside.

Last winter Winjer went astray but after three or four days came
home, meowing plaintively as usual. Katie and Maurice were
delighted, and stroked her head. Winjer purred. Then her ears fell
off.

"There they were," said Katie, "lying on the kitchen floor like two
furry mice..."

The frost-bitten cat purring cosily on my lap after I had eaten
roast caribou (juicier than venison, more stringy and leaner than
lamb) with the Cloughleys, as Eskimo children stared at us through
the double-glazed windows, was a reminder of how fragile was the
capsule of existence in the Arctic. Eskimos had lived in harmony
with their environment and perfected a technology that com-
plemented Nature without exploiting it, while enabling them to

Winjer, the Resolute cat, whose frozen ears fell on to the kitchen floor.

survive its harshness. White Society has merely conquered the cold, without learning to live with it.

In the new polar stockades of suburban comfort ordinary life is barely touched by the cold: one experiences it from time to time, mainly when walking briskly from one building to another, or between vehicle and porch, but it is not necessary to wrestle with it in a personal way unless something goes wrong. There is much to go wrong, because all we have done is to bring in various kinds of engines to keep the cold out and declare a truce in what Vilhjalmur Stefansson called "the trench warfare with cold". But it is no more than a truce. If the power goes off, if your vehicle breaks down or the plane makes a forced landing the cold awaits – the silent enemy.

If the cold gets you, as it did poor Winjer, you can be lucky if it is only your ears that drop off. Cold sears like white heat. It turns lubricating oil to the consistency of butter, freezes condensation in fuel to form ice crystals that block carburettors, makes electric wires as brittle as glass. In deep cold, steel snaps like porcelain when dropped on a hard surface. Propane gas lighters are useless because the cold turns gas liquid and smokers in the Arctic rely on Zippos that flare like barbecues. Liquid fire extinguishers freeze up, batteries do not last ten minutes, and a snow machine seat crackles like Cellophane and tears as easily. If Arctic cold can do this to durable materials like steel what effect does it have on humans? Questions like this are much in your mind when you fly north in a passenger jet for the first time and, in its hand basin, find scented sachets of tissues instead of running water – because its water tank freezes, not while it is in the air, but during the short time it is on the ground.

The accounts of polar explorers and others who have lived with the Eskimos paint an alarming picture of misery and discomfort. No clothing is proof against Arctic cold. Frost nips are common and you must be alert for white spots indicating freezing flesh on the faces of other people. Eskimos do not blow on their hands to warm them because the vapour of their breath freezes and does more to chill than to warm.

In calm conditions the first serious confrontation with cold can require no special protective clothing if you are careful and quick. With breath snapping and smoking round your ears, you walk briskly from heated aircraft to heated "terminal" be it hangar, tent, or a pick-up with its engine running, and as soon as you reach the warmth, condensation pours at once from the tip of your nose; the extremities which have gone numb spring instant pins and needles; spectacles mist up maddeningly.

Let there be just a breath of wind, however, and a quick dash through polar cold becomes an experience to remember. The cold tattoos your skin and drives blunt needles through the bones. There is no question of gritting the teeth and seeing it through like a brave boy scout. It is an onslaught against which a human being stands about as much chance as a stalk of wheat in the path of a combine harvester. If there is no shelter immediately to hand you have to be smart enough to do exactly the right thing very quickly – or perish. It can happen in mundane and routine circumstances: if you go out in a vehicle without protective clothing and it gets stuck in the snow a few hundred yards from home you could be dead before you make it on foot. Death does not come at once; it is the lethargy settling on you like a cloud of deadly gas that makes it certain.

If you are constantly out of doors as a scientist or oil-patch worker, getting to grips with cold is a matter of training and self-discipline demanding a strict regime of behaviour. Once acquired by education and experience it becomes second nature, but you must never drop your guard: like a sly dog, the cold waits until your back is turned, then it gets you. Technical adjustments take you most of the way; dressing in the Arctic is a science.

The insulation value of clothing is measured in "clo. units": an ordinary business suit has a value of one unit, while a traditional Eskimo winter outfit made of caribou furs varied between seven and twelve. Sleeping at −40°F (−40°C) the body needs about twelve units to be comfortable, but if you are active in this temperature, in calm conditions, you need only four.

At first afraid of the cold, one is tempted to over-dress and button up tightly, which often results in increased perspiration. It is not cold that tips the arrows of a grisly frozen death in the Arctic, but sweat. As long as you have good clothing the main problem is not keeping warm, but keeping cool. If you work up a sweat your clothes become damp and they lose their insulation value.

Dressing in heavy boots, quilted leggings or "wind pants", and a bulky Arctic parka, then struggling with unfamiliar zips and toggles, works up an old-fashioned sweat in no time, especially as most houses are kept at nearly tropical temperatures. With practice you get the job done quickly and step out into the cold at once, before you boil. At first the cold air wraps around you like a clammy sheet but comfort depends on the layers of air in your clothes being warm so you have to turn on your generator – and get moving.

The body itself is a furnace that puts out a lot of heat. When standing still it uses about one hundred watts of power obtained from the metabolism of food. Output can be boosted up to ten times by conscious physical activity, otherwise the body automatically takes over and provides more power by shivering. Without realising it, a warmly dressed but inactive person can suffer a debilitating cold injury in the same time that an inadequately clothed active person suffers severe discomfort and shivering but avoids injury. If the body is kept on the go to generate heat its core will always be comfortably warm even if arms and legs are chilled and shivering; when there is ice to be chopped for drinking water, fuel drums to be loaded into an aeroplane or snow to be shovelled, the first rule of Arctic survival is that it pays to volunteer. At the end of the day you will feel nothing but tiredness, while the shirker is chilled to the bone. Research and engineering in the Arctic is tough because carrying out the laborious, precise, patient work of science is seldom sufficient to keep the body's generator going. Hands working without mittens on tiny adjustment knobs have to be warmed frequently: in an emergency your own crotch or a colleague's belly is the best source of heat.

Once you are on the move the problem is how to stay cool. Wrapped up in the most advanced clothing that technology can devise, you step smartly into the crisp sunshine of a bitterly cold Arctic spring day, boots crunching in the crumbly snow, and within minutes your armpits run like hot butter. It is essential – truly a matter of life and death, when out in the wilderness – to take off some clothes or slow down. Having started well buttoned up, you gradually loosen off, unzipping the parka to let some heat out, throwing back the parka hood. The instant you stop moving it is necessary to close up again, trapping residual warmth now that the generator has been shut down. After a time it all becomes automatic.

In modern Arctic communities and work camps engines of various kinds keep buildings, tents, workshops and vehicles at a temperature of about 70 °F (21 °C) so people can walk around comfortably in shirt sleeves. So hot are the buildings, in fact, that you are more likely to experience real discomfort from warmth and stuffiness than Arctic chill. As a nomadic hunter the Eskimo carried his central heating system around with him, maintaining the same cosy heat within his winter suit made of two layers of caribou skin back to back. It was a wife's chore to chew the skins daily to soften them, which explains why the smile of an old Eskimo woman reveals teeth as straight and level as those of a zip fastener. Caribou skin lasted only a year, and in warm weather had a certain "air" about it, but it provided clothing that hung loosely around the body, automatically providing insulation while the hunter stood still, and ventilation when he was on the move.

Eskimo parkas were designed so the arms could be pulled inside for extra warmth. They were also buoyant, acting as life preservers if you fell into the water while hunting on sea ice. Although modern Eskimos wear mostly Army surplus clothes or jeans it is thought their habit of bending over stiff-legged may be due to the stiffness of traditional skin clothes. Though more functional and comfortable than any clothing imported from the South, fur parkas are now hardly ever seen.

The first parts of the body affected by cold are those furthest from its inner core, the hands and feet. In the Arctic mittens are preferable to gloves because the fingers help to keep each other warm. Canadian Forces – "Grunts" (army), "Hairy shirts" (navy) and "Crapfats" (air force) – are equipped with special mittens with a trigger finger, and a woolly patch intended for wiping goggles but generally used as a nose wiper. Working on the layer principle, the idea is to wear gloves inside thick mittens which are thrust into gauntlets that extend halfway up the sleeve, for frostbite is as likely to hit the wrists as the face or fingers.

Feet must be dressed for where they are, not where the head is.

Rooftops are the adventure playgrounds of the Arctic settlements — skating rink, football pitch, riding track, wrestling mat. Most children, like these at Chesterfield Inlet, now wear clothes trimmed with artificial fur, rubber or plastic boots, blue jeans, nylon quilting.

Commonly the air temperature five or six feet above the ground is several degrees warmer, particularly when the feet sink into snow. In windy weather the effects are reversed and the feet, protected by snow, may be warmer than your head stuck out in the wind. A woolly cap that comes well down over the ears and forehead prevents much heat loss.

Eskimos traditionally wore roomy *kamiks*, soft sock-like boots made of caribou hide with soles of waterproof sealskin. In Greenland they were padded with dry grass to provide insulation, and in North America liners of caribou fur were worn. Today these are seldom seen, the new generation of Eskimos preferring Army surplus "bunny boots" or mass-produced Skidoo boots worn several sizes too large with liners of thick felt.

Working in cold the body requires more fuel to keep its inner furnace blasting out heat. You find an unexpected appetite for fats; steak trimmings are no longer left on the plate. While British Commonwealth countries issue lightweight ten-day food rations for long-range military patrols having a value of 1,900 calories a day, in the Arctic increased energy output requires at least 3,000 calories so the Canadian soldier's ration pack is one-third heavier.

But it is water, not food, that is the main problem in Arctic living. The air is so dry, due to the inability of cold air to hold moisture, that the body transpires great amounts of water vapour into the atmosphere. Most of it is lost at the rate of up to one (US) gallon a day through the nose and breathing passages as the body automatically humidifies the incoming dry air. The USAF reckons that a 2·5 per cent loss of body water results in a twenty-five per cent loss in working efficiency, and that dehydration is a greater problem in polar regions than in hot deserts. The fact that you don't feel thirsty makes it worse. For some reason thirst centres in the body do not transmit the usual signals, and by the time you do begin to desire a drink the body is already moderately dehydrated. The more you dry out the less thirsty you feel, until you become groggy. The heart jumps at the least exertion, and fainting or heart attacks can result.

During the first couple of days in the Arctic you tend to urinate more often. One reason is that the cold makes the body shut down peripheral blood vessels so its core temperature can be preserved. This means the blood must flow in a smaller system, the body feels there is too much blood and gets rid of some in the form of water. Ordinarily, loss of water makes the blood saltier so you feel thirsty but in the Arctic the salt is excreted as well, along with potassium. Salt and potassium are vital to keep the nervous system and muscles (including the heart) running properly.

All that moisture which smokes out with your breath must be replaced, but more than a gallon is a lot of water to drink in one day, especially in some settlements where hepatitis due to water pollution is rife and refrigerators are full of pop. Fruit juice does not cure dehydration because it must be digested while tea, coffee or liquor increases urination and adds to loss of fluids. When working in a field camp in winter getting water is what experts call "a low-yield, time-consuming endeavour". In plain language, getting water in the Arctic is a pain in the arse. Chipping ice or cutting snow blocks, carrying it, melting it over a fire, is all a great deal of work when you are listless and not a bit thirsty. Eskimo hunters sometimes obtained water by turning the stomach of a freshly killed caribou inside out, filling it with snow, and returning it to the carcass where the snow was melted by residual body heat. Arctic snow is not soft and fluffy like it is in the sub-Arctic forests, requiring snowshoes to stop yourself floundering up to the hips, but granular and so hard that boots barely leave a mark and a five-ton tractor sinks only a couple of inches. It is half the density of water, compared with snow in southern regions which is only one-tenth as dense as water, so you don't have to gather so much for melting down.

Beards are no trouble in summer, and serve some purpose in boosting the image of polar fearlessness among young men returning home after working in the Arctic, but in winter they collect moisture from the breath which builds up into stalagtites of ice next to the skin. A close-cropped beard may permit you to avoid shaving while providing a modicum of insulation, but USAF survival instructors at Fairbanks say it is better to wear a warm scarf so any ice that forms can be snapped away. Eskimo men have little facial hair, which may be a physiological adaptation to the climate; in their early twenties a few hairs sprout on their upper lip and chin but otherwise they are mostly smooth skinned.

Those who work only occasionally in intense cold have many pet theories about how to "take it" but the real experts admit there is no system and the cold can never be beaten; the only remedy is to get on with a job until it is done. No clothing is ideal for bad conditions, and its inadequacy can be made up only by grit, persistence and a "think warm" attitude. During a season working in a scientific camp on the sea ice Fred Alt, of the Canadian Polar Continental Shelf Project, lost so many layers of skin from touching cold metal that when he returned home he was unable to supply fingerprints for a security pass. Seismologist Tony Overton told me how the cold makes objects dance in your tears when you look through instruments such as theodolites; while adjusting tiny focusing and levelling screws with bare fingers you have to stop breathing so they are not frozen up by moisture – "You soon learn to curse a lot and it's not the sort of thing you can force yourself to do; you have to enjoy it to stay with it."

Physiologists doubt whether the body acclimatises to cold as readily as it does to heat. Eskimos certainly seem to feel the cold less than Whites, but this may be due to stoicism: they tolerate the cold better, hardening themselves to it mentally and accept as they come any other Arctic environmental insults such as dampness, murderous terrain and long hours of boredom. In fact Eskimos freeze just as fast and easily as any human, but the Arctic is not a laboratory and in real life Eskimos are more likely to survive because they are experienced at dealing with cold and their mental attitude treats the whole problem as one of normal living rather than as an emergency that could cost a life. The metabolic rate of Eskimos is about twenty per cent higher than that of Whites, but according to Dr Fred Milan, a physiological anthropologist at the University of Alaska, it is not known whether this is due to diet – the Eskimo being "the most exquisitely carnivorous person on earth" – or physical adaptation. It means their body furnace runs hotter although their temperature remains the same, like turning up the thermostat in a room but leaving the door open. Eskimos have better blood circulation to the face than Whites, and many more sweat glands around the nose and upper lip but fewer on the forehead, normally covered by a thick lock of hair, and on the trunk. But this is an adaptation to heat, not cold, for the Eskimo's thermal problem occurs during prolonged bursts of activity, while hunting, when he has to remain fully clothed: he does not sweat under his clothes but is able to dissipate the heat through the parts of his face that are exposed to cold air. Hypothermic adaptation of other native races, like Australian aborigines and African bushmen, is greater because they live nearly naked. In cold conditions their skin protects them by cooling down so the body loses less heat and they drop into a torpor. Eskimos are always adequately clothed, and rather than shutting down blood supply their bodies respond with high heat production and blood flow to peripheral tissues, which explains the Eskimos' warm handshakes that astonished early explorers.

One measure of an individual's ability to withstand cold is cold-induced vasodilation (CIVD), the ability of the body to heat itself locally to prevent injury from cold. The first reaction of blood vessels in the fingers to severe cold is constriction, and this causes the muscles around them to become paralysed so they relax, the blood flows again, and they become warm once more. It is an on/off reaction that can last for about three hours before serious discomfort is felt. Some people do not have this ability to recover from initial cold and maintain a certain manual dexterity. Good CIVD is present in older Eskimos who have been hunters and trappers, and in people who have worked for long periods as fish filleters or cold-store workers, but it is less marked in younger Eskimos who have led softer lives, and in Arctic-hardened troops after two weeks of living in tents and hauling sleds around the frozen tundra. This suggests the body is slow to adapt to cold conditions in the short term, but ultimately does adapt in part.

Habituation is a different thing to acclimatisation. Many things influence ability to withstand cold. Part of it is simple stamina, a self-selection process in which those who can't stand it do not return to the Arctic. There are those who may not feel it so much because they have good CIVD or, if they feel it, do not scream about it. With experience you learn little tricks, like turning your fingers to the sun when doing delicate work, and avoiding shade. The main things are learned in the first weeks – how not to sweat, how to stay cool and dry and resist the temptation to dress too warmly, how to drink all that water you don't want.

Frostbite is less of a problem in the Arctic than in the sub-Arctic and South because you are less easily caught off guard. Accidents and stress conditions can contribute to frostbite which would not occur for climatic reasons alone. Injury and shock reduces the body to a passive condition so its own internal generator barely ticks over. The most violent and rapid cases of frostbite have occurred not in the Arctic, but over Germany during the Second World War when frostbite injuries in US heavy bomber crews during the winter of 1943–4 were greater than all other casualties combined.

Frostbite happens when part of the body shuts down, sacrificing an extremity rather than risking death of the whole organism. To prevent the body core temperature falling below the danger point the blood refuses to go into the cold area. Tissues and nerves freeze up and are deprived of nutrition and oxygen. Ultimately the affected parts drop off, a prolonged and messy business when it affects fingers or toes, quick and clean when it is the ears.

Frost can nip the face and cause sudden whitening of the skin which is normally noticed by other people before you feel it yourself. It is treated by holding a warm hand firmly against the spot. The most reliable sign of frostbite is cessation of feeling cold or discomfort. Once your feet *stop* hurting, watch out. Mere numbness of fingers and toes, followed by tingling as they are warmed up, is just frost "nip". Even in its mildest form true frostbite damages the flesh and is always serious. In emergency, once a person's feet are frozen he can walk a long way without further injury, and perhaps reach safety without burdening companions. As soon as a frozen foot is re-warmed the patient becomes a cot case and raves with pain. Often people are seriously burned by placing frozen feet too close to a fire, because they have no feeling and do not realise how hot it is.

Worse than frostbite is hypothermia. It happens more often in cool temperatures than cold because it steals up on you, and first to be affected is the brain. Hypothermia is the lowering of the body core temperature. When it gets cold the body cuts off circulation to the extremities to keep its internal organisms going, constricting the small blood vessels – and the brain is all small blood vessels. First your judgement cools: in a survival situation this is dangerous enough. Then vision blurs, you stumble, hands and feet stiffen, and you lose consciousness then die. While frostbite is rarely fatal but always serious, hypothermia is frequently fatal. Treatment is difficult because the body can only be warmed (usually in a tepid bath) from the outside inwards, so the heart must cope with great quantities of warmed blood while it is still cold and weak.

Nothing rekindles the élan quicker than first glimpse of the returning sun on some day in January or February, depending on latitude. When explorers' ships over-wintered in the ice, crews took turns climbing to the crow's nest for glimpses of the sun. Today, across the breadth of the Arctic, people mark the magic day on their calendars and climb the nearest high point for the pleasure of seeing the sun on its way back into their lives. In places like Pangnirtung, lying in the shadow of a great fjord, the sun itself is not visible but each day the band of light on the peaks of the mountains opposite gets excitingly broader and deeper until, one miraculous day, it floods the entire settlement.

Extreme darkness exists only *at* the North Pole, but even there the sun shines for twenty-eight weeks of the year, you can read a newspaper out of doors for thirty-two weeks, and there is twilight for another eight weeks. Its three-month night shortens as you head south until, at the Arctic circle, the sun can be seen for at least part of every day. Overall there is more light in the Arctic than in the tropics. The North Pole has 140 hours more daylight than the Equator, and the Arctic Circle 230 hours more.

The long light is wearing on schoolteachers. Eskimo children go to bed only when they feel tired, and after a long dark winter it doesn't hit them until the early hours. They stumble fractiously into class in the middle part of the day, and tempers wear thin. At Inuvik a siren is sounded at nine-thirty every evening as an official curfew to remind children under fourteen it is time they were in bed, (it is not enforced because some children stay outside to avoid drunken adults in their homes). CBC television programmes beamed to the Arctic by satellite run public service advertisements at ten o'clock saying, "For children who have lessons tomorrow, now is a good time for bed."

Added to extremes of cold, loneliness, and long hours of winter darkness are other factors like the wind. Chinook-like winds rolling off the ice caps of Greenland and Baffin gain speed and intensity as they are channelled into the fjords. At Pangnirtung, the rooftops are held down by wire hawsers anchored into the frozen ground, and anything that could take off, even sledges which you would think had the sailing qualities of a ladder, are weighted down by rocks. One winter storm in one night blew away the nursing station, the community garage and half the Hudson's Bay store. At Auyuittuq National Park ("The land that never melts") thirty miles up the fjord, wardens advise you officially to expect "nothing but a gruelling experience". Savage squalls of freezing rain, blizzards and gales that roll boulders like bowling balls can strike without warning at any time. It is a place where humans walk at an angle, as if hammered into the ground like tent pegs.

The coldest spot in the Arctic is central Greenland, on the exposed ice cap two miles high, where the annual mean temperature is $-27\,°F$ ($-33\,°C$) compared with $-9\,°F$ ($-23\,°C$) at the North Pole, and around $-11\,°F$ ($-24\,°C$) at settlements like Barrow and Coppermine. Even the lowest temperatures at the North Pole are probably not much worse than those of coldest winter days on the fringes of the Arctic in Ontario and Manitoba, and occasionally during cold snaps as far south as Chicago. The polar climate is not so much characterised by extremely low temperatures as by the long duration of cold. Barrow, for example, experiences below-freezing temperatures 324 days a year, and below $0\,°F$ ($-18\,°C$) for nearly six months.

People in the Arctic are less concerned about thermometer readings than the strength of the wind. For it is the combination of cold and wind that is the greatest threat to survival and the true measure of climatic harshness.

You can dress comfortably for a temperature of $-20\,°F$ ($-28\,°C$) and work steadily for long periods in shirt sleeves. But when there is the faintest breath of a breeze you find out what it is like to be massaged by Brillo pads. The eye-cutting wind sucks heat from your body by constantly changing the air around it, intensifying the feeling of cold. This effect is known as "windchill" and you cannot be long in the Arctic before you know a lot about it.

Although the concept is not rigorously defined by physiologists and there is a lot of room for subjective error, windchill is factorised in terms of loss of kilowatts per square metre per hour:

Windchill factor	Description	Actual temperature	
		In calm air	In 20 mph wind
1000	Very cold	$-20\,°F$ ($-25\,°C$)	$32\,°F$ ($0\,°C$)
1200	Bitterly cold	$-29\,°F$ ($-34\,°C$)	$21\,°F$ ($-6\,°C$)
1400	Travel hazardous	$-44\,°F$ ($-42\,°C$)	$10\,°F$ ($-12\,°C$)
2000	Exposed flesh freezes in one minute	$-76\,°F$ ($-60\,°C$)	$-22\,°F$ ($-30\,°C$)

Windchill is also expressed in "equivalent" temperatures, indicating how cold you feel. At −20 °F (−28 °C) it takes only a 15 mph breeze to reduce the effective temperature to −60 °F (−51 °C). On a typical early spring day, with the thermometer reading −40 °F (−40 °C) a breeze of only 10 mph plunges the effective temperature to −70 °F (−57 °C); in a 40 mph gale the air feels as cold as −115 °F (−82 °C), and that is more than any human can bear. Such figures look more alarming than they really are, however, because the windchill chart can be misleading. In Arctic communities people whizz around on snow machines with faces uncovered and although it brings tears to the eyes they do not suffer from frozen flesh. Windchill factors make no allowance for blood nourishing the face, the warming effect of clothes, the influence of the sun when you can find it, and human capacity to ignore discomfort. But the mean monthly windchill of the coldest months does illustrate vividly local differences in real living conditions:

Location	Mean monthly windchill
Verkhoyansk (Siberia)	1471
Thule (northwest Greenland)	1605
Point Barrow (Alaska North Slope)	1705
Churchill (west coast Hudson Bay)	1820
Resolute Bay (Arctic archipelago)	1940
Baker Lake (Canadian barrens)	2030

In the heart of Siberia far from the sea, yet on the same latitude as Inuvik, Verkhoyansk experiences some of the coldest temperatures ever measured in the northern hemisphere, ranging between annual extremes of minus ninety and plus ninety degrees (−68 °C to 32 °C), but its deepest cold occurs in utterly still conditions. At the North Pole the ocean warms the ice which warms the air, and mean monthly temperatures have a small range between freezing point in summer and −29 °F (−34 °C) in winter. But at Chesterfield Inlet winter winds are typically 15 mph from the north producing a temperature that feels as cold as −56 °F (−49 °C) and windchill is in the "danger" zone three days in four.

It is the sea ice of the polar pack, in winter covering ten per cent of northern seas, which makes the Arctic so cold. In the first place the sun is weak because it is low, and its rays are scattered over fifty per cent more area than at the equator. Also the ice reflects at least seventy per cent of the sun's light and heat back into space, so that overall the Arctic loses more heat than it gains. The sea ice is a lid, in winter preventing the sea from warming the air and in summer preventing the sun from warming the water. In this way it acts as the main shock absorber in the earth's northern climatic engine. In other regions the sun heats the water and the water heats the atmosphere, the circulation bringing weather. In the Arctic the ice cover reduces the heating of the atmosphere to almost nil, creating a "heat sink" in the form of vortex of deeply chilled air. In winter the vortex is not quite round but is pinched at the centre between the Bering Sea and the North Atlantic, and lengthened towards the frozen regions of Hudson Bay and central Siberia. Its inner core, circulating in at very high altitude from the equator and sinking over the ice-covered Arctic Ocean, is sluggish and moves only slightly. Now and then a tongue of its super-chilled polar air breaks out, is turned eastwards by the spin of the earth, and blasts across the prairies to make the corner of Portage and Main streets in downtown Winnipeg feel as cold as the North Pole itself.

Low pressure areas form around the rim of this polar heat sink – the Arctic front – and travel across the continent under the influence of westerlies, but are seldom felt in the Arctic where characteristic winter weather is settled with clear skies and long periods of steady, intense cold. During the coldest months – December, January, February, March – the mercury lingers around – 30 °F (– 34 °C) nine days in ten. As the air is so cold any clouds that form are very light; thunder and lightning, and cumulus clouds, are almost unknown.

The extent of polar ice has a critical influence on weather in middle latitudes – approximately the eastern US and Canada between Cape Hatteras and Newfoundland, and most of western Europe – because it controls the route of weather systems. When the ice retreats, as it did between the World Wars, the middle latitudes come under the spell of a zone of westerlies that brings a regular pattern of predictable and non-extreme weather. When the ice is extended by a cooling trend, the causes of which are not yet understood, this ordered procession of westerlies is disturbed. Instead, cyclonic activity moves randomly into high and low latitudes while in the middle latitudes anti-cyclones bring prolonged spells of hot weather and often droughts punctuated by periods of persistent cyclones, so the result of a bigger Arctic ice pack is greater frequency of extreme weather.

Meteorologists conclude that the new cooling trend has levelled off but there is no sign yet of a warmer regime. The Climatic Research Unit of the University of East Anglia believes this halting of the slide into another Little Ice Age – when the world was cooler, damper, stormier and pack-ice extended further south than Iceland – may not be natural but may have been caused by the great amounts of carbon dioxide and waste heat released into the atmosphere by industry. At present it is thought that natural events still dominate the side-effects of Man's all-consuming lifestyle, but this may not continue long into the next century. The World Meteorological Organisation has warned that a drastic warming of world climates from accelerated industrial production might already have begun, leading ultimately to the disappearance of Arctic sea ice, melting of ice caps, a rise in sea level that could flood most ports, and great shifts of the natural vegetation and crop-growing belts.

As the ice reflects nearly three-quarters of the sun's warmth it persists long after the sun is so high in the sky that darkness is reduced to a brief midnight gloaming. Although March and April have more daylight than darkness, climatically the circulation patterns are still those of the Arctic night, and their days are brilliant, clear and cold. It is the best time for Arctic travel and getting work done because land and sea are frozen solid and you can land planes or drive vehicles almost anywhere. By May much of the sea ice begins to "rot" and becomes dangerous but it remains in large floes long after the snow has melted from the land. Spring comes with a rush: the moment dark-coloured soil appears beneath the snow, or pools of melted water collect on the ice, the sun's warmth is not reflected but is absorbed, and melting accelerates rapidly. Transformation from winter to summer is completed in a few days – "When you can see the garbage under the snow it's spring, and when we've cleaned it up it's summer" – but the summer brings an end to the crisp, bright and settled weather. On the foreshore at Godthåb, Finn Lynge, director of Radio Greenland, had taken an afternoon off and was painting his boat in the sunshine. "Summer here can be so beautiful", he sighed. "The fall is just terrible, winter is so long, and spring – just isn't."

In summer the polar vortex retreats to the vicinity of the tree-line so that storms track further north. The pack ice shrinks by about ten per cent and most of the shorefast ice, and ice in straits between the islands and in Hudson Bay, disappears. Without its icy lid the water evaporates into the warm air. The land itself is covered in bogs, lakes, ponds, and braided streams which add to the moisture in the air. Almost continuous local fog or low stratus cloud hides the sun and keeps temperatures to a low and damp 45 °F (7 °C) which in turn brings cold drizzle, light snow and sometimes freezing rain. Some places get a hundred days of fog during a summer barely 120 days long. In winter aircraft and even herds of caribou can make their own fog. Air which is below 0 °F (−18 °C) at ground level can be as warm as 55 °F (13 °C) three hundred feet up, so when a Hercules aircraft takes off, its four thirteen-foot props creating tremendous turbulence, the stirring of the air brings warm air to ground level where its moisture condenses in the sudden cold, causing convection fog that commonly lasts an hour and in extreme conditions "socks in" all day.

Coastal weather is so erratic that every year forty thousand travellers have to wait an average thirty-two hours in the (very expensive) transit centre at Søndre Strømfjord in Greenland. The record is held by a group who waited twenty-nine days to make a ninety-minute flight to Sukkertoppen, but delays of two weeks are common. Schedules are booked up more than half a year in advance – "But really," Greenlandair's traffic manager warned me, "our schedule is just something to divert from."

Although much of the Arctic in summer is a brown desert lapped by sea passages as blue as the Mediterranean, any impression of having landed by navigational mischance in Iraq or Somalia is rapidly dispelled by the chill, which somehow comes as more of a shock in summer than in winter because you are not ready for it and not wearing the right clothes. In fall continuous storms, fogs and lashing drizzle are made even more miserable by the rapid retreat of the sun, darkness gaining at the rate of about ten minutes a day. More than anything it is the mid-winter darkness that puts out your inner fires. In their old way of life Eskimos coped with it by going on holiday at home, staying in their igloos and socialising until the returning light allowed the resumption of hunting. The White man's nine-to-five regime makes no such happy allowances.

3

SUB-ZERO SUBURBIA

*The nuts and bolts of the polar
wilderness – ordinary life on the top
shelf of the world*

Baffin Island! Like the Amazon River or the Sahara Desert, its very
name smacks of high adventure. When the jet drops its left wing to
turn up Frobisher Bay the snowy, boulder-strewn peninsula below
has the blood-tingling name of Meta Incognita; a skerry on its south
shore is called Isle of God's Mercie. To this day Baffin is one of the
least explored and violent environments in the world. Bigger than
any European country except France, it has only eight small communities of which Frobisher, with a population of 2,300, is about
four times bigger than any other because it is the administrative
centre of the eastern Arctic. It lies at the head of a long bay near the
island's southern tip, and the sight of the ice-covered sound thrills
the imagination; already you are as far from Toronto as Cuba is, but
this is only the gateway to the Arctic. You look out for dog teams, and
perhaps see an Eskimo hunter threading a snow machine between
the pressure ridges on the sea ice, trailing a loaded *komatik*.

From the starboard windows there is a glimpse of a few score of
bungalows and shacks set around the foot of a grim-looking eight-
storey tower. Two large windowless white structures, like big plastic
picnic boxes, are schools. As the plane settles for the last three
hundred feet of descent you might glance out of the port windows,
and on the rocky crags across the bay from the village is a remarkable

sight: a wall of bright orange polythene bags poised like an avalanche about to happen, with long ribbons of rusty brown seeping down to meet the sea ice. Next moment the wheels touch on the paved strip built by Strategic Air Command in the mid-1950s and it is only later that your romantic notions are shattered by the significance of what you have seen. It is known locally as Shitbag Hill.

When speaking of the North it is tempting to evoke images of the indomitable Eskimo hunter standing motionless with spear poised over a seal hole on the ice, or to picture the fearless polar bear that adorns every badge and crest from vehicle number plates to coats of arms and official letters. In fact, few people in the Arctic have ever seen a living polar bear in the wild, and hunters blaze away at seals with high-powered rifles. The true symbol of the North, one which flavours every aspect of daily life, is the ubiquitous polythene bag lining a tin pail in nine out of ten Arctic bathrooms – the "honey bag". And one of the first things you find out about the Arctic is that there are no holds barred when it comes to getting rid of your honey bags.

In the Canadian Arctic and Greenland most honey bags are collected and replaced regularly by council workers. In small settlements the daily progress of the honey truck comprises about one third of the vehicular traffic, the remainder being trucks delivering water and heating fuel. The system works well enough most of the time. Indoors the odours are contained by the throat-cloying camouflage of Misto-Van or Pine-Sol disinfectants. When the honey trucks break down, as most machinery does in the Arctic, or are prevented by snowdrifts from making their rounds, householders tie up their honey bags (failing to leave sufficient overlap for the bag to be gathered and tied is a mistake the Arctic pioneer makes only once) and put them outside where they freeze hard. It is common to see walls of honey bags stacked up like bricks outside every house. While frozen the contents are sterile and inoffensive but they tend to be buried by snow, the polythene becomes brittle in the cold and at the touch of a dog or child, or when the collector appears wearing a rubber apron over his parka, the bags split.

In Frobisher the honey trucks tip their contents from the top of the ridge making an orange blaze on the dark rock directly opposite the village. The bags are biodegradable in sunlight, and after the first few days of summer a winter's worth oozes down the slope into the bay where it forms a scum that drifts a few hundred yards across the harbour to the low tide sand and mudflats where children play, summer hunters and campers load freighter canoes, and barges unload bulk goods shipped north in the summer sea-lift.

Greenlanders are more sophisticated about it. Some communities have large incinerators for the purpose, others have special ramps built over the sea like lifeboat houses in English seaside coves where honey bags are slashed so their contents spill into the sea and the plastic is burned.

In Barrow, Alaska, the honey bucket system is combined with one using pails. Bathroom pails are emptied into an open-ended gas barrel (fuel drum) on the roadside in front of the house. Once in a few days a tanker truck comes along and the barrels are baled out by hand, an operation which a blind man can detect from a mile distant. Until recently the tundra around Barrow was dotted with thousands of barrels. People collected them for use as sewage tanks; when full they were dragged out on the sea-ice where they were carried away to Russia, sank, or were returned to the town beach by storms. In summer and fall barrels had to be abandoned on the land, and it became increasingly difficult to find ones that were not partly filled. Sewage from the school and hospital is emptied into a lagoon in the centre of town; the lagoon is separated by only a few feet of shingle from the town's water reservoir.

The honey bag is a symbol not only of the Arctic, but of White society's inability to come to terms with living there. We can use satellites to keep tabs on polar bears wandering over sea-ice, build a pipeline to carry hot oil over frozen tundra, and bring self-dial telephones to remote communities of only a few hundred people. When all is said and done, the civilisation which Whites have brought to the Arctic is only a plastic bag ahead of the traditional squat in the snow.

The reason the Arctic is one of the few remaining parts of the Western world yet to be "saved" by the Great American Bathroom is the permanently frozen condition of the ground, known as permafrost. The steady temperature of the ground, below surface influences, is approximately the same as average air temperature. At the tree-line, where the mean air temperature averages freezing point, permafrost becomes continuous and gets deeper as you go north; at Resolute the ground is frozen 1,300 feet down. In some places the ground comprises huge wedges or sheets of ice, as solid as rock until it melts. Permafrost is impervious to water, so a cesspit simply freezes as it fills and does not allow the contents to soak away. Even if you can dig the iron-hard ground for a pit privy, that standby of frontier life is made rapidly obsolete by its contents rising in a perfect stalagmite.

At Barrow, Alaska, in an operation a blind man could detect at a mile's distance, municipal workers bale out raw sewage from the open-ended drums at every front gate.

In fact, future archaeologists will probably conclude that people of today's snow-go culture worshipped body wastes, since they preserved them so carefully and tidily in the permafrost. One of the little pleasantries of life reserved for Arctic archaeologists excavating middens outside dwellings of prehistoric Eskimos is the smell. As the top layer of the excavation is thawed and carefully scraped away, human and dog wastes and old meat are exposed along with artifacts, and the researcher will always be found sitting on the up-wind side, frequently with notebook in one hand and the other holding a handkerchief over the nose.

Icebergs of bath and dish water released on the ground are a distinctive feature of any Arctic settlement. Waste water builds up beneath the houses then stretches in wide slippery tongues – streaked with ketchup and spaghetti – across the road. In Pangnirtung the iceberg outside the hotel was so big that kids were using it as a hockey rink.

The only satisfactory system of dealing with sewage in permafrost is by using heated pipes (which also have to be insulated to prevent the heat from melting the permafrost), or using a "utilidor", an insulated wooden trunk which carries pipes for water and sewage that are prevented from freezing by a third set of pipes bringing hot water for central heating. The utilidor often criss-crosses the village in long wooden tunnels, raised above ground on piles, like a second network of streets. Roads climb over it on hump-backed bridges and steps are provided for pedestrians. Costing five hundred dollars a foot to install and one million a year to run, it is more expensive than the houses it serves. In Barrow the new utilidor will cost thirty thousand dollars a connection. Most of the eighty-odd Quonsets of the Naval laboratory there are connected by a white-painted, coffin-like utilidor at power-pole height. This means all wastes have to be pumped up to it, and to carry out repairs you need a very long ladder which is no joke in a bitter Arctic wind. Worse, it dominates the sky as the bleakest industrial monument in a place that already has the air of a Siberian labour camp, and people spend their lives literally in its shadow.

The commode crisis discommodes Whites in the Arctic far more than the cold does. If you were really roughing it the discomforts would be part of the adventure and at least would furnish raw material for your memoirs, but such discomforts are hard to accept in the setting of a centrally heated modern house, in a bathroom well stocked with such miracles of consumerism as striped toothpaste, soap on a rope, and scented tissues, which these days can be purchased at any Arctic trading post worth the name of a supermarket. But this is just one example of the inadequacies of the ill-adapted technology imported from the South and expected to make life tick over in the Arctic as blissfully as it does in city suburbs.

Although they are large on the map and accessible only by hours of travel, Arctic communities are strikingly small. An office building in downtown Toronto contains more people than any community in the Canadian Arctic. Populations are counted in hundreds rather than tens of thousands, and more than half the people in the Arctic are either at school, should be at school, or are coming up to school age. The North Slope of Alaska for instance, administered as a borough, is larger than any but nine of the states in USA. It has a population of about nine thousand of whom 5,500 are oil-patch workers on shift at Prudhoe Bay, 2,200 live in Barrow, and the remainder live in nine villages of which Point Hope (population 402) is the largest. In the Canadian Arctic only Inuvik and Frobisher have more than two thousand people and most communities north of the tree-line have fewer than six or seven hundred.

Despite its great size Greenland's communities are small and crowded. One-third of the population lives in apartments, at a density nearly as great as that of resettlement blocks in Hong Kong. Built on steep rocky slopes around harbours sheltered by outlying skerries and islands, Greenlandic communities in summer have the air of Cornish fishing villages. Centre of each village is the quay with its official buildings, relics of the colonial days when Greenland was a closed country. Here you find the barn-red buildings of the Royal Greenland Trade Department (warehouse, store, fish-plant, travel offices), the slate-blue buildings of the Greenland Technical Organisation (power plant, workshops), and the mustard-yellow health clinic or hospital. Some of the early warehouses and timber dwelling houses are two and a half centuries old, and in every village one official building has a large number written in mosaic tiles on each side of its steeply pitched roof, to aid aircraft navigators during the Second World War. Around the long-standing official buildings small wood-frame houses are perched everywhere on the rocks. Painted bright colours they are knitted together by a maze of pipes carrying cables for power, telephone, television and – for the few rich enough to pay for it – water, fuel oil and sewage. Supported on wood blocks the rickety pipes criss-cross everywhere. Long and tortuous flights of wooden stairs serve as pavements. If more than three houses are served by one wooden walkway or stairway the snow and ice is cleared by local council workers, otherwise you do it yourself.

Hanging out in the chill air from a window in each house is a plastic shoping bag containing butter and cheese, and racks of drying fish. Unlike Canada, people in this part of the Arctic seem to manage without refrigerators. Every village has a wooden church of elegant simplicity, painted barn-red and roofed in wooden shingles coloured a vivid old-copper green. The cottages are pretty to look at but awful to live in, for they are badly insulated and water has to be obtained from tap houses. Yet the vast blocks of apartments have the air of a refugee camp, and make the place seem one to which you are sentenced.

While Greenlanders inhabit rocky niches in a vertical landscape people in all but a few communities of the North American Arctic live in a world of flatness – a landscape, wrote Robert Service, "rubbed and licked and smoothed as smooth as a shaven pate". For eyes not yet adjusted to the values of Arctic distance and scale it hits

Perched on bare rock with no water, no drains, heat only from oil stoves and poor insulation, this meaner type of cottage is typical of many in Greenland which generally speaking has the best housing in the Arctic.

you as a vista of unremitting monotony. Unless you get to grips with the landscape personally, and slog over it on foot or by snow machine, its nuances are hidden.

Greenland villages at least have a natural orientation towards the sea: the fishing boats in the harbour and dog-teams pegged out on the green slopes are used at different times of year in the same business of supplying the fish factory on the quay. But North American Arctic communities – a few rows of matchbox-like houses joined by pencil lines of trodden snow – have no visible means of support. The people do not seem to be busy at anything, and when a plane comes in many of them take a ride out to the airstrip to see who is coming in.

Until the early 1970s an Arctic traveller was greeted at an airstrip by howls and yips of dog teams wreathed in steam from their panting. Now, in Canada, true Eskimo dogs have declined almost to the point of extinction and when the plane's engines shut down the sound you hear is the mutter of idling two-stroke engines from a troop of El Tigrés, Sno-cats, Panteras and other "iron-dog" snow machines parked haphazardly beneath rising plumes of exhaust smoke.

The largest building in any Canadian Arctic settlement is invariably the school, centrally situated among houses in close, straight lines because that is the way the powerlines were laid out. The oldest building, with white-painted weatherboards and a red roof, is the Hudson's Bay Company store with its satellite warehouses (separated in case of fire) and houses for manager and clerks. Established as trading posts in the first half of this century, the stores became the nuclei around which settlements evolved, preceding even the missionaries, and the company was known from its initials as Here Before Christ. Every settlement has its nursing station, and a garage where snow-clearing graders and bulldozers, and trucks or half-tracks that deliver water and collect honey bags, are kept warm. The powerhouse is identified by its smoke-stacks and the rumble of Caterpillar diesel engines, while nearby are the large steel fuel tanks filled up once a year by tanker.

Houses are identical in every settlement because they come from the South complete, or in kit-set form. The largest ones, of two floors, belong to the schoolteachers who comprise the majority of about twenty Whites in any settlement, the others being Hudson's Bay staff, policeman, priest, game officer, government services officer, power man and a couple of nurses. Snowdrifts reach almost to the roofs which provide the only snow-free playgrounds and are used for storing such things as frozen caribou carcasses and bicycles. Pink cards in house windows are signals for the water truck to call: sometimes it comes twice a day if the operator can start the engine. Powerpoles stand like withered pot plants in large tubs made of corrugated iron filled with rocks, because the ground is too hard for holes to be dug for them.

In the clinical whiteness of the blanket of snow that covers everything with a sterile shroud, the communities resemble hospital wards. Houses in tidy lines, like beds. Everything provided, from television brought in by satellite to shopping trolleys and (in schools) boot laces and Kleenex. Whites serve the community in custodian roles and tend to remain apart, like ward nurses. Due to the weight of clothing, and the biting air, people walk in unnatural attitudes, hunched or shuffling like geriatrics. At night, lights radiate softly from frosted-up windows like diffused bed-head reading lights, the red fire alarm lights on the power poles glow brightly, and, like a ward at midnight, the Arctic silence is ever restless. When settling down to sleep you can identify the different engine noises that sustain life in the Arctic suburbs – the roar of the space heater, the clatter of the fan pushing warm air through galvanised air ducts running through every room at ceiling level, and the ticking as the heat expands the metal; the rattle of the water pump when a tap is turned on, the hum of fridge and deep-freeze, the distant mutter of diesels in the powerhouse.

Day and night the aimless driving of snow machines irritates like the sound of lawnmowers on a peaceful southern Sunday. The high-pitched whine of over-revved two-stroke engines, some without silencers, hardly ever stops. When hunters come in from the land their wives and kids drive round and round for the sheer pleasure of movement, like teenagers with new motorbikes.

A snow machine is a motorised toboggan driven by a wide rubber belt and steered by a pair of runners. You sit astride the engine, steering by handlebars and sheltered by a windscreen as if riding a motorcycle on skids instead of wheels. Known as the Skidoo or snowmobile in Canada, snow-go in the Yukon and parts of Alaska, and universally as snow machine, it was developed initially as a toy, a recreation vehicle for winter sport. For the Arctic it has done what the Model T Ford did for middle America, though with some disastrous results. Rapid transport has killed the art of building igloos and other traditional Eskimo skills, permitted over-hunting of caribou, changed a hunting lifestyle irrevocably into one of cash and carry, and has caused the near extinction of sled dogs bred for power and endurance rather than speed. Like any other engine a snow machine can break down, and when this happens far from home travellers cannot eat it, cuddle up to it for warmth, or let it find its own way home as they could a dog team. Breakdowns have caused a number of deaths and now wise hunters travel with lots of spare parts on their sledges, and also escort each other.

Designed as fun machines, for speed and dash at the expense of power, towing ability, sturdiness and reliability, few modern snow machines are appropriate for the job they are expected to do in the Arctic: it's like using a sports car as a jeep. Suspension is very hard and with legs bent almost double it is difficult to cushion shocks to the spine. Travelling long distances with broken mufflers has caused many cases of deafness. In the Arctic a snow machine costing about $2,500 rarely lasts more than two winters.

The Hudson's Bay store provides all the essential support of a suburban lifestyle, from frozen food to birthday cards. Prices are set when goods arrive in bulk by barge in summer and remain unchanged for a year. If the store runs out of an essential commodity it undertakes to fly in stock without passing on the very high cost of freight. Fresh produce, like tomatoes, lettuce, oranges and apples are flown in when possible and snapped up immediately. Everywhere in the Arctic, prices are horrifying. Ten pounds of sugar costing $1.86 in Washington DC cost $6.69 in Barrow, a 33¢ tube of toothpaste costs $1.44, and a $1.62 pound of steak costs just under four dollars.

A lot of housekeeping money can be saved by purchasing bulk supplies once a year and having them freighted north by ship or barge. Janet Lidstone, wife of RCMP Corporal Barry Lidstone* who polices forty thousand square miles of Arctic territory from Igloolik, sends an order south in early April and in August Barry collects it from the beach where it is unloaded down a ramp by fork-lift. Goods are supplied at cost plus ten per cent. Janet's summer order includes frozen meat worth seven hundred dollars, which is kept in three large freezers along with seven cases of frozen French fries, cases of ketchup, corn starch and peanut butter, three of pineapple chicken balls, four of blueberry muffins and – to last their two baby girls for the year – a whole case of marshmallows.

Nobody can be long in the Arctic without feeling disturbed by the image of junk in which the place and its people are being developed – junk food (every child seems to have its mouth full of potato crisps or candy), junk reading (Bay stores display "adult" magazines alongside comic books and pulp Westerns), junk clothing, junk entertainment (low-grade films hired from the South, or one-channel television). This problem does not affect only the Arctic, of course, but its effects are sinister because there are no alternatives. When the all-concealing snow begins to melt in spring Arctic communities are exposed – literally – as the junk heaps they are. The sight is scarcely credible.

In the space of about two weeks during May or June the icebergs of dishwater drain away or form sludgy lagoons with a scum of soap suds. Eight or nine months' worth of dog droppings deposited on successive layers of snow make a single pile. What truly staggers the imagination is the tide of litter. Every house is surrounded by tons of it: old snow machines and motorcycles, obsolete machinery such as washing machines and refrigerators, caribou antlers and uncured sealskins from winter hunting, pop cans by the million and masses of packing materials, off-cuts from building timber, and piles of soggy insulation padding which lie around like the entrails of whales. Litter

---

* A few months after I met him Cpl Lidstone was transferred to New Brunswick where he was murdered by a gunman on his first night of duty.

fills the roadside gullies and streambeds, and is scattered over the surrounding countryside as if a bomb has exploded in the centre of a municipal garbage dump and a few spaces have been cleared in the debris for building houses. On the day summer comes, and the community has its annual clean-up, the tide is reduced from knee to ankle depth, and everyone begins to yearn for winter freeze-up because the hot Arctic stinks.

In summer the top few inches of permafrost – the "active layer" – melts. Water collects in big pools because it cannot drain away, and unless the ground is gravelly it is invariably as soggy as a marsh. Yet there is scarcely enough water to drink. Nobody dies of thirst in the Arctic; at worst you can suck a piece of ice or go out on the tundra with a cup. But water is in extremely short supply, especially for services such as flushing and fire-fighting. If water is obtained from beneath the permafrost it can be so heavily mineralised it turns whisky black. Rivers tend to be shallow with braided channels where collecting water is difficult, and are dry most of the year except during the few days of break-up.

Most communities have to collect water by truck from a nearby lake. In summer the lakes are prone to contamination and the tea-coloured water has a high organic content that defies chlorination. In winter water can usually be obtained from beneath the surface ice, otherwise chunks of ice have to be sawn out. When delivered to houses the ice cakes are stacked outside where they are soon braceleted with collars of dog urine (hence the old Arctic saying, "Don't eat the yellow snow"). In a temperate zone a person uses about one hundred gallons of water a day. This would require eight hundred pounds of ice to be quarried, carried and melted. The melting alone would consume 1·1 gallons of fuel. The total effort for a family of six, requiring a couple of tons of ice a day, would be enormous.

In some communities with shaky water supplies, like Barrow and Eskimo Point, hepatitis is rife. Most Whites and many Eskimos go several miles out to cut their own ice for drinking, using delivered water only for washing and at the same time keeping their fridges full of pop.

Fierce cold, pitiless winds, dust, dryness, intense light, long darkness – in no context is the manner in which environmental conditions magnify the inadequacies of technology more evident than in design of houses. The perfect house can be designed and built but nobody will live in it, so every design must be a compromise between what you know won't work and what helps you to cope. For example, in terms of heating costs a window is ten to twenty times more expensive than an insulated wall panel, and the cost recurs annually for ever, but could you live without it? Even with *eight* panes of glass a window loses three times more heat than a six-inch insulated wall.

Besides losing heat in winter windows are almost useless in summer because the low sun shines straight in, day and night. Glare is intolerable and heat intense, so the windows through which you can see nothing during the dark winter are curtained off during the sun-lit summer.

The ideal Arctic dwelling has been in use for centuries. The snow house, or igloo, had a minimum ratio of surface area to volume, exactly what is needed to conserve heat. Within an hour the snow walls of an igloo sintered to provide a small fortress against wild animals and storms; a polar bear could walk over the top of it. An igloo was so sound proof that dogs could not be heard snapping outside but vibrations, from a dog fight or an approaching bear, could be "heard" from afar even when a gale was raging. The largest igloos could sleep twenty or more and had annexes opening off. Economising on seal-fat fuel rather than the inadequacies of snow houses themselves was what made the igloos cold. Technically, the domed igloo was perfect because if it had a window at all it was a tiny one made of seal membrane or transparent lake ice, and as it was entered by tunnel, virtually from below, the dome trapped and retained warm air. Stefansson told how he had to strip to his pantaloons and sit with sweat pouring off him, mopping it up with moss and sipping iced water.

In Frobisher an architect commissioned by ITC (the Eskimo native organisation) tried to adapt igloo technology and designed a two-floor domed house with a diameter of twenty-eight feet. But it was not easy filling a round house with square furniture, the upper floor became too warm while the lower floor was too cold, and tall people could not walk near the walls. Now it is not inhabited by Eskimos, for whom it was intended, but by a White staff member.

The door of an Arctic house should be like that of a walk-in deep-freeze, fitting over the outside of the frame. Conventional doors which continue to be used distort or break because snow and ice packs through the cracks, and the hinges act as cold conductors and on the inside grow mushrooms of ice. Arctic snow is hard and granular like gravel, and is as hard to push against, yet many doors open outwards. Little thought is given to wind or blowing snow. The north wall is coldest and darkest, and ideally should be used for storage with no openings. But most houses are designed and prefabricated in the South. On arrival they are installed on gravel pads to protect the permafrost and there is no way they can be oriented to

suit prevailing conditions, usually because the powerlines go in first
and houses have to be positioned with connection points nearest the
poles. Positioning is important because the storm wind – not necessarily the prevailing wind – is the one which clears the snowdrifts.
But in the North you are stuck with what you can get. Houses come
with windows on four sides and doors on two, and that's that.

Often the gravel pads have insufficient time to settle so prefabricated panels do not interlock, floors buckle, pinholes develop letting
in cold air and snow, and repairs are difficult and more expensive
because of the prefabricated mode of construction.

In the Arctic a vapour trap in the wall is essential, as is proper
ventilation. Air at 70 °F (21 °C) holds ten times as much moisture as
air at 10 °F (–16.°C), and a family of four produces twenty-five
pounds of moisture in cooking, washing and breathing. Also, burning a pound of fuel produces a pound of water as "ash"; consuming
350 gallons of heating fuel over a winter produces a ton. All this
water will stay in the house as ice unless there is proper ventilation.
Water vapour migrates towards cold until it reaches a cold wall
where it condenses. A single window pane, for example, is the same
temperature as the air outside. Steam in the air inside the house
touches the cold glass, condenses to water, then freezes. Within a few
weeks a large cauliflower-head of ice grows into the room. The same
thing happens when a child puts a foot through an insulation panel,
causing the entire panel to become saturated with ice, or when air
seeps into the attic through cracks in the ceiling lining. Snow
accumulating on the roof acts as insulation so an ice-filled attic
begins to warm up and the ice melts, leaking through the ceiling.
Residents then suppose the roof is leaking and clear the snow. The
attic gets cold again and the ice freezes so the leak stops. But all the
time the trouble is caused by *internal* leaks – allowing moist air to
reach the attic. In most houses the polythene sheeting that serves as a
vapour trap is an exercise in futility because anything fitted to the
walls drives a nail right through it, and the sheeting itself is fitted
with staples; in the attic you find an inverted icicle over every nail
hole, and in summer this ice melts, seeping into the insulation.

The contempt which architects seem to reserve for the Arctic is
particularly evident in Alaska where most houses provided for
Eskimos by the Bureau of Indian Affairs are designed in Albuquer-
que, New Mexico. Glass buildings are chic in most parts of the world
but you can't live with them in the Arctic because the windows have
to be curtained to keep them warm in winter, and covered with
aluminium foil to keep them cool in summer. Yet they are erected in
the Arctic as if architects thought it was part of California. In the

A municipal problem in the Arctic is how to get rid of the dead. In Greenland graves are chipped out of granite with pneumatic hammers or (as shown here) a small patch of swampy ground is available. Plastic flowers are scrubbed once a year with Daz.

high-rises of the University of Alaska, in Fairbanks, every south-facing window is covered up with newspaper, curtains or foil. No concessions are made to winter: few of the buildings are connected by passageways for pedestrians, and parking lots are a long way off, yet tunnels do exist to carry central heating pipes. Many private homes have been designed on ranch-style lines with floor to ceiling windows and open beam ceilings: nice, cool houses for Texas or Florida, but in Alaska so totally unsuitable that owners have to cover the windows with thick bricks of expanded polystyrene during the winter, and lower blinds to cover them in summer.

Architects are also contemptuous (or ignorant) of permafrost. Time and again houses with heated basements have been built on permafrost, and within a few months the ground has literally melted away from beneath them. In Apex, a satellite community of Frobisher, melting permafrost excavated a six-foot hole beneath the concrete floor of the fire station and one day the fire truck just dropped into it. Other problems can afflict fire trucks. At Resolute there was a slow leak in its fire truck's water tank which was not noticed until there was a fire call and the vehicle couldn't move because it was frozen to the ground, hub-deep in ice.

Fire burns better in the Arctic because materials become dry. Many fires are caused by over-enthusiastic efforts with a blowtorch to thaw unlagged water pipes (a hair dryer or reversed vacuum cleaner is better). Once fire starts it is hard to stop due to lack of water and the fact that fire extinguishers are useless in deep cold.

Another municipal problem is burial of the dead. Upward pressure in the permafrost due to accumulating water, called frost heave, tends to pop the coffins back up. On Herschel Island, used as a whaling base at the turn of the century, long-dead whalers have had to be reburied several times. At Inuvik graves are dug in summer, when the ground is soft, and bodies are covered with a six-inch slab of concrete to keep them down. In Greenland the graves chipped out of the granite with pneumatic hammers are decorated with plastic flowers which fade in the sunshine.

Outside Frobisher and Inuvik cars are rare in the Canadian Arctic. The average life of a vehicle is only two or three years because cold splits vinyl and plastic fittings, makes flat spots on tyres and affects the engines. A vehicle might have a few miles on the clock but thousands of hours of unregistered running because engines are often kept going all winter. When some visiting Ford engineers asked a rental truck operator in Inuvik whether he had winter starting problems they were told, "Oh no, the engines went fine when we started them – four months ago."

Telsat brings colour television and long-distance telephone to most places in the Canadian Arctic, although the system is split between two commercial companies and east–west calls are routed several thousand miles by way of southern Canada. Oil companies in the Arctic keep permanent lines open via the satellite so they can direct-dial anywhere in North America from drilling rigs on the polar ice. In Greenland telephone and radio services have long been delayed due to interference caused by the vertical nature of the geography and national networks are now being set up. Television is available in most communities, provided by "pirates" who record programmes on cassettes in Copenhagen and airmail them to TV and radio shops with transmission equipment in Greenland. The operation is strictly illegal but the government turns a blind eye because a service is provided at no public cost. Every night the names of those who do not pay their fees are broadcast on the screen between programmes.

Alaska has made the least electronic progress of all. Until 1971 the only communication was by way of HF radio. Then ordinary taxi-cab radios were converted to bounce signals off the NASA applications technology satellite and a network was established to link health centres in twenty-six villages. Today villages are being equipped with a new RCA satellite communications system and the State government is planning to install a vast computerised communications system, with satellite-linked data terminals in every village which can be used for telephone, television and telex, plus village business, administration records, health records, library and information services and education – it would enable, say, a child with a skin complaint to be treated via satellite by a specialist in Seattle, or a senior student in one small community to link into an appropriate education course without having to leave home. At this stage it seems to be a case of technology gone mad, because only five of the nine North Slope villages have a power supply.

When Bob Pilot, now an official in the Government of the Northwest Territories, first came to the Arctic in 1953 it was as a young RCMP constable stationed in Frobisher. At that time there were seventeen Eskimos and a run-down military base with a gravel runway. "When the ship sounded its siren and left, that was it, for a whole year," he says. A Mountie was then a kind of government granny and nursemaid, helping babies into the world, pulling teeth, dispensing medicine, helping with income tax forms, paying old age pensions and welfare cheques to widows, organising search parties for missing hunters, issuing hunting licences, running a Post Office (the service was at most a monthly one), and registering births and

deaths. In ten years as an Arctic Mountie Bob Pilot never had to deal
with a criminal case.

Then the airstrip was extended to take SAC bombers, Eskimos
flooded into the settlement and a government centre was established.
In the late 1950s architects drew plans for a domed town centre
surrounded by thirty-six apartment towers in groups of three, the
centre to be heated to a comfortable temperature and laid out with
tundra gardens. Frobisher promised "to be a town which will make
all Canada – all the world probably – think again about living and
working in the North".

Today Constable Ted Kelly, aged twenty-three, is one of a dozen
policemen in Frobisher. There had been a distemper epidemic
amongst the dogs kept as pets in the village, and because the bylaws
prohibited discharge of firearms within village limits the Mounties
were being called out ten or twenty times a day to collect an animal,
take it to the garbage dump, and put a bullet in its head. "Shooting
dogs and putting drunks to bed isn't police work but that's what we
spend most of our time doing," he said "Once we were an important
person around here. Now we're just that cop."

The jobs which Bob Pilot and other solitary constables like him
did for small groups of Eskimos like those in Frobisher are now done
by about two hundred civil servants who administer a region of
fourteen small communities scattered over an area larger than western Europe. The futuristic domed city once visualised for Frobisher
has developed into an eight-floor high-rise inhabited by administrators, teachers, policemen and their families, a dreary luggage-
locker existence in a small complex containing a cinema, swimming
pool, stores and a few small shops including an ice cream parlour
(who said you couldn't sell ice cream to Eskimos?). The dim yellow
corridors are haunted by listless children and teenagers and covered
with graffiti (*Itetsaaq was sik here, R. Kadlutsiak was here today*). The
place is seedy, smelly and stale, and its windows overlook the Eskimo
houses, the sound, and that visual reminder of a half-baked and
inadequate lifestyle which White people have imposed on the Arctic
– Shitbag Hill. There may be romance and adventure in the Arctic,
but it is not found in the places where Whites have made their mark.

4

HELL FOR BREAKFAST

*... With maple syrup for
the chosen frozen: White people
living and working the Arctic*

For seven hours we drilled through the white sky northwards from Winnipeg. The Hudson's Bay men read *Penthouse* and ate boxed lunches – prawn salad, homogenised milk, after-dinner mint. Polished like a new car and emblazoned with the company's logo in old English lettering, the Twin Otter was taking regional manager Ed Spracklin on a tour of his stores in the central Arctic, and travelling with him to new posts were two clerks. Refuelling stops had shown the gradually changing nature of the terrain: Thompson, where feathery snow fluttered into deep soft drifts between gaunt, black conifers, and Churchill, where snow eddied like dust between trees stunted and twisted by the rigours of near-Arctic cold. Now we seemed to be landing in the middle of a cloud. There was a reassuring glimpse of an oil drum suspended in the blur of whiteness, apparently marking the edge of a runway. Then a bump followed by a lurch as the props reversed, and after swaying over ridges of snow we stopped and switched off. Outside the window the one object on which to focus was the plane's own wheel, its shallow track already being built into a row of patterned pyramids by the blown snow skimming along at hub-cap height. With his three-piece businessman's suit only slightly rumpled, Ed Spracklin zipped his legs into quilted wind pants, thrust his shoes into fur-lined over-boots, and zipped a bulky down-filled parka right up to his chin.

Roofs are tied down with steel hausers anchored in the frozen ground at Pangnirtung, near the southern tip of Baffin Island, one of the loveliest spots in the Arctic; a recent storm blew half the Hudson's Bay store over the sea ice.

Then, shoving his hands into deep fleecy gauntlets he nodded to the co-pilot who opened the rear door.

The breeze came in like a spray of razor blades. The bleary warmth vanished in an instant and because I had been slow in following Ed's example the sub-zero chill caught me in a breath-taking clinch. Through the window I glimpsed Ed sidling round the aircraft keeping his back to a wind which was producing a chill factor equivalent to about −65 °F (−54 °C). Only his nose, rather pink, and his eyes, three-quarters closed, were visible in the circle made by the fur trim of his parka hood. Shaken by the intensity of the in-rushing cold, and moving clumsily in bulky boots and padded clothes, I stumbled after him out into the burning Arctic. The wind brought a tart tingle to the skin, like a body-rub with horse liniment. A bar of fierce cold, burning like hot metal, lay against my front where the wind came through the zip of my parka because I had failed to fasten the flap over it. My wrists wore hot bracelets because I had not tucked my cuffs into the tops of my gloves. I stood numbly outside the aircraft and like a radar scanner rotated on the spot.

The snow lay in hard runs and ripples, like a sea petrified in mid-squall. On the far side of the plane a shed was banked up with snowdrifts and the pilots were trying to get in to find an electrical connection to keep their engines warm overnight. Nothing else was in sight except a single incongruous street light. During the long flight I had been cynically amused at the differences between image and reality: where was the dog whip over the shoulder, the wolf-skin coat, the pemmican? One of these heroes of the frozen north had actually used the jack-knife on his belt when opening the vacuum-sealed cheese in his lunch box. Now, totally humbled and moving stiffly with face averted from the eye-cutting wind, I prayed we wouldn't have to walk anywhere.

Out of the skim-milk haze a covered truck appeared and backed up. Though bound for stores farther north all our cargo had to be taken out of the aircraft, the cases of Carnation milk in case they froze up, boxes of bullets and bags of cash for security. Alan Robertson, a burly Scot who managed the store at Eskimo Point, loaded the truck with his hood thrown back, no gloves, and the wind blowing drips off the end of his pink nose. Lending a hand as best I could I learned my first lesson of the Arctic, that heat is more difficult to handle than cold. A few minutes of exertion turned up the thermostat inside my clothes but when I unzipped my parka the cold wrapped in like a stainless steel vest. Needlessly frightened of it, I zipped up to my chin again, and cooked. When we came to the big cardboard boxes that had been in the tail the young clerks, Tom and Chris, handled them through the wind-whipped snow with the gingerliness a fur trader might once have applied to his year's supply of whisky. These modern adventurers were proofing themselves against polar solitariness in a different kind of way, for the boxes bore the labels of Sony and National Panasonic – amplifiers, tuners, turntables, speakers, tapes, records. Today the call of the North comes in stereo.

The compartment on the back of the pick-up was insulated, like a walk-in freezer. This was not to keep produce frozen while Alan ferried it from airstrip to store, but to *prevent* it from freezing. It was through the narrow crack of its back door held open with an out-thrust boot, as the vehicle slithered over the snowdrifts and dish-water icebergs, that I had my first sight of an Arctic settlement. Only the black meat speckled with frost on the rooftops, and the pyramids of yellow ice decorating the foot of every powerpole, like border gardens of wallflowers, made it real, otherwise it could have been a Lego village set out on a flat counterpane. A snow machine zoomed up behind, a hooded Eskimo, wearing sunglasses and chewing gum, driving erect, one knee on the seat steadying a carry-bag from which a six-pack of Coke and a bundle of frozen TV dinners protruded. Blipping the throttle impatiently he tried to overtake, changed his mind, then bounced over a snow ridge and took off across country.

The store manager's house on the foreshore over-looked a vast expanse of furrowed ice only a little harder and glossier in texture than the pasty, darkening clouds. There was a big unheated porch where we took off our boots and parkas, and brushed the snow out of our hair. The lounge had a colour TV in front of a black padded swivel chair, and a blue chesterfield that was to be my bed for the night. Ed Spracklin's men knew their manager's whims: Alan had a leg of lamb ready roasted in the oven and a packet of instant mash in his parka pocket. Within five minutes Ed himself had the potato whipped up, a jug of hot gravy on the table and the roast ready to carve. Setting the pattern that he was to follow at each of the seven places where we stopped for two or three nights, he had also gone directly to the fridge and removed the half-dozen opened and half-used tins of Carnation growing grey stuff round their rims. Ed learned his Arctic house-keeping the hard way: at the age of fifteen he had been put ashore at a trading post on Baffin Island in 1950 by a ship that stayed a day and did not come back for a year. Apprenticed to a trader, he spent two hours a day learning *Inuktitut*, the Eskimo language, well enough to transmit and receive in Morse code; he mined his own coal, set his own trap lines, hunted seal and caribou for his own survival and to feed his dog team, and traded packets of sugar, tea, flour and tobacco for seal and fox pelts. At that time Eskimos visited the posts by dog team, built an igloo outside, and spent two or three days doing their shopping. Now Ed runs a chain of Arctic supermarkets selling everything from rifles to custard powder, carburettors to buckets of ready-cooked chicken, and Eskimos came shopping by snow machine sometimes two or three times a day.

With darkness the wind died and the blowing snow settled; the night was black but clear, the snow a luminous grey beneath a speckle of stars. At the furthest reach of the house lights three parka-clad figures were industriously digging a large hole in the snow, and every few minutes during dinner Alan looked out at them and shook his head in disbelief. Fifteen minutes before the store closed three young Eskimos had come in with enough cash to put down as deposit on a $2,000 snow machine. Alan had five of them in crates which had drifted up outside, and told the lads he would have one dug out and assembled for them in the morning. But that wouldn't do. "They had the cash and wanted a Skidoo," said Alan, "so I took the money and gave them a shovel." It was midnight when the crate was finally cleared sufficiently for the sides to be ripped off and the snow machine assembled on the spot then fuelled, oiled, started up, and driven out of the hole.

"You'll be selling refrigerators to the Eskimos at this rate," I said to Ed next morning, when describing how my illusions had been pricked by the discovery of what you might call a snow-go culture.

"That's not likely," he replied, fitting a cigarette into a short black holder. Then he snapped his lighter and added, "but not for the reasons you might think."

"Why then?"

"Well, most Eskimo families already have refrigerators, provided free by the government. But swimming pools – now there's a selling problem!"

Walking around the settlement for the first time I encountered other people on foot who beamed friendly though frankly curious welcomes from within the cocoons of beautifully embroidered traditional-style duffel parkas trimmed with soft white fur of Arctic fox or stiff orange and brown mane of Arctic wolf. They wore hand-sewn tasselled *mukluks* or sealskin *kamiks* on their feet. These people were not Eskimos but Whites, usually schoolteachers. Their parkas cost around three hundred dollars in craft shops. They wear rings of walrus ivory carved in shapes of polar bears or seals, ivory toggles around their necks, and the mantelpieces in their homes groan beneath half a hundredweight of soapstone carvings.

The Eskimos were the people driving around on snow machines, wearing quilted nylon parkas, Levis, Army surplus boots, plaid shirts, and brightly coloured baseball caps bearing trade-names like Honda, Caterpillar, or Chevrolet. The Eskimo dresses like a Canadian working man because that is what The Bay sells him. While teachers ape traditional Eskimos, young Eskimos live in the image of what they see on television, wearing jeans, hockey shirts, wind cheaters, and Indian-style headbands.

Eskimos nod in a friendly way and steal sidelong glances as they go by. Kids playing on the roofs and sliding on the snow-drifts shout "Hi John!" whatever your name might be and don't mind posing for pictures but adults bristle visibly at sight of a raised camera and react with a stolid dignity that somehow commands more respect than ordinary shyness or hostility: when snatching pictures you have to be thick-skinned not to be discouraged by such formidable reserve. It dissolves a little with time, especially if you can be introduced by somebody they know well. In their minds I was never the visitor from England but "the guy who came in with The Bay" and in this role it was easier to be accepted. The Arctic has become such a goldfish bowl for different kinds of social scientists that it is commonly said a typical Eskimo family consists of Mum, Dad, four kids and an anthropologist. Yet it is the Eskimo way never to demonstrate curiosity. In their eyes inquisitiveness is the height of discourtesy and one reason for their reserve might be that they know only too well a stranger opens his mouth only to ask questions.

It doesn't take long to discover that Eskimos are not as interested in you as you are in them, and you never really overcome the image of the usual White "instant expert" who flies in, makes a screw-up, and flies out again. Eskimos neither initiate contact with strangers nor invite them spontaneously into their homes, although they are by no means inhospitable or unwelcoming if you take the initiative and go visiting. After trial and error I found I could make contact best by asking outright if I might visit at a certain time – "I'd like to come and see you around three o'clock, will you be at home?" – and did not confuse them with explanations about my purpose: it was better to play the role they expected and be flagrantly curious and naïve. They answered questions willingly, and offered cups of tea, but seldom volunteered a remark. It is the Eskimo way not to be frightened of lapses in conversation, but even making allowances for this a conversation is invariably one-sided. Whites are proud of the way they bend over backwards to accommodate the differences but Eskimos do not pretend to do so, as if they were saying, "You don't realise how different we really are."

Eskimos are among the most studied people on earth, any library containing a wealth of literature about their traditional way of life, but it is a way of life that has been transformed within a couple of decades, as explained in Part III, and no literature is up to date. Consequently many Whites who bone up on the subject before arriving to work in the Arctic have a romantic, unrealistic and distorted picture of what they will find. The titles alone suggest a stern, unforgiving and rigorous way of life: *The Howling Arctic, Hell on Ice, Land of Ice and Darkness, Land of the White Death*, to name but a few.

At Hall Beach a small Eskimo plays with a toboggan on the edge of the frozen sea on a typical early spring day. At temperatures of −40° children happily play outside. One in three children suffers from chronic ear infection and in most settlements it is safer to drink pop than water, due to risk of hepatitis.

The types of Eskimo described in such books no longer exist. In fact, modern Eskimos are better fed, better schooled, better housed and are healthier than poor Whites in the South, and if they don't feel like paying the rent they don't. Also, people get a misleading picture of actual living conditions. The gold-panning poet of the Yukon, Robert Service, wrote glowingly of the deathly cold, stillness, brilliant beauty and toughness of life in the North and people go there with his words ringing in their ears: "It's the hell served up for breakfast that's hard..."

In this respect most Whites are disappointed. Faye and Ross Janusaitis, schoolteachers at Igloolik, were warned by the education department official who briefed them to expect snow blowing through their windows and a hard life pitted against the elements. So prepared were they to confront the wilderness at its worst that they brought colouring books for the native children, and household necessities like rubber bands. What they found were Eskimos with transistor radios, snow machines and pocket calculators living in square houses with hot and cold running water. There was no snow blowing into their apartment, which was furnished down to the last drape, and the only disaster during their first winter occurred when The Bay ran out of toys a week before Christmas and the DC3 chartered to fly in an emergency consignment was socked in at Churchill.

"We were almost hoping to get hell served up for breakfast," said Ross, a Latvian-born Canadian, "but all we got was maple syrup."

"And only one brand to choose from," added his Australian wife drily.

Until the mid-1950s – the "old days" – White people in the Arctic lived on the fringes of Eskimo life and left behind them everything but a few modern comforts like matches and warm underwear. Now it is Eskimos who live on the fringes of an urban style of life, while the Whites who come to the Arctic bring everything with them. Teachers and other civil servants posted to the North are allowed to bring three hundred pounds weight of baggage with them on the aircraft, plus a couple of tons forwarded free of charge by ship or barge at the first summer resupply. Once inside a typical White house you could be anywhere in suburban North America. The diet of a schoolteacher or store-keeper in the Arctic is no different from that of a person in Ottawa except that fresh fruit and vegetables are harder to obtain.

The Arctic has always been a magnet exerting a mysterious force on the spirit of adventurous men: in the past it presented a challenge to the courage and endurance of the individual whose commitment to it had to be total, for once winter came there was no going back. Today it has something of a new-style gold rush about it where all that glisters is found in government and oil company pay packets. Survival is no longer in question, unless you speak in terms of corporate finance, for the real risks are run in company board-rooms. The overwhelming majority of Whites are in the Arctic for money or science, and only a small proportion for the fun or challenge of it. Outside the settlements it is a stockade existence, like living in a barracks, where some people manage to spend months at a time without ever going out of doors, winter or summer. The chain of Distant Early Warning radar stations (the DEW-line), where several thousand men are scattered in remote outposts across the breadth of North America and Greenland along roughly the 70th parallel, is the classic example. Men are flown in by their own airliners for four months of duty, with one off, and lead a reclusive existence in electronic ghettos so quiet and private, and distant from the real life of the Arctic, that (apart from the mess they leave behind them) you can forget they exist. Their lives are so quiet, one man told me, that the biggest problem is finding something to say in letters home – "A plane woke me at 2am . . ." One supervisor boasted that in thirteen years he had never been out of sight of the buildings.

The oil industry presents a more vigorous image, especially in publicity and advertising in the South, perpetuating the Victorian concept of an Arctic environment to be conquered, endured or resisted – a harsh life at the very frontier of survival. In fact oil men are superbly insulated from all the qualities that made the old way of life in the Arctic so demanding, such as hard travel, unremitting toil, long periods of loneliness, monotonous food and time periods measured in months, not days. It can be tough getting the job done, certainly, but it is not especially difficult to survive.

The modern oil man spends at least one or two weeks at home every month, is supported by every conceivable engine and technological device, and many men working in camps never have to don a parka until it is time to walk out to the plane flying them home. Even in sunny and warm weather off-duty crews seldom take an opportunity to walk about on the tundra or to do a little fishing, preferring to watch films in a stuffy, smoke-filled "rec" room and count down the days until the jet arrives. The Arctic is a place to beat, boast about ("It's hell up there!") and make money in – a place to be exploited, than abandoned.

Every summer scores of scientists fly north to carry out research but few come in contact with Eskimos. Bases for scientists tend to be removed from communities. Typical scientific field camps – sleeping tents dotted around a larger cook-tent, generator running in a shelter, flag rippling from the radio pole, Twin Otter strip marked out with bags of rocks – are as much a White stockade as the oil camps. There are half a dozen different Heinz dressings on the table and, if not a deep-freeze, there is at least a hole in the permafrost filled with frozen steaks. It is many years since a scientist has had to hunt seal or caribou for his dinner, but the Arctic remains a huge scientific adventure playground where you can live rough, enjoy wild country, and get paid for it while also furthering a career. Camping in the Arctic in summer can be harsh and uncomfortable, with mist, freezing rain, and marauding polar bears: hypothermia is as much of a risk in summer as frostbite in winter.

Scientists are nursemaided by fleets of helicopters and STOL aircraft which take them where they want to go without any kind of struggle against the environment. You can always pick out first-timers in the land of the midnight sun because they have flashlights in their kit. When the going gets tough and the place begins to freeze up practically all scientists pack their gear and fly home sporting beards, jack-knives, and movies of majestically desolate country.

The small number of scientists who do tackle the Arctic in its frozen state wait for the settled weather and returning daylight of early spring, then work with massive technological support that ensures their comfort and safety. Many scientists who have become authorities on aspects of its environment or ecology admit that despite many seasons of experience in polar regions they have never actually been there in winter. While there is no reason to sneer at scientists taking advantage of modern equipment to live more comfortably and get their work done, or to denigrate the importance of their work, it's true that as individuals they are merely using the Arctic as a laboratory or as a microscope slide. They are not committed to the Arctic. Their homes are invariably in the South. Like the oil man, who doesn't really care if he is in Timbuktu or Tuktoyaktuk as long as the air conditioning works and there is a plane to take him home at the end of his shift, or at the epitome of monotony-worshipper, the DEW-liner, who seeks and relishes barracks life, scientists are merely Arctic migrants, flying in and out like the birds. The story is told of a pair of Eskimos watching a party of social-scientists unloading their baggage at the airstrip one April. "My word," one Eskimo said to the other, "the sociologists are early this year."

Sociological research among Eskimos is not easy because they resent questions and, being anxious to please, or to get rid of you, are likely to provide the answers they think you want to hear. And they have a wicked sense of humour. "Innocents come up here and get such a story handed out to them by Eskimos," says Dr Andy Rode, who runs the Eastern Arctic Research Lab in Igloolik. "The turnover is so great that the Eskimos get fresh victims every year." Researchers are so eager to find something new that they tend to see things which don't exist. Like the social-anthropologist Dr Rode took hunting with a couple of Eskimos. The hunters wore caribou-skin parkas that shed hairs everywhere, as did the caribou skins on the floor of the tent. "The scientist asked me in all seriousness," said Dr Rode, "what was the significance of putting caribou hair in the tea?"

One game Eskimos play with wide-eyed Whites "trapped" in a tent is offering something disgusting from the cooking pot, such as a boiled seal's eye. The luckless visitor, loath to offend his hosts, chokes it down, and says, "How lovely..." Once it may have been the politic thing to do, but now most Eskimos themselves eat corn-flakes for breakfast and steak and sweet corn for dinner, and know only too well how sick their visitor is feeling. But Whites who find themselves victims of this behaviour can only blame themselves for being patronising and not totally honest. The same kind of distressing patronising shows up in the attitudes of Whites, usually those in ivory towers in the South, who lament the passing of traditional Eskimo ways and say, "Of course, life expectancy was shorter in those days, but *for them* life was so much more valuable..."

When the migrant scientists have flown south with the geese at the onset of winter, and if you discount the stockaded oil men and DEW-liners, the Whites who remain are those who reside in the Arctic. They live in suburban-style houses, just as they did in the South, and raise their children in the image of suburban life. A very small number make energetic forays into nearby countryside, running their own dog teams for recreation, or taking their children camping in the wilderness, but this is done for fun, not out of necessity.

During mid-summer, the best months of the year when Eskimo families camp and hunt for whales, or fish, most Whites head south for holidays with relatives, or trip to Hawaii. Even at this level commitment to the Arctic is transitory. Careers might be committed to the Arctic, temporarily at least, but it is hard to find a single White person who is so at home in the Arctic that he plans to retire there; even priests, devoted to the well-being of Eskimo people, wish to rest their bones not in the Arctic but in their homelands of Brittany or Quebec.

In any Canadian Arctic settlement teachers comprise roughly half the White resident population, and on average they stay only one and a half to two years. Their motivations for coming at all are diverse. There is the missionary type, the do-gooder who wants to do the work because it is worth doing, among whom one finds the very best of teachers as well as the not-so-good. Then there are the tourists, who come to look at the Arctic and experience a different way of life; they arrive with guns, fishing rods, snow machines and all the paraphernalia of a major expedition, but tend quickly to lose interest. Another type is the escapee, husbands running away from wives, wives running away from husbands, both running away from mothers-in-law or city life. But it is the group which education director Brian Lewis calls the pragmatists – "those motivated by benevolent self-interest, perhaps because they are not romantics" – who perform best as teachers. The pay is good without being marvellous. Teachers get a living allowance which is absorbed by extra living costs, but pay less for accommodation and heat than they would at home, and there is little opportunity to spend.

In the oil business take-home pay is better in the Arctic because workers are guaranteed ten-hour days, seven days a week, with lots of overtime because they work twelve-hour shifts. Once a worker gets on the plane everything is provided so it is not necessary to spend a cent. One young fork-lift driver I met had arrived in the Arctic with a dollar in his pocket and after six weeks still had sixty-five cents left, having bought one tin of pop. A lot of houses, farms, cars and boats are paid off by the oil operation.

The Arctic is also used as a stepladder to greater things – young journalists and broadcasters trying to make their names, or young pilots working for low wages to clock up air time that qualifies them for better jobs in the South. A number of people live in the Arctic to take advantage of government incentives; a mother of four children, widowed by an air crash, who worked in Frobisher because her children were entitled to almost unlimited education free of charge, including air fares, tuition and living costs at southern universities, and trips home for Christmas and summer vacation. But achievement in an Arctic settlement is artificial – White children are at the top of the class and, figuratively speaking, at the top of the heap. Often, when they go south many get the shock of their lives and simply can't cope.

The turnover of government staff is a little over one-third every year, so even those who stay have to keep changing jobs to fill the gaps. Anyone who does a job half properly either does not stay, because he is disillusioned, or cannot stay because he is promoted. Constant changing of personnel is disruptive, especially when you consider that the Northwest Territories, where in 1901 the total White population was only 137, now has two armies of civil servants, three thousand working for the territorial government (of whom six hundred are teachers) and two thousand for the federal government. The turnover means Eskimo communities are littered with half-baked projects. People come into the Arctic with good ideas, get them half going, and are then promoted out of the job. Those with real ambitions for the Arctic become disenchanted and leave for areas where they have wider scope for their ideas and will see quicker results.

A typical example of bureaucratic misfiring was the saga of the freezer built for the community of Savoonga, on St Lawrence Island between Alaska and Siberia. A freezer was needed for storing walrus meat but there was no electricity in the village so Lee Leonard, a Fairbanks engineer, designed one based on the heat-exchanger principle, using the temperature of the air to chill the compartment. In order to get an economic development grant to build the structure, the people had to be in business. With the intention of selling extra walrus meat, the freezer was made twice as large. Then the Sea Mammals Protection Act stopped the sale of walrus products so only half the freezer was used, and because it was too big for the job it didn't work. Now the Eskimos use domestic freezers running on oil that costs dollars a gallon.

There is also a tendency to use the Arctic as a social laboratory. Whites who really understand the Arctic are scornful of consultants far away in Ottawa, Washington or Copenhagen, who work out ideas on paper and try to impose them with no knowledge of the real issues, like the Danish administrators who, as described in chapter twelve, moved Eskimo hunters out of foreshore huts into massive apartment buildings with no preparation. The "instant expert" is a figure of scorn in the Arctic, like the intense and dynamic young scientist I met in a plane in Alaska who was planning to put desk-top computers linked by satellite into villages where the single telephone did not survive vandalism for more than a few hours. Another example is the way Whites have mixed up Canadian Eskimos over the use of dogs. The true Eskimo husky, or *Qimminik*, had been even more important to the polar Eskimos than the horse was to Whites. It carried packs, hauled sleds, hunted, sniffed out seal holes in the ice, provided fur, and had instincts that could look after you in an emergency. Sturdier than the Alaskan malamute and Siberian husky though not as fast, the *Qimminik* is probably the most powerful dog for its size in the world, and the most stoic, able to pull its own weight for many miles a day, for days on end without food. In camps out on

The new Greenlanders: Henning Meyer is a Danish-born engineer, his wife Maria is the daughter of an Eskimo hunter who speared seals from his kayak; she is now president of the powerful Greenland Women's Institute. Every summer for five or six weeks, with their children Tina (14) and Peter Oluf (10) they go camping to shoot three or four caribou for the deep freeze and catch a lot of fish. Maria makes their own tent and they sleep on a caribou skin, but this is spread on top of an air mattress.

the land dogs could run free and nobody cared, but it was less welcome in settlements run by Whites, particularly when dogs were allowed to go hungry. To help preserve numbers of caribou, Eskimos were told by government game officers that it was prohibited to feed caribou meat to dogs. When lots of young children were bitten by hungry, free-running dogs the Eskimos were told to tie them up or they would be shot. Then other well-meaning Whites from the South, ignorant of the pressures Eskimos were under, visited settlements and passed round leaflets saying it was cruel for dogs to be tied up all day. Eskimos took the line of least resistance and got rid of their dogs so quickly that when Yellowknife game biologist Bill Carpenter realised what was happening and gave up his job to devote himself to saving the *Qimminik* from extinction it was almost impossible to find pure-bred dogs to breed from. Now the Eskimos are criticised by Whites for using snow machines ("You can't eat a Skidoo if it breaks down . . .").

Besides those in flight from some kind of southern foul-up such as bankruptcy, a bad marriage, or just a feeling of inadequacy, Whites in a small polar community can play roles that in influence and importance far exceed their real level of ability, or they can lead a reclusive existence, answerable to nobody. One of the most famous examples of just how deeply you can bury yourself is the story of an Italian, hired as chief surgeon in Inuvik in 1974, who operated on more than a hundred people, including a policeman, before it was discovered that although he was highly trained he had no qualifications. It was only when Mounties were puzzled by his findings in a post-mortem conducted on a murder victim that they ran some quiet checks and the true facts about him came to light: Interpol, too, wanted him for posing as a doctor.

However, one makes allowances for "the northern factor". Any inefficiency which could easily be avoided is covered by the explanation, "Don't forget, you're in the North now." In a funny way people do slow down and act in a more fuddled way. It is evident everywhere you look, even in the oil camps. Our two Hudson's Bay pilots, for example, were having trouble with a slow leak in a tyre but every time we were scheduled to take off it was not until the plane was loaded with cargo and passengers and ready to go that they set about trying to rustle up an air cylinder.

The proportion of Danes among Greenlanders (about one in five) is higher than that of Whites among other Eskimos, and many Danes are of an older generation whose commitment to the country is in the tradition of old style colonists. Hearts might be set on retirement cottages in Denmark but careers are committed to Greenland and they make homes there in every sense of the word, fishing, camping, and using the country as Greenlanders do. Greenlanders accept Danes more readily because they have lived with them for two and a half centuries and because there is a high proportion of mixed blood. There is also a high degree of trust between the two races, a quality which is conspicuously lacking in Canada and even more so in Alaska.

On the North Slope of Alaska, where Eskimos now have the political freedom, the cash and the desire to run their own affairs, they would like to thumb their noses at Whites but dare not do so because Alaskan Eskimos have neither the experience nor the education – so they hire Whites to do technical and administrative work for them as consultants, at fees of around fifty dollars an hour, including travel and all expenses, counted from the moment they get on a plane to fly north. Hardly one of the many consultants lives in Alaska, let alone on the North Slope, most flying up from cities like Seattle in the Lower Forty-eight. Many of the consultants tend to be young, fresh out of college, sent on assignments in the Arctic partly because they are least in a position to complain about being sent frequently away from home, and partly to prove themselves professionally, as many do – "You've got to be a fool not to make money out of the Eskimos."

Alaska is the rawest edge of American feeling for immediacy. The whole State is regarded as a frontier, where a person can make a bundle and go. There are groups of imagined frontiersmen at several different levels. The imaginative, bearded young biologist concerned for the ecology and adept at the kind of political in-fighting required to stop or control the industrial development that is threatening it. The cowboy-hatted, four-wheel-driver up from Colorado or Montana ("Where things are kinda squeezin' in") who wants the wildlife preserved so he can shoot it and cook it on a camp fire; pro-development on idealistic grounds, he is disenchanted with its effects and might be called something between Daniel Boone and James Audubon. Then there are the homesteaders who carve a niche for themselves out of the wilderness, as their grandfathers did in Iowa and Illinois, and fill it with all kinds of junk in case it is needed one day. And the boomers, who really do make a killing from big projects like pipelines, whether their line is prostitution or welding, but seldom save the money. People do not plant trees in Alaska because nobody thinks they will be there long enough to see them grow, and the same attitude dominates such things as community planning and local government. There is no cooperative spirit except in the face of adversity: if your house burns down or you get stuck in a snowdrift your neighbour will stand by you every lick of the way, but there is no chance in the world he will agree on a joint boundary fence.

Meeting people in the Arctic is mildly shocking, literally. On the North American side they are prone to the hearty handshake and so-glad smile, but polyester fibres are all the rage and in the super-dry air these build up voltages of electricity that has no escape until you touch something. As you reach out to shake hands a spark half an inch long arcs from fingertip to fingertip with an audible snap. It's enough to make you begin to snatch your hand away, as if you've been stung. Meeting pet dogs indoors has the same alarming effect and you soon learn to pat a dog through its fur to dissipate any voltage build-up and avoid the bolt of lightning that would otherwise leap from the tip of its wet nose.

In small Arctic communities invitations to visit the private homes of Whites are left unsaid, in Eskimo style, because it is taken for granted you will come if you want, but you are especially welcome if you bring a bottle. In most Canadian Arctic communities liquor can only be bought by mail order, for which "permission to import" must be obtained from Yellowknife. Often people in a community combine to charter a light plane to fly in a cargo of liquor. In Greenland liquor is sold in stores except on Fridays (pay day) and Saturdays, but can be obtained at double price by ringing certain taxi companies. In Alaska liquor is available when stores are open.

Canadians are not as spontaneously hospitable as Danes or Americans in the Arctic, nor do they seem to be as successful at coming to terms with their lives there. Those who settle down best to a polar life, and make a real contribution to it, tend to be non-Canadians. The fact is strikingly obvious and is reflected, for example, in the visitors to Auyuittuq National Park of whom more than half reside outside the country.

In their own "Artik" (as they call it) Canadians are constantly upstaged by those from outside the country. Unless it is something to do with switching into four-wheel-drive, at which they excel, Canadians are generally slower to adjust to difficult or different conditions. Nurses who come from other Commonwealth countries to work in the Arctic, for example, roll up their sleeves within minutes of walking in the door and ask where the work is, while Canadian-born nurses seem to require time to "recover" from the flight and often put their names right away on the transfer list so they can get out of the place, although by the time the request is granted they often change their minds and settle down. Non-Canadians are more interested in the Arctic as an experience, rather than as a place to which they have been sentenced.

Corporal Barry Lidstone, RCMP officer in Igloolik for three years, policed 40,000 square miles and collected a year's groceries from the beach; here with his wife Janet and their two children outside their house.

Outsiders can see the Arctic more easily for what it is: small-time colonies spread very thinly over a great area. Canadians, especially those from the prairie provinces, tend to be small-town people bent on developing the Arctic in the image of home and are less able to see how the Arctic could be developed with a different and more suitable style of life without prejudicing all good things Canadian. In Eskimo communities that have voted to prohibit liquor it is principally Canadian-born Whites who have lobbied most strongly to prevent prohibition.

The typical Canadian home in the Arctic is a fingerprint of suburban civilisation with mock ranch-style decor. No concessions to the environment are made, and not even the conversation touches on issues of the Arctic unless it is to do with village gossip. Many Canadians seem to suffer from permafrost of the mind: neither curious nor contentious, they simply don't discuss things much, as if born and bred into such material comfort that they have never had to think about it.

It is rare to find people living in the Canadian Arctic who are not supported in some way by government or big business. Rent, heat and other living costs are prohibitively dear, and you need a lot of money just to get there, let alone set up a business.

The fact that Eskimos live in square houses and eat cornflakes, as Whites do, makes it tempting to suppose they also think like Whites. The typical Canadian is inclined to judge progress by suburban skills alone, and is likely to persuade you how brilliant Eskimos are because in no more than a couple of decades they have made the leap into civilisation which took White society ten thousand years. But those with a broader experience of the world are alert for more subtle nuances of behaviour, and suggest that just because Eskimos have been trained to cut up their seals elsewhere than in the bath, to send their children to school, to vote in local elections, and to eat ketchup with their French fries, does not mean their hearts and minds have followed so far along the same road. Practically every Eskimo over the age of twenty-five was born in an igloo, sod house or skin tent, into what was little more than a primitive, nomadic way of life hardly coherent enough to be called a culture, but it allowed a community to have a dignity and sense of continuity, qualities which today are largely absent.

The contempt, indifference and *differentness* of the Eskimo was illustrated in an experience of Hank Kiliaan, a Canadian Wildlife Service technician studying polar bears. He hired two hunters at Grise Fjord to take him on a month-long denning survey by snow machine. Akpaleeapik ("little murre") and Ningyou ("old woman") – amazing names for two stoic super-hunters – imposed only the condition that Hank did no sledge-loading or camp work. The month was March, when temperatures are coldest, skies bright and clear, days become longer than nights with dumbfounding speed, and the High Arctic is at its most dazzling.

Living in a house with central heating and a ready supply of store-bought food had not dulled the wits of the two middle-aged Eskimos, and the little expedition moved at a steady rate among the areas of deeply compacted snow where sow polar bears tunnelled dens like shallow rabbit warrens in which to suckle their young. By observation of footprints Hank was able to build up an accurate picture of bear populations. Being an energetic and resourceful Dutchman, he chafed at the enforced limitation on his activities and one morning loaded up his own *komatik*. His guides chatted and smoked, watching him. When he had tied the last knot the Eskimos sauntered over and without so much as a look of reproach kicked the load into the snow and started again.

Another day Hank thought the Eskimos looked a little surprised when he got out of his sleeping bag as usual but thought nothing of it as they packed up and got going – until evening, when they did not stop to build an igloo. Instead, they made Hank continue travelling and working until the early hours of next morning. Only then did Hank realise he had inferred that they should work through Easter Sunday. The Eskimos were too polite to say anything, but – in their own way – taught him a lesson he would never forget.

Every evening, when the igloo had been built and the Primus pressure stove was started, sugar tin, biscuits, tea and butter were set out on a wooden board along with a large, lidless peach can that served as a communal piss-pot. Every evening, with increasing disfavour, Hank watched the accumulation of frozen golden globules melt down the sides of the can and dribble across the food board. Finally Hank decided to open a second large can from his provision box and when the meal was over he cut off the lid, set the new can on the board, tossed the old one out through the ventilation hole in the top of the igloo and said with a grin, "Let's have a new piss-pot, eh!"

Akpaleeapik and Ningyou reacted without so much as a flicker of expression, but continued their quiet conversation until Akpaleeapik reached the end of his cigarette. Then he stubbed it out, and in his normally congenial manner proceeded to cut a hole in the side of the igloo. The hole was so big that he could walk through it without stooping: half the igloo was demolished. He went out, retrieved the old peach can, brought it in, and painstakingly rebuilt the wall. It took an hour, and not once did either hunter betray with a look or a murmur the least sense of displeasure or annoyance.

When the igloo was again sealed up Akpaleeapik tossed the new peach can through the ventilation hole, lit another cigarette, and carried on chatting as if nothing had happened.

This is not a tale of the "old" North: it happened five years ago and Hank, continuing to study polar bears but now travelling by helicopter, is still haunted by the crushing sense of shame inflicted on him by his beaming, friendly companions. For him it was an object lesson in Eskimo behaviour. In this case Akpaleeapik and Ningyou had been able to deal with one uppity White man. Today the hottest question in the Arctic is how a whole new generation of modern Eskimos can make that supreme gesture of contempt, cut their way out of the avalanche of good intentions and – without denying themselves the peaches – chuck White Society's new piss-pot out through the roof.

Part II

SCORCHING THE ICE

5

POLAR WILDCATS

*How technological adventurers of the
Arctic frontier use cold to beat cold
in the race to find new energy*

For the typical Arctic oil-patch worker the quest begins once every
three weeks, generally at some ungodly hour, at a shed on the
perimeter of Edmonton International. He drives up in his new car or
pick-up, pecks his wife on the cheek as she slides behind the wheel,
and waves at his kids who gaze at the Boeing floodlit on the other side
of the chain-link fence, its front end being loaded by fork-lift with
bags of drilling mud. An ordinary-looking, settled sort of bloke, he is
likely to be wearing well-curled boots, jeans with a silver buckle,
plaid shirt, digital watch: could easily be cowboy, ditch-digger or
trucker. In the shed he thumps his kit on the scales, collects a
boarding slip, and makes for the coffee machine while lighting a
cigarette with a Zippo bearing the legend: "Happiness is a 727
heading south."

This is not his happy day because he is heading north, commuting
nearly two thousand miles for a two-week shift rather nearer to
mainland Russia than to his wife and kids. On this day he had
already enjoyed an unexpected bonus. Up north the Arctic breeze
had picked up the light, dust-like snow and with nothing to break it
the snow had been whirling over the landscape in a low, smoking
blanket that reduced horizontal visibility to nearly zero. Take-off
scheduled for 7 am had been postponed twelve hours, but it was

midnight before the pilots got reports of improving visibility. In front of me as we boarded a worker with shoulders like a rolled-steel beam and a Mitchum swagger was following the footsteps of great men into the Arctic with a bottle of shampoo in one back pocket and a pink-handled hairbrush in the other.

For more than two centuries oil for the lamps that illuminated the civilised world was hunted in the Arctic by whaling ships. Today, the same ice-infested waters are again the scene of urgent, competitive, dangerous scrabbling for energy. The lurching sailing ships have become giant corporations. Their harpoons are drilling rigs, their whaleboats "thunder-belly" transport aircraft and helicopters. The body juices they seek are not those of blowing whales but of tiny organisms buried millions of years ago by sediments washed downriver, debris from the sculpting of the world. The new frontier is not geographical but technological. As if the magnetism of the North were not confined to the compass needle but exerted its power over the slide rules of engineers and geologists, we are pitting the best technology the modern world can devise against the severest, harshest, most testing environment Nature can provide. For the sake of our lifestyle it is not a match we can afford to lose. The end of the oil era is in sight, and if the Arctic exploration crews like these men now fastening their seatbelts ultimately come home "clean", like a ship without a whale, the effects will be calamitous and sudden.

It is often said that one airport in North America is like any other. Not this one. At the end of the four-hour flight, the figures as massively dressed as deep-sea divers clumping up the aisle to unstrap the cargo hinted at what was in store. Tears of cold had frozen on the mufflers covering the lower parts of their faces. The small patches of flesh visible around their eyes were pink and chapped. Frost and icicles framed their noses and mouths, and they wasted no time greeting their pals. The cold swept in behind them like a surf wave of liquid stainless steel that locked the body in an armour of knife-points. Outside, the air itself was white with tiny chips of blowing snow and ice. It was a fifty yard dash across a tarmac eerily lit by the headlights of pick-ups and fork-lifts gleaming on ice, every vehicle trailing horizontal plumes of exhaust steam. The wind snapped at our legs like a pack of frenzied terriers and it was hard to see what we were running to, for the complex of single-storey huts linked together in a series of H formations was almost completely drifted over. An adit had been shovelled out for access to a small orange door in a blank wall of snow and beside it a palm tree flapped its tattered plastic fronds. Luggage was chucked out on the snow and if you didn't know to collect it yourself it would be buried before daylight. As it was, in the few minutes my kitbag was exposed to the elements the toothpaste became so cold that after the first searing touch of it on a hollow tooth I had to warm it under the hot tap.

Inside the camp it was another world. Men strolled around in slippers and shirt-sleeves. There was a pungent aroma of socks, Juicy Fruit and Old Spice. New arrivals queued at the coffee urn then scanned the blackboards to see when the Twin Otters were scheduled to lift them out to the drilling rigs and work camps. But it was to be a long wait. Minutes after the Boeing roared away with a happy south-bound shift the wind piped up. Fine granules of snow lifted like powdery desert sand and formed a skein of near zero forward visibility and Panarctic's base camp at Rea Point, on the east coast of Melville Island, was "socked in" for four days.

Eighty men slept in the passageways, "hot" bunked, or spent the entire time in the smoke-filled recreation room where the same four dreadful movies were shown in constant rotation. When, for my benefit, a half-hour documentary about Panarctic's frontier exploration was put on, the bleary, sleep-sodden "modern heroes of the Arctic" greeted themselves on the screen with jeers and slow handclaps. Outside, in the white haze of blowing snow, a Hercules "thunder-belly" transport aircraft, trapped by the weather, had to keep one of its four engines running constantly to keep the others warm. There was a brief alarm when the engineer in its cockpit sighted the wraith-like figure of a man in a track suit, a towel wrapped around his head, running down the runway. A pick-up truck sent to investigate returned with an abashed new hand who had gone for a keep-fit jog. With the wind behind him he might have lasted ten minutes, but it is doubtful he would have made it back. With windchill, the effective temperature was $-98\,°F$ ($-170\,°C$).

In eight years camp boss Tony Durant has seen only one man – who kidnapped an entire Herc crew with a butcher's knife – "go bananas". Weather permitting, nobody works more than two weeks without going home for one week or two, depending on rank; those unable to get on with the Arctic don't come back, and those who do come reckon to spend more time with their families, overall, than most of their neighbours. There is a continuous telephone link, by Anik satellite orbiting over the equator, direct from the camp radio room to Panarctic's office switchboard in Calgary. Navigation computers in the Twin Otters allow pilots to punch in coordinates of a series of destinations then simply follow the dials, so they do not have to rely on chancy compasses. Fire is a threat but the accommodation units are on skids, linked together with hooks, and caterpillar tractors stand by in separate heated garages to pull them away from any outbreak. Once the Boeing waited a couple of hours while a specialist brought up from the south on a day-trip reconditioned the pool table, so there is little to complain about. Ironically, unlike the explorers who pioneered winter survival methods while searching for a passage through these islands a century and a half ago, the whole sophisticated technological oil-hunting operation can be locked in by what the old-time whalers used to pray for – a stiff breeze.

A hundred miles inland, where visibility was perfect, a seismic party was down to its last drums of fuel. All but a couple of vehicles, and the generator providing heat and light, were shut down and getting cold. When the grains of snow finally fell out of the air at Rea Point the Twin Otters were mobilised instantly. We landed on a rough airstrip marked with flares, their flames lying horizontally in the cutting wind. Lumbering Nodwells – tracked vehicles with box-like cabins – converged on the little plane as drums of fuel were chucked out and I followed, to climb immediately into a cab when its door opened as if by magic in front of me.

A seismic camp is an ever-rolling scientific wagon train. Geologists draw straight lines on the map and seismic men follow them exactly, crawling across-country for scores of miles, every hundred yards or so pausing to set off dynamite charges buried deep in the ground. The sound waves travel down through the sediments and bounce back from the granite twenty thousand feet below. These echoes are picked up by geophones laid out on the ground in long strings in front and behind, and are recorded on tape. As sound waves travel at different speeds through materials of differing densities, computer analysis can produce a map showing a cross-section of the ground below. From this geologists determine the nature of the materials and whether they are likely to contain hydro-carbons. Seismic is the sharp end of oil exploration: physically hard, technically painstaking. Iron-hard frozen ground in winter and spring makes the going easy and saves environmental damage by the tracks of the eighteen Nodwells, cats, and fold-up trailer cabins for fifty-one men. But the cost in discomfort is fearful.

Seismic crews wrestle with the cold in a way that would stagger the imagination of the majority of the oil men who had flown north in the Boeing. The surveyors, laying out the route far ahead, must operate delicate instruments without gauntlets to protect their fingers. When using a theodolite and looking into the wind your eyelid can freeze to the eyepiece, objects dance in your tears and the heat of your eyeball can mist up the lens. If you make the mistake of breathing on the instrument it is instantly covered in a glaze of ice: you have to be like a pearl diver, and survive on a long breath exhaled slowly. In winter darkness survey poles are marked with fluorescent tape and picked out with spotlights. The consolation is that working out front you encounter some rare Arctic sights, like a patch of snow on the ground which suddenly moves away: a herd of hundreds of white Arctic hares. Recently a man had caught one by the ears and put its shrill protests over the vhf radio that links all vehicles; the driver of the Nodwell who picked me up was still laughing about it.

Now the seismic train was in a huddle, as if coralled against the cold. High drifts had formed over the cabins and snow had heaped into ridges between them. It was a surreal scene with bulkily clad figures lying in scooped-out hollows beneath the vehicles warming the frozen engines with propane torches while other men heated the propane cylinders to get the gas flowing. Steam lit from beneath by the flickering torches made long contrails from the exhaust pipes of those engines that were running. The men wore masks of frost, as if foaming at the mouth. "Welcome to the Fukawi tribe," the camp chief said, thrusting coffee into my hand. "It's our motto – where the fuck are we?"

The radio operator answered him drily, "In the shit as usual, I expect."

Arctic oil patch workers are blunt, forthright, courteous, reserved. There is nothing of the edgy temper found in a construction gang. A new man must display a lot of assertion to learn the routine of camp life because nobody tells you anything unless you ask, but then you get all the help you need. Parka hoods can be adjusted to protect the face from the burning wind so you peer down a fur-rimmed tunnel and cannot see right or left without swivelling the whole body, and it seems the physical attitude has become the mental one. But out of doors there is an automatic camaraderie. If you are waiting in the cold, cab doors open and welcome you into the warmth; if you are walking, the first vehicle to come by will stop, you can bank on it.

Oil is not a subject of conversation. They are wheels and guns men, who believe Mankind was born to travel in four wheel drive. The talk is of getting the job done, but hardly anybody in the entire camp is concerned with the wider implications of an oil discovery. Even a tool-pusher, whose job is to get the hole drilled, is remote from the consequences of what he finds. He is concerned only with pressures and logs and what they might do to the column of wet mud sitting on top of his drill-bit.

To find out about *oil* you must go to what Arctic hands call the banana belt. Edmonton, self-proclaimed blue jean capital of the world, provides most of the brawn for the work in the Arctic, but the brains are found two hundred miles south in a Stetson-wearing

cow-town called Calgary. Every July the week-long whoop-up of
steer-wrestling and chuck-wagon races of the Calgary Stampede
evokes the dream-time of flapjacks and campfire-grilled bacon. But
it was not the cattle business that paid for the city's 626-foot exclamation of pre-stressed concrete, capped with a revolving restaurant,
which pins it to the Rocky Mountain foothills like a giant nail.

The city's Yellow Pages directory lists six hundred oil and gas
companies (Globe Oil, Gobles Oil, Gold Lake Resources, Golden
Eagle Oil and Gas, Gottfred Oils ...). There are eighteen four-
column pages of oil consultants (Adair R. to Woofter), oil-field
mappers, oil-well corers, oil-well loggers, plus many more pages of
geochemists, geophysicists, and geologists. After Houston and
London, Calgary is third largest oil centre of the world, but as far as
Arctic oil exploration is concerned, Calgary is number one.

When maps of the Arctic were unrolled in Calgary in the mid-
1960s geologists recognised fabulous potential. What they look for is
a sequence of historical accidents, beginning long ago in geological
time with countless little sea creatures building coral-like reefs
higher and higher as the oceans became deeper. Then, in a process
that ended around 400 million years ago, great rivers loaded with
sediments from inland erosion had to bury the reefs thousands of feet
deep. Over great ages of time, and under intense pressure, the body
juices of organisms in the reefs, and other animals that died in the
sludge on the sea-bed, are squeezed out but will not collect and
remain unless the newly formed rock containing them is porous.
Then, to prevent it dissipating, the fluid must be trapped by a
geological fault or an upper layer of impervious rock, such as shale. If
all these things happen an oil field is created, and all you have to do is
drill a hole in precisely the right location, to the right depth, and find
it. This is what oil men call "wildcatting".

The sedimentary rocks of the world lie in five hundred basins of
which only three contain half the world's oil and gas and less than a
hundred contain significant amounts. The remainder contains none.
In Canada's Arctic, geologists identified four major sedimentary
basins; others were on the north coast of Alaska, between Baffin and
Greenland, and on the continental shelf off Labrador. In the Arctic
Islands alone the size of the basin is greater in area than that of the
five major US oil states (Oklahoma, Texas, California, Wyoming
and Louisiana) combined, six times bigger than that of the North
Slope of Alaska, and four times bigger than that of oil-rich Alberta.

Having identified sedimentary rock capable of forming oil, geologists commission seismic surveys to locate underground traps
where oil might have collected. What they are looking for is a

Author at Beechey Island graves of the Franklin Expedition.

(Overleaf) A land that looks as if it has frozen to death: the Canadian Arctic Islands at dusk.

Blue ice is hard ice, because it is frozen melt-water rather than snow.

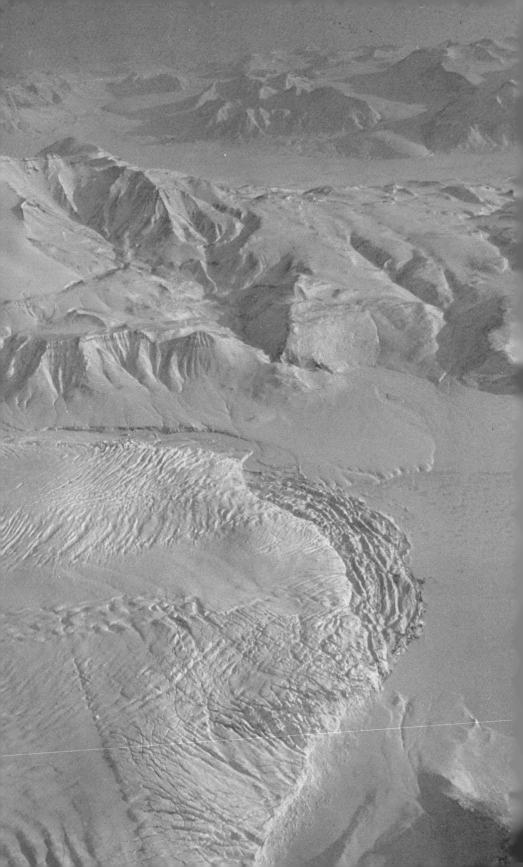

Fishing cutter wends among the giant icebergs of Disko Bay in Greenland; hulls are protected against ice by sheathing.

West Greenland's 100 tidewater glaciers, the largest 60 miles wide, annually carve 15,000 icebergs into the sea.

Gone is the dog whip over the shoulder, the bear-skin coat, the frozen moustache and the tins of pemmican. For today's young Hudson's Bay men, unloading their hi-fi from the Twin Otter, the call of the North comes in stereo.

A shattered mirror of lakes heliographing messages to passing aircraft as they catch the sun, the Mackenzie Delta is a vast, wet sponge of great biological vitality.

Greenlanders inhabit a near vertical landscape; a summer morning at Godhavn.

(Preceding page) *Dwarfed by a floating cathedral of ice, the village church at Jakobshavn, Greenland, north of the Arctic Circle.*

Cottages crowd close to the water's edge, at Godthåb, Greenland.

Airport 'bus' arrives in near white-out at Coral Harbour, Canada.

(Overleaf) Wild flowers and Eskimo skulls: ankle high Arctic fascination.

Arctic suburbia at Barrow, Alaska, northernmost point of USA.

reservoir with a lid on it but the only way to find out whether it holds anything worthwhile is to drill a "wildcat" hole.

When Panarctic Oil was launched with forty-five per cent government ownership in 1967, to find out with the drill what Canada's oil and gas potential really measured on the Arctic frontier, the Canadian Petroleum Association reckoned the 50,000 square miles of the Sverdrup Basin in the northwest islands could hold three times as much oil and gas as had already been found in the rest of continental Canada. At the same time Imperial Oil, the Canadian subsidiary of Exxon, and other companies like Gulf, Mobil and Shell, commenced major programmes of exploration in another potentially exciting sedimentary basin, the Mackenzie Delta. It was thought the lands fringing the Arctic Ocean at the top of the world could contain a vast storehouse of petroleum – so big that the focus of world supply would shift from the Persian Gulf to the Arctic.

On the North Slope of Alaska the dream did come true.

Exploration started there by Standard Oil in 1921 had been shelved indefinitely when large discoveries were made in Texas and Oklahoma, but 37,000 square miles of Alaska were designated a petroleum reserve for the US Navy. An eight-year exploration programme started in 1944 yielded several modest oil and gas wells, one of which now supplies the town of Barrow, but the problems of transporting oil and gas then seemed insurmountable. In the mid-1960s twelve wells drilled in one structure were dry and by 1967 only one wildcat rig was drilling, in a much less promising structure at a remote place called Prudhoe Bay. The hole had taken sixteen months to drill and the partners, Atlantic Richfield (Arco) and Humble Oil (a subsidiary of Standard Oil New Jersey) were growing disenchanted. British Petroleum (BP) had bought exploration leases in Prudhoe Bay and, being squeezed by Britain's Labour government to cut down on dollar expenditure, was within an inch of selling out. At the eleventh hour the drill struck oil. The follow-up well drilled seven miles away proved an enormous oil-field had been discovered, the largest in USA and the sixth largest in the world. So far, 9·6 billion barrels of oil and 26 trillion cubic feet of gas have been *proven* – a third of the nation's oil and a tenth of its gas.

Encouraged by this fabulous discovery, oil companies expected similar big finds in the Mackenzie Delta and the Arctic Islands. But what has been on paper a much better bet than either Alberta or Prudhoe Bay has not fulfilled one-tenth of expectations. Oil in the Canadian Arctic, except in the difficult conditions of the Beaufort Sea, is practically a write-off. Gas discoveries have confirmed the

Direct from Edmonton International Airport, a Boeing 727 touches down on floating sea ice six feet thick, in the Canadian Arctic archipelago, where Panarctic is drilling wells from rafts of artificially thickened ice.

problems rather than the advantages of frontier development. All the gas fields discovered so far extend offshore, and some are expected to lie wholly offshore. Companies must face not only Arctic conditions with its long logistical chain, difficult access, and harsh environment, but also drill from platforms in ice-covered seas.

A rig move that costs $12,000 by truck in southern Alberta costs $500,000 by aircraft in the High Arctic. A wildcat well drilled for $50,000 in southern Alberta costs up to $12 million in the Mackenzie Delta and something like $45 million in the deep water of the Beaufort Sea. Once an oil or gas field is discovered, the costs of developing it in the Arctic are around one hundred times higher. Despite these handicaps, in the Delta alone $500 million has been spent sinking about 130 holes with a remarkably good one-in-seven

success ratio, but the actual amounts of oil and gas found have been small. In the High Arctic Panarctic has spent about the same huge sums finding an average two trillion cubic feet of gas a year plus one small oil field; another $200 million is committed over the next four years. Several "elephant" fields – oil parlance for the big ones – have been found, but through an unlucky quirk of geological history have been empty of oil.

Though giant in dollars, the scale of Arctic exploration is comparatively small. About one hundred holes have been drilled in the huge area of the Arctic Islands but in the North Sea, another hostile and treacherous environment, five hundred dry holes have been drilled. Of 6,438 wildcat wells drilled in Canada in 1976 only twenty were in the Delta and Arctic Islands. At this rate the Arctic will be considered virgin territory for years to come.

Ask any oil company head office executive whether it is really necessary to spend such large sums on making so little progress and you are treated to a one-man version of the Calgary Stampede. First the howl of outrage, then a procession of PR graphs in glossy slabs of colour, their red sectors yawning wider towards the right-hand edge signifying a cornucopia of trouble before long. Grabbing the steer by

Sea ice under enormous pressures of up to 200,000 tons piles up in concentric rings around this drilling rig on an artificial island in the shallow waters of the Beaufort Sea; in 1976 two oil men were mauled to death by polar bears.

the horns, Imperial's Arctic manager Roland Horsefield laid out his graphs on a low coffee table bearing an eskimo whalebone carving of a snowgoose and presented an utterly convincing case for the certainty of petrol rationing in North America – he said by the mid-eighties, but recent events have shown that even he seriously underestimated society's vulnerability to oil shortage.

Despite higher prices, conservation and slower growth, world oil and gas demand would nearly double by 1990. Allowing for synthetics (one per cent of total demand), hydro-electricity, geothermal and solar energy (six per cent) and coal (nineteen per cent), oil production must increase by 165 per cent to meet demand. By that date a third of world oil will have to come from supplies that are not yet discovered – supplies which, to be in production at that time, *must* be discovered in the next five years. You can play with the figures in all sorts of ways, but the looming energy crisis is bound to begin the demise of the petrol engine, give our economy the jolt of its life, and rip the fabric of our urban lifestyle. The question is not *whether* there will be an energy crisis at the end of the coming decade, but how soon it will arrive and how bad it will be.

The facts are as starkly uncompromising as an overdraft statement. During 1976 (in round figures) the US discovered 1·6 billion barrels of oil, produced 3·0 billion barrels and *consumed* 6·2 billion barrels. Canada produced 584 million barrels but *used* 653 million barrels. About forty-three per cent of North America's oil had to be imported and by 1980 the proportion was expected to rise to around half. For all its tremendous size the reserves of the North Slope field are sufficient to meet total US demand for only a year and a half. The North American oil shortage is not a domestic problem but an international one, because competition for available supplies will intensify and political considerations will become paramount.

The same alarming picture is reflected in the gas industry. North America uses half the world's output of natural gas but contributes only one-eighth; gas heats half of all American homes and drives forty per cent of US industry. All other forms of energy are less convenient, more expensive, more difficult to extract, harder to handle and most have a far greater environmental impact, requiring larger installations and enormous capital investment. Solar energy is promising on a small scale but is not available in the enormous quantities required.

When blizzards all but buried the Great Lakes and eastern states in the winters of 1977 and 1978, causing acute gas shortages that closed down hundreds of factories and put millions out of work, Calgary oil men hoped it would at last bring a sense of personal urgency to the energy crisis. They prayed Ottawa and Washington DC would freeze solid, for a dose of spartan living would be worth all the PR charts in the world. The irony is that due to political uncertainties and lack of firm government leadership since the first oil and gas discoveries were made on the Canadian Arctic frontier, exploration has not accelerated but slowed down; with the new Conservative government this may change.

Three months after Imperial made its first discovery in the Delta the federal government cancelled drilling and land-use regulations. Since then it has been unable to decide how the whole thing should be handled and companies have hesitated to spend money without firmly specified terms under which they might get it back. Under *proposed* regulations, the government could take a quarter of any discovery without absorbing any of the great costs. Also, the Canadian content of any company making a discovery could be queried and its permits declared void on the whim of the Cabinet. Exploration companies are supposed to be one-quarter Canadian, but the definition is open-ended and ultimately at the discretion of the government. Only recently have tax incentives to encourage exploration have been restored. The result is that in the Canadian Arctic current exploration is being carried out only by Panarctic, which has had steady if unspectacular success (seven gas fields with marketable reserves of 12–16 tcf), and is nearly half government owned; Imperial Oil which hardly dares walk away from the $300 million already invested in the Mackenzie Delta; and Canmar's costly, environmentally risky and technologically adventurous operations amid the polar ice in the Beaufort Sea (see next chapter).

Following the Prudhoe Bay discovery, Imperial's hopes were high for a similar find in the Delta, only 300 miles away. But – in the words of one Calgary geologist – it proved to be "a fantastic disaster". Imperial found only one per cent of the 10 billion barrels of oil it hoped for. Instead of finding enough to make Canada self-sufficient in oil for decades to come, it found enough for fifty days. Its gas find of five million cubic feet would meet Canada's domestic requirements for barely two years. But that's oil business. When the guile, guesswork and good luck of a geological team happens to spud a well on the precise location of a sequence of fortunate geological accidents it could change overnight.

So far, drillers have been taking no more than first crack at the big picture, and the same thing has been happening in other areas of Alaska's North Slope. In 1969, soon after Arco and BP had made a second big strike in another geological structure northwest of

Caribou browse among the derricks and pipes of the Prudhoe Bay oil field. It is only exploration for oil and gas that consumes landscape and this is a temporary phase. Despite its importance, sitting on a third of US oil reserves and a tenth of the nation's gas, the actual size of the Prudhoe Bay development is only twenty miles by ten.

Prudhoe Bay, the State government auctioned further exploration leases for a fantastic $900 million. The meagre discoveries made subsequently show that the companies lost their heads in the excitement. In 1971 the huge petroleum reserve designated in 1923 was transferred from the Navy to the Department of Interior and tagged National Petroleum Reserve (NPR) Alaska. Its potential is estimated at 10–33 billion barrels but recent exploration has found only two small fields hardly worth developing. When the programme ends the US Congress will decide whether this federal asset should be leased to companies, explored more closely, or designated a wildlife reserve as a trade-off to permit exploration of the Arctic Wildlife Range, between Prudhoe Bay and the Yukon, which has an estimated 20-billion barrel potential.

Now the hunt for Arctic oil is shifting offshore. On the North Slope the State of Alaska has been selling exploration leases for areas of shallow inshore waters and the low marshy islands near the coast. Federal sale of drilling leases on the offshore continental shelf were scheduled to begin at the end of 1979. So great is the confidence of finding vast reserves offshore that some authorities predict Alaska will provide a quarter of US oil and much of her gas within the decade, requiring at least two more pipelines in addition to the gas line now under construction. State officials predict the ultimate yield of the North Slope to be at least eight times more oil and sixteen times more gas, half the oil and most of the gas lying offshore. But drilling has hardly begun. So far, predictions rate with Imperial's hopes for the Mackenzie Delta as wishful thinking.

Denmark permits summer operation of three drill-ships in Davis Strait, between Cape Dyer in Baffin Island and Holsteinborg in Greenland; drill-ships are also working with high hopes in Canadian waters off the Labrador coast. In both operations powerful tugs stand by to push away icebergs that drift down on the drill-ships and, as a last resort, the ships must be able to close down and abandon the holes at short notice.

To drill the seabed from the surface of a sea covered with heavy ice that can crush an ordinary ship, and which is constantly moving en masse, is an engineering challenge that makes North Sea drilling look a picnic. The different techniques depend on the depth of water and type of ice.

The muddy waters of the Mackenzie Delta are less than twenty feet deep for miles offshore, and it is here that since 1972 Imperial has been pioneering a unique programme of drilling wildcat wells from artificial islands. Twenty islands have been built by cranes, dump barges, and suction dredgers. To build Pullen Island a hole 225 by 375 feet was cut in the ice with a ditch-witcher, a cutting machine like a five-foot chainsaw on wheels. Five-ton chunks of sea-ice were lifted out by crane, each one, said the PR man, big enough to chill 100,000 martini cocktails. Then a convoy of trucks hauled tons of gravel miles over the sea-ice and filled the hole. Rig and supplies were also delivered by truck. When the sea-ice melted it left an island. The drilling islands self-destruct after a few years and are protected from vicious summer storms by sandbags, from the pressure of ice by false shorelines (electronic pressure sensors are linked directly to a computer in Calgary), and from marauding polar bears by a double electric fence and a watchdog.

When flying over the level plain of snow-covered ice to visit an island rig it is difficult to believe you are crossing the open sea.

Rea Point, Panarctic's base camp on Melville Island in the High Arctic, is connected with Edmonton by twice weekly Boeing 727 and is plugged in by satellite to the head office telephone switchboard.

During the late Arctic dawn of a February morning the ice is as grey as cement. Then, touched by a watery sun with barely enough bounce to clear the horizon, it becomes a delicate shell-pink etched with fluted mauve shadows where the sharp ridges of blown snow peak like real waves on the point of toppling. Occasionally, in the middle of nowhere, you suddenly look down on a slowly moving geyser where a snow plough is clearing the long straight ice-roads on which tankers and "turkey trucks" bring fuel and supplies over the sea to the rigs that stand out on the level expanse like red lighthouses. From the air the drilling island, three hundred feet in diameter, looks like skin on your knuckles because it is surrounded by concentric rings of wrinkled ice where pressure has forced it to fold and pile up.

Thousands of miles of seismic survey over the sea-ice between the islands of the High Arctic have shown the largest structures to be offshore here also. The Geological Survey of Canada estimates potential at 17 billion barrels of oil and 300 trillion cubic feet of gas. Panarctic's problems differ from those of the Delta because the water is hundreds of feet deep. But there is the same runway smoothed flat on the ice, a red and silver derrick spangled with hoar-frost and heavy nylon drapes, to protect the driller and his men from the wind, orange cabins hooked together to provide comfortable living with meals of steak, apple pie and ice cream as good as you will find anywhere in the world. And the same kind of tidy, courteous, self-contained men among whom the ultimate sin is wearing wet or dirty workboots in the camp.

When the wind finally dropped at Rea Point and normal flying operations resumed, I hitched a ride to a drilling rig called Drake Ice P40, off the coast of the Sabine Peninsula. From a mile-high Twin Otter the grand vista of level white stretching away to a paper-edge horizon was dauntingly immense. When the pilot pointed ahead with a gloved finger my eye searched out the rig's derrick but all it found, after a time, was a tiny outline like the imprint of a pale exclamation mark. This was the mile-long runway. When the derrick finally became evident to the eye it was as a solitary map pin stuck in the dead centre of a single enormous sheet of flat, white paper. So tiny was it, on such a vast plane of distance, that you had to marvel at the elaborate process of geophysical deduction that singled out that particular spot in the cross-hairs of the geological target-shoot.

Amid the humming of diesel generators, compressors, mud-pumps and shakers beneath the drilling platform, I stood with an engineer on wooden boards gazing at what looked like a dirty ten by eight-foot swimming pool. A ten-inch pipe came down from the platform above us and vanished into the murky water, the surface of which lapped within a few inches of our toes. The pipe was supported by thick wire hawsers which very slowly rose and fell about six inches. No, the pipe was stationary. It was the entire rig moving up and down with the imperceptible rise and fall of the sea-ice itself. In fact the oblong patch of water, known as the moonpool, was 1,200 feet deep. Everything around us – pick-up trucks, camp buildings, aeroplanes, the rig itself – was afloat on the frozen Arctic Ocean.

Then a sleek brown head popped out of the water and regarded us with a blank, innocent stare: a seal, treading water and sniffing the air, its whiskers twitching. After a moment it vanished, and I wondered what the whole 450-ton rig would look like from a seal's point of view; a skid mark on the translucent sky, perhaps.

In shorefast ice which does not drift with the current but remains attached to the land like a skirt, Panarctic has pioneered a remarkable new way of drilling. Like the old-time galley sailors who feared wind until somebody invented the sail, oil men who once dreaded the deep cold of mid-winter have learned to harness it and make it work for them. In early winter, when sea-ice is still only a few inches thick, surveyors on snow machines mark out the site. When the ice is just over a foot thick a construction crew gingerly drives out a light tracked vehicle, called a skidozer, towing a sled with tents and equipment.

When the camp is established, a hole is made in the ice and for two months pumps suck sea water from below and jet it over the surface. The water runs away and finds its own level then freezes. In total darkness, at temperatures of $-45\,°F$ ($-43\,°C$), the air is a great deal colder than the water which creates its own cloud of fog. The operation has to be done with care, to ensure that no hollow patches develop. At the rate of 2·4 inches a day the ice pad grows thicker, forming an oval four or five hundred feet in diameter. As it becomes heavier the ice settles deeper into the water, forming a large, self-stabilising bulge averaging twenty-three feet thick in the centre and tapering off towards the edges. At the same time a second island is made about three hundred yards away, to serve as a platform for drilling a relief well in the event of a blowout.

When the floating ice platforms are ready the sea-ice itself is four or five feet thick and strong enough to take a bulldozer that makes a runway for a Hercules which flies in the drilling rig. Drivers of heavy trucks and graders must remember not to park their vehicles in a bunch when going in for coffee, in case the ice fractures beneath their weight, but although the ice has a structural strength of only about fifty pounds per square inch (thirty pounds allowing for safety factors) compared with steel's twenty thousand pounds, the ice is supported from below by the water it floats in.

An artificial island costs up to $1 million per foot of water depth but cannot be built in depths greater than about fifty feet. A floating ice platform costs as little as $500,000 but cannot support rigs capable of drilling further than about 6,500 feet, and the drilling season is only four months long. Although it is attached to the shore, the ice is nevertheless constantly edging around. For drilling safety the rig is allowed to move a distance no greater than two per cent of the water depth. At an earlier well in two hundred feet of water the rig was able to move only ten feet: when the ice had carried it 9·7 feet the 3,000-foot hole was abandoned and started again. Panarctic was $2 million down the drain with no guarantee that the ice wouldn't keep shifting.

Once a week the Boeing "three-piper" extends its trip beyond Rea Point and brings a new shift direct to the rig, landing on the ice. Homeward-bounders run a dollar sweepstake on the precise minute of touch-down as they wait in the warmth of the camp corridor wearing Calgary street clothes. The husky watchdog kept to warn against polar bears – "When it hides under the table, watch out!" – ran out to greet the 727 as it taxied over the ice. Stewardesses came out for a stroll on the Arctic Ocean. A new selection of four films was put on the front seat of the camp chief's pick-up. The dog wanted to go south with the men and had to be kicked out from under the seats where it was hiding. Then the big jet roared down the strip and climbed into the bottle-clear air: five hours from Arctic sea to Edmonton International.

6

THE BLACK DAWN

*The horror of an oil blowout beneath
the polar pack-ice: weighing
calculated risks against potential
rewards*

The helicopter was full of groceries and even the pilot's foul cheroot
could not mask the reek of lettuces dying in the blast of the cabin
heater. Beside me a master mariner flying out to relieve a drillship
captain, the dial of his watch giving the time in twenty-four world
capitals, spent the flight knotting elaborate turkheads in a rope's
end. Like the other four men squeezed on pipe and canvas seats, we
sweated in bulky flotation jackets. A couple of thousand feet below
was the same patch of Beaufort Sea where I had seen snowploughs
clearing roads over the ice for the turkey trucks carrying supplies to
Imperial's artificial islands. Now it was late summer, the ice had
gone, and the job was done by boat. From this height we could see
distinct patterns where the grey, turbid, fresh water of the great
Mackenzie River blended with the clearer, bluer salt water. In this
deep, blue-green Arctic sea nearly a hundred miles offshore oil men
were pioneering the most risky, costly and difficult exploration
adventure the industry has ever seen.

As the helicopter circled head to wind to approach the landing pad
on the bows of a red drillship lurching in choppy water it seemed a
routine offshore drilling enterprise. Only the nip in the air as we
dodged beneath the whipping rotor blades suggested we were not
aboard one of scores of drillships operating in similar geologically

promising offshore areas such as the Mississippi or Niger deltas, or
the North Sea. There was the usual air of determined functionalism.
Men were either sleeping or working, never wasting time. The apple
pie was marvellous and complaints were quickly radioed ashore
about the dead salad. The captain had gone on a week's leave and
the London *Daily Mirror* he left on his bunk for the new skipper was
only six days old; if nothing else, the oil business made the world
seem awfully small. The ship was a strange mixture of professional
seamen and professional oil men. "You ring the bells for lifeboat
drill," said Captain Colin Meiklejohn, "and along comes some
cowboy with his thumbs in his belt saying, "What's up, Cap?"

What made this drilling operation different was visible from the
ship's bridge. It was enough to turn any ordinary mariner's backbone to jelly. Beyond the tall lattice tower in the waist of the ship you
could pick out through binoculars a glint of white on the knife-edge
horizon to the north. Above it, the washed out appearance of the sky
signalled it was not merely a fragment of ice advancing out of the
north but a huge mass that might extend all the way to the North
Pole and beyond. It was the edge of the polar pack.

The ice could drive down on the ship in a matter of hours,
requiring hasty abandonment of the hole. It could break into many
pieces which would drift around the ship and be pushed out of the
way by tug-like, ice-reinforced supply ships. Or it could retreat again
beyond the horizon. Meanwhile its movements were monitored and
reported hourly by telephone to head office in Calgary.

The polar pack is seventy-five per cent multi-year ice averaging
nine feet thick. It is very hard ice because the salt has had time to
drain out of it. Only five per cent is open water and the remainder is
first-year, relatively soft ice. The whole mass of floes, mashing
against each other to form pressure ridges, and breaking away to
create leads of open water that emit clouds of steam until new ice
once more seals in the warm sea, circulates clockwise around the
Arctic Ocean every seven to ten years. Daily movement of the ice
varies between two and sixteen miles. The line where the moving
pack rubs against the stationary shore-fast ice is called the shear
zone. Vital to wildlife such as seals and birds, because the shear zone
is where most open water occurs, it is a battleground of smashing and
splitting ice as leads open and close, sudden fogs clamp down, and
pressure ridges grow in great tumbling blocks before your eyes. It is a
fearsome place where Eskimos hunting for seals in open leads can
suddenly find themselves on rafts of ice breaking away from the
shore-fast ice and being whirled out into the shifting, deadly wilderness of the polar pack.

This is the environment in which Canmar – the Canadian Marine Drilling Company, a subsidiary of Dome Petroleum, one of Canada's largest independent oil companies – has elected to drill for oil and gas. The potential of the offshore Beaufort Sea is rated at 36 billion barrels of oil and 300 trillion cubic feet of gas, well over three times Canada's total existing reserves. According to Dome Chairman Jack Gallagher, Canada will require twice the existing supply of energy by the turn of the century and the Beaufort Sea offers the best chance of providing it. With three drillships and ten support vessels, Canmar has stuck its neck out to the tune of $235 million in capital costs plus running costs of around $50 million a year.

Due to the ice conditions, the drilling year for Canmar operations has been restricted by government regulations to a basic sixty days. Deep drilling must stop by 25th September, although ten-day extensions can be granted in good ice years.* After that date new holes may be drilled only to 1,600 feet and all ships must leave for winter anchorages by 20th October. In 1976 the ships got in with hours to spare, thrusting through a thick custard of new ice growing stickier around their hulls by the minute and thickening at the rate of four inches a day.

The drillships, two converted US Navy freighters and one purpose-built in Norway, are strengthened to cope with ice and fitted with four thrusters to push away encroaching floes. From the bridge the captain can press a button and blow apart the massive shackles linking his vessel to eight anchors holding her square over the drilling hole. The ten supply ships are seven thousand horsepower, Class II icebreakers capable of bashing through ice ten feet thick; one had just rammed an ice floe but the ice had refused to break and the ship rode up, momentarily high and dry, until the ice rolled and she slid off with damaged propellers. These are waters in which "congested ice conditions" are normal. In 1973 the drilling season could have been twice as long; in 1974 the ice was so bad that none of the ships would have reached its drilling site. The only certainty is that no two years are alike and there is no pattern. When half the sea is covered with ice four inches thick an ice-strengthened ship doesn't have much to worry about. But a single floe drifting down with the polar pack, five feet thick and 110 yards in diameter, weighs about 120,000 tons and has the momentum of a loaded supertanker. Drilling in the offshore Beaufort Sea is like digging a hole in a highway with your back to the traffic.

* Shallow drilling was allowed until Christmas in 1978 when the company chartered the icebreaker *John A. MacDonald* from the coast guard as a support vessel.

From the cockpit of a helicopter bound for Canmar's base camp from a drillship in the Beaufort Sea, the hamlet of Tuktoyaktuk seems to be more water than land; even most of the land rests mainly on a bed of solid ice. The consequences of an oil slick drifting along these low-lying shores then being carried inland by a storm surge are horrendous.

While the captain may be confronted with a $2 million decision on whether to cut loose from the hole to avoid an iceberg, the drillers also face ice problems that have never before been encountered in the oil exploration business. Down to seventy feet the sea-bed is constantly scoured by keels of icefloes. Sometimes they scrape along the bottom like immense bulldozers, scarping out ravines like railway cuttings eighteen feet deep which scientists have photographed and measured with echo-sounding equipment. To avoid the possibility of the well-head being ripped away by an iceberg the drill is spudded in at the bottom of a forty-five foot "glory hole" sucked out by dredger.

For more than a thousand feet below the sea-bed, permafrost exists. A warm drilling pipe going down through this permanently frozen ground can melt the ice so the casing becomes unstable and there is no firm seal, allowing water and gases to bubble up around the outside of the pipe. This has been a regular problem in other parts of the Delta but is that much more difficult to deal with under the sea and against a stiff time schedule. Also, because the area is geologically new, a "rubbish" of unconsolidated sediments and vegetation extends at least four thousand feet down, unlike the North Sea which is solid after about one thousand feet. In the shale shakers, where the cuttings and debris brought up from the drill face are separated out, drillers find chunks of green twigs buried many thousands of years ago in the permafrost and almost perfectly preserved. The vegetation also creates pockets of a kind of marsh gas that builds up very high pressures and can be encountered suddenly. Powerful gas "kicks" are common in Delta drilling. If gas or quantities of hot water bubble up around the outside of the drill casing a bigger hole will be reamed out and the integrity of the blow-out preventer (BOP) could be affected.

Canmar reckons its $2 million blowout preventers installed at the head of every well are capable of controlling any pressure likely to be encountered in any offshore drilling anywhere in the world. If the highly trained driller, one of the best in the world, sees by his instruments that the weight of mud in the drill-pipe is insufficient to hold back the pressure of gas, oil or hot water encountered far below the ground, and that the whole thing is on the way up, within seconds he can shut off the top of the well by operating powerful hydraulic rams that cut through the drill pipe. Once the well is shut down the immediate emergency is over and he can consider what to do with it. One simple method is to circulate heavier mud to overcome the pressure, which is like putting an extra weight on a pressure cooker. the BOP 'stack' of a typical Arctic well has as many as nine different systems, connected one above the other.

The possibility of blowout, when oil or gas comes roaring up the pipe and cannot be stopped, haunts every oil man. A gas blowout can be ignited by the smallest spark and become a fireball, consuming the rig and everything around it. Oil can jet scores of feet, spitting out drill-pipe as if it were a toothpick; breaking out on the sea-bed it would rise to the surface in a plume and form an enormous slick. The damage caused by an uncontrollable oil slick on the sensitive Arctic environment could be catastrophic, and for this reason it is not only oil men but politicians, ecologists, native organisations and ordinary people concerned for the welfare of the polar environment who are haunted by the spectre of an offshore blowout. Once it started, a blowout may be impossible to control until the following year because the ice pack could close in, driving the drillships away from

the scene. As the pack-ice moved steadily over the up-welling foun-
tain of pollution, it would package the stuff, dispersing it far and wide
over a period of many months. The Arctic could awaken from its long
winter night to a horrifying black dawn.

The frequency of offshore blowouts in wildcat drilling depends on
how you read the figures. Canmar says the chances are less than
one-fifth of one per cent, or one in five hundred. The Canadian
government says one in 425 blows out, but of those which have
occurred nine have required relief wells to be drilled and only four
have caused major oil pollution. This might not be so bad if Arctic oil
exploration to date did not have such a poor record. One of Panarctic's first holes, on Melville Island in 1969, struck hot salt water that
blew out of the hole at high pressure and formed an ice pyramid 225
feet high; the rig had to be shifted because it was in danger of being
encased in ice. In October 1971 a Panarctic well on King Christian
Island blew out during a crew change. Gas shooting up the drill-pipe
was ignited by a spark and burned in a pillar of flame, its base one
hundred feet above the ground and its peak as high as 340 feet. The
column of flame burned for four months throughout the mid-winter
darkness and became the beacon of the Arctic; one British Airways
captain on a polar flight saw it from his cockpit and radioed in a
report of an Arctic bush fire.

What would happen if such a blowout occurred beneath the Arctic
sea-ice? While it would be disastrous perhaps for the oil men, it
would not be an environmental catastrophe because gas disperses
relatively cleanly into the atmosphere. If it ignited the heat would
melt a big hole in the ice but pollution would not be significant. It
would be a different story if it was not gas that gushed out of the
seabed, but oil. Opponents of Canmar's drilling operations hold that
existing technology is simply not capable of coping with a blowout in
ice-infested waters. In the first place, drilling in sub-sea permafrost is
risky and new. Secondly, drillers are inevitably involved in a race
against time because their season is so short. Thirdly, if a serious
blowout did occur there might be no way of dealing with it until the

*The black dawn – smoke rises from a small experimental oil-spill burn-off on
the Arctic sea ice. The consequences of having to set fire to crude oil lying in
hundreds of such melt pools scattered along a swathe perhaps two hundred miles
long simply defy the imagination. Photo: David Dickins, NORCOR*

following season, and even then the three-in-ten chance of a bad ice year could hamper operations.

Canmar's application for drilling permits reached the Canadian government at a particularly bad moment because it was arguing at the Law of the Sea Conference that the Arctic was a special case deserving of its own regulations, and was trying to assert dominion over Arctic seas and passages in coastal waters beyond the twelve-mile limit by imposing strict anti-pollution measures. Prime Minister Pierre Trudeau had told Parliament the Arctic ice pack was the most significant area of the globe – "Its continued existence in unspoiled form is vital to all mankind. The single most imminent threat to the Arctic is the threat of a large oil spill ... (which) ... would destroy effectively the primary source of food for Eskimos and carnivorous wildlife throughout thousands of square miles."

To determine the precise effects of an oil blowout in the Beaufort Sea a two-year environmental study costing $12 million, of which a third was financed by the oil industry, was initiated. Called the Beaufort Sea Project, it involved nearly two hundred scientists, naturalists and specialists whose forty-six detailed reports scotched the principal fear of an Arctic blowout echoed by Trudeau, that an oil-blackened polar ice pack would alter the climate of the northern hemisphere. But the reports did paint a devastating picture of environmental damage that would be all the worse for the Arctic's unique sensitivity and slow time scale. Pollution would not persist for a few months, as in the English Channel or California, but for decades. Microbiological organisms are active only a few weeks a year, evaporation is slight due to cold, and ice floes tend to act like a breakwater so there would be little wave action to stir up the oil and assist dispersal.

The Mackenzie Delta is comparable with the Everglades as a huge wet sponge of enormous biological vitality where many animals spend a critical stage of their lives. The wildlife most seriously affected would be birds, millions of them converging to nest in the western Arctic from wintering grounds scattered over a third of the globe. About one hundred species migrate to the Beaufort Sea and its coastline to feed, nest and moult. Two-thirds – swans, snow geese, white-fronted geese – fly in by way of the prairies and the Mackenzie Valley. Others – geese such as Pacific brant from Mexico and California, eiders, guillemots and gulls from the North Pacific – come along the northern coast by way of Alaska. Among them are Arctic terns migrating from the Antarctic, so the only time they ever see darkness is briefly during their 12,000-mile transit between polar regions. Some birds pair and copulate before they arrive so the shortness of the season is no disadvantage. Such is the concentration of birds that during one six-week migration period 240,000 birds of fifty species were recorded passing just one spit on the north Yukon coast. On arrival, birds are concentrated by geographic features such as open leads in shallow water which are popular stopovers for diving birds: during one spring week in 1974 175,000 loons, oldsquaws and eiders were counted in a single polynya (area of open water in the pack ice).

The delta and its coastal fringe are the major Canadian nesting grounds of all ducks, geese and swans. Brackish shallow waters make ideal summer feeding and moulting grounds for 600,000 scaup, oldsquaws and scoters. Barrier beaches and sand bars are important nesting grounds because they are island barriers against predators like foxes. It is all these areas vital to birds that are likely to be the final resting place of any oil released into the Beaufort Sea, and the scale of the disaster could be greatly magnified because the oil would remain in place for years.

If oil drifted into the delta beaches periodic storm surges would carry it scores of miles inland in a tidal wave of pollution. Oil stirred by wave action into the shingle and sand bars and spits would emerge years later and lie on the surface. Clean-up of mudflats, shingle beaches and cliffs would probably not be possible: the areas of low-lying tundra flooded occasionally by the sea are sensitive to foot traffic, let alone vehicles, and most of the inshore waters are too shallow for any but the smallest boats. If oil was burned off the vegetation might not recover by natural means for fifty years. Protection of most of the low, estuary-like coast would be impossible and the Arctic environment makes practically every known clean-up technique useless.

Due to the muddiness of the Mackenzie water, and the coldness of its temperature, the Beaufort Sea is a biological desert when compared with other waters on the same latitude such as Davis Strait, which produces ten times as many organisms, or the North Atlantic which is forty times more productive. Biological activity, when it does occur in the Beaufort Sea, is rapid and effusive because constant daylight allows photosynthesis to take place without interruption. Zooplanktons are adapted to a life of short feast and long famine. Oil pollution would directly affect this productivity which in turn would affect birds and also the five thousand beluga whales that in summer seek the shallows of warm river water in which to nurse their calves; even if they avoided the oil, their routine would be disturbed by the activity of boats and machinery cleaning it up. In one polynya only twenty miles from a Canmar drilling site 1,500 belugas were counted. Bowhead whales also push through the cracks and leads of the shear zone feeding on invertebrates attracted by increased light and food. It is estimated that about thirty per cent of the fifty thousand seals hauling out on the ice to moult in late June would encounter oil, and oiled seals would in turn have an effect on polar bears and Arctic foxes.

How many of these birds and animals are at risk of being affected from an offshore oil blowout is unknown. A large slick remaining at sea would have little effect, but a small slick inundating an ecologically critical area could be disastrous. Nevertheless, any "disaster" of this kind must be put in the perspective of the total ecological picture. Natural disasters are routine, such as the late spring in 1964 which froze over the open leads and caused the death from starvation of about 100,000 king eider ducks. Hunters in Canada and the US shoot about one and a half million swans and geese a year, most of them reared in the Arctic, plus hundreds of thousands of ducks, a kill ratio unlikely to be exceeded by any single oil blowout.

Basing their calculations on the fact that the geology is similar to that of other delta oil fields such as the Gulf of Mexico, government and oil industry scientists have figured that a "typical" blowout occurring in the Beaufort Sea would release 2,500 barrels of oil a day during the first month, and 1,500 barrels a day thereafter. The blowout could in fact be ten times bigger, or insignificant. Many oil men remember the Atlantic No. 3 well near Edmonton that blew out in 1948; for six months it spewed out ten thousand barrels a day plus huge volumes of gas, and when it caught fire the flame shot eight hundred feet. In Saudi Arabia blowouts flow at anything up to thirty thousand barrels a day.

Accepting these official figures as little more than something to go on, what would be the effects of a blowout occurring just as a drillship was preparing to close its well in late September?

By the end of May total output of the blowout would be around 40,000 tons. If it lay in a single slick one-tenth of an inch thick it would cover about eight and a half square miles. In the event, it would inevitably be broken up into fragments by gas and carried away by drifting ice. Had a blowout occurred on Canmar's number one drill-site at the end of the 1976 season, according to Beaufort Sea Project scientists, about 2,600 tons of oil would have been carried to the innermost reaches of bays and lagoons along the shoreline by a storm surge that occurred the following month. Some oil would have been carried northeastwards towards Banks Island and some trapped in the growing apron of landfast ice. By early May about 17,000 tons of oil would have been distributed in pockets along the northern edge of the landfast ice for 250 miles to the west. – "A harpoon pointed at our hearts", say the North Slope Eskimo leaders. However these estimates of the extent of the swathe of oil were based on observations of an ice island; further work has suggested its rate of drift was atypical and that in the course of a winter the oil would be carried only twenty or thirty miles.

The silent slaughter occurring in the globs and tentacles of the black dawn would contrast markedly with the noise and frenzy it would cause on shore. When the Canadian government decided at Cabinet level that it could live with the risks and drilling should go ahead, it also signalled the start of a bureaucratic bonanza. An inter-government task force prepared oil-spill contingency measures under the game-name of Operation Toxin Tocsin. An army of civil servants would be mobilised, and if the consequences of an Arctic offshore blowout seem appalling, they are nothing compared with the bureaucratic foul-up that seems likely to ensue. Despite the glibness of the contingency plans the whole thing is speculative and embryonic because nobody has ever seen – let alone contended with – a major oil slick in ice-infested waters. The picture that emerges is one of a riveting technological drama, best described as a back-to-front version of fighting a great forest fire, in which the aim is to set alight to as much as possible.

In open water, floating oil can be contained easily by special Arctic booms, floating barriers constructed so small ice floes can slide over the top of them. Booms would also be deployed to protect the most ecologically critical parts of the shoreline, which vary according to the time of the year. Unlike the North Sea, where waves are seldom less than five feet high and swells can be ten feet high on a "calm" day, clean-up would not be hampered by high seas because of the damping effect of the floating ice; Beaufort Sea waves are usually less than three feet high, eight feet at worst. Nevertheless, mariners would be struggling against great difficulties due to lack of reliable weather forecasting, long periods of fog as the season drew in, and the fact that September and October are the windiest and stormiest months of the year. In 1975 a "25-year storm" and a "50-year storm" threw probability factors to the winds by striking the Beaufort Sea in the same week. Chemical dispersal of oil would be limited by cold and lack of mixing by waves.

The real problem begins when the sea freezes over, and massive ice floes from the polar pack drift over the blowout.

When the oil drifted beneath landfast ice, teams of workers would follow it, drilling through the ice with mechanical augurs to relieve the gas pressure and allowing the oil to bubble up. As the oil was burned off, the ice would melt, creating pools in which more oil would collect and be trapped. Trenches for trapping oil could be blasted out, then allowed to freeze over; one shot of thirty-five tonnes of TNT is calculated to create storage for eleven days' worth of oil. Once the oil was collected it could be pumped out. In the shear zone, which varies in position according to the strength of landfast ice, oil would collect in narrow leads. When floes pressed together the oil would ooze over the top and saturate the snow. Black pressure ridges would erupt like volcanic larva, a spectacle of dread horror in the deep darkness of the long winter night.

Pack ice moving with the current over a wild well would be like a ceiling gliding over a paint brush. If the ice moved an average one and a half miles a day, the oiled areas could travel more than three hundred miles during the seven months of winter. As it moved, the ice would collect a ton of oil every thirty-eight feet, spread in a band nearly a hundred feet wide. Once the oil was trapped in the hollows beneath the moving floes the ice would begin to grow around it. First an ice lip forms and after about a week grows beneath the oil pool – "encapsulating it like chocolate sauce in an ice-cream sandwich".

Once its covering of snow melts in late spring the ice begins to decay first through its brine channels. The oil would gravitate upwards at a fast rate, forming pools on the surface. Its blackness would absorb heat from the sun and hasten the melting. Because it was so perfectly packaged, the oil would retain most of its volatile elements, and burn easily. In average weather conditions there would be a period of five to eight weeks between the oil emerging and the ice becoming unsafe to work on, when burning operations will be possible; as it will take two weeks for the pools of oil to grow large enough to burn, and bad weather is likely to restrict flying for at least one day in five, the total operational "window" is only fifteen to thirty days. During this time the Arctic will be a macabre scene as helicopters skip from pool to pool, setting each one alight with a cupful of gasoline and a flare fired by pistol. Most pools will require burning at least two or three times. The sky will fill with dense black smoke along a broad front scores of miles in extent. There will be loud cracking and hissing as the oil atomises, the water boils, and ice floes fracture. Temperature inversions that prevent hot air from rising are characteristic of the Beaufort Sea in spring, so the smoke will hang about for hours, perhaps days, until a brisk wind clears it away. If it drifts inland it could affect lichens (important food for caribou) which die out so rapidly with contamination that they are used as biological indicators of air pollution.

Thick, multi-year ice floes of the polar pack have no brine channels through which oil could reach the surface in the first spring. Multi-year ice melts on top in summer and grows from below in winter, so it could be ten years before the oil trapped within actually reaches the surface. Polluted ice floes would have to be tracked by placing radar reflectors on them as they drifted over the blowout, and followed as they circulated around the Arctic Ocean.

Even if burn-off was successful a gummy residue of at least ten per cent (possibly fifty per cent) of the total volume would be left in tens of thousands of pools and eventually wash up on the shoreline. To collect all five thousand tons of this material in the available time would require a work force of up to 1,200 men deployed along the coast by fleets of helicopters; disposal of the debris would also be an immense logistical problem.

What is happening in the Beaufort Sea is just the beginning, for at the end of 1979 the US government was planning to sell exploration leases for the off-shore continental shelf north of Alaska. Drilling is also being planned for the deep waters of Lancaster Sound, a part of the Northwest Passage which happens to be the principal wildlife oasis of the eastern Arctic. It is so important that the International Biological Programme recommended its designation as a major ecological preserve, and it was selected by the Department of Environment as a desirable site for a maritime national park. Before drilling starts the government will await the findings of three to five-year environmental study similar to the Beaufort Sea Project, but this time a hypothetical blowout of ten thousand barrels a day will be the basis of calculations.

What really concerns serious environmentalists is lack of decent rationalisation between the development of the Arctic, and logical preparation for it. In 1979 Canmar was building a new kind of icebreaker that would be a prototype of the biggest icebreaker in the world, to be launched within a couple of years, which would provide a year-round base for clean-up operations while extending the drilling season immediately to at least two hundred days; in 1978 it chartered the Coast Guard icebreaker *John A. MacDonald* for $17,000 a day to extend the season to December. Environmentalists argue that the icebreaker should have been provided *before* any drilling was started. They also say the icebreaker itself is typical of the lack of preparation prior to technological development, because it is not known how a new vessel powerful enough to operate year-round will affect distribution of wildlife by creating leads of open water.

A blowout that blackens the Arctic ice for hundreds of square miles is an easy catastrophe to "sell" to the public because, like the clubbing of baby seals, it is something they can get their emotional teeth into. But it is by no means the most critical question. In the unlikely event of it happening, a blowout would indeed be a disaster but the Arctic would ultimately recover. The recovery might take many years, but it would happen.

More sinister is the possibility of a large oil field being discovered and of continuous small spills causing steady, undramatic but pernicious damage. If the Beaufort Sea oil field was a quarter of the size of Prudhoe Bay between thirty and sixty barrels a day would be spilled. How much of this kind of certain punishment could the Beaufort Sea take? The possibility of pollution from a blowout can be rated at between one in 500 and one in 5,000, and everyone is anxious about it. Steady but small-scale pollution from oil production is certain, yet the question is largely ignored.

In 1977 and 1978 drilling seasons, Canmar's drillships found substantial quantities of oil and gas, though just how much was being kept a close secret. Share prices rocketed and Dome Petroleum President William Richards forecast partial production of the wells by 1985. The worst fears of environmentalists appeared to be confirmed in July 1978 when an ice floe broke the anchor ropes of *Explorer III* and in her hasty retreat from the hole the well-head was damaged. It was not oil that leaked up from the hole, but water. But it was a caution. The government tightened its regulations but attached no blame to the company or its procedures, except that the risk from the ice was not recognised early enough.

In drilling the Beaufort Sea Canmar is shooting from the hip. It claims to have the best shots and the best guns in the business, and the sheriff, in the guise of the federal government, is providing cover.

You could argue that the shortness of the season creates unnecessary human stress which leads to short cuts and accidents, but the need for energy is urgent and there is no reason to suppose the air of forcefulness and enterprise aboard any drillship would change if the season was made longer. When it comes down to discussing drilling problems with the top men in the world, outsiders are anyway in the position of the nervous Concorde passenger who asked the pilot how he found his way so high above the ground and was told: "You see those lights on the wingtips? I just fly right between 'em". For the oil men Beaufort Sea drilling is a technological adventure in which expertise gained today will be applied in other parts of the Arctic tomorrow. For the government it is a calculated risk. For environmentalists it is an unlimited horror, but after three not-so disastrous seasons even they are learning to live with it.

7

PIPEDREAMS AND NIGHTMARES

*Why the march of pipelines bringing
Arctic oil and gas to southern
markets is the ultimate environmental
insult*

"Square dancing – all welcome!" The advert in the daily *News-Miner*
I was reading over steak and chips at a 24-hour diner on the airport
road promised a livelier way of spending a first evening in Fairbanks,
Alaska, than watching TV in a motel room. I imagined a typical
North American bar with lots of dark corners where I could twitch
my toes to some country-style music and see how these Alaskan folk
kicked their heels. But it wasn't quite like that. It turned out to be a
typical rural community hall, brightly lit with a bare-board floor and
home-made posters of musical notes pinned to the walls above hard,
wooden benches. The men, noticeably tall, had sweat towels on gold
loops slung from their belts, while even with bouffant hair styles and
bouncy petticoats their wives seemed small. The crowd was predom-
inantly middle-aged, rather formal but very friendly, and once I
got through that door there was no way of backing out. My name was
taken. As the song number ended and the dancers bowed to the
centre with a lilting "Thaaan-kyou!" the caller made a special
announcement welcoming a new friend from London–England to
The Nugget Squares. Clutching my paper cup of cherryade I made a
flustered bow.

During the evening nearly every couple made a point of coming to
shake my hand and I was able to meet a cross section of Alaskan

society. Not "boomers" here for the oil industry's mega-buck but those who called the place home. In this unlikely setting I met research engineers, scientists, chief of a NASA satellite tracking station, air force people, university staff, city officials. Many were connected with work in the Arctic and later gave me all kinds of help: like others before me I had come to Alaska and immediately struck gold. Meanwhile, every conversation turned back on itself as neatly as the sets being called to the foot-jigging music. These plain, pleasant, homely folk were having to live with the consequences of the biggest and most controversial construction project in the history of the free world, and it was evident the Alyeska oil pipeline would be on their minds for a long time yet.

There are those who cringed at the pipeline's existence. Who see it spoiling and interfering with the beauty of the rugged terrain and the wild rivers for which the country is famous. On the other hand, there are those who can't be upset by the pipeline, especially while driving home from the great wilderness. Flying over the pipeline in a small plane one wouldn't know it was not a road or stream water catching the light. In reality the pipeline is much less intrusive than, say, a freeway or high tension cables on pylons. When I first saw it, the pipeline did not diminish the landscape but was a yardstick by which the eye could more easily measure its true scale.

Evidently a pipeline was not something about which you could have mixed feelings. It was a monument to the ingenuity of Man; it was an aesthetic abomination. You loved it or loathed it. There was no middle way and the whole issue had become one of emotional reaction, far beyond rational discussion. A few minutes' drive out of town, where it zig-zags out of a thick aspen wood and marches across a stony stream-flat on high stilts capped with radiator fins, the pipeline is a tourist attraction. Campers, pick-ups and sight-seeing buses turn off the road to look at it. Tourists pat its burnished fuselage as if trying to sense the hot oil slicking southwards at a steady four and a half miles an hour. The brave and agile clamber on top, photographing each other in defiant poses like hunters on a dead elephant. *Bill loves Nancy, Charley Fredericks was drunk here*: once a thing like a pipeline is in place it seems there is nothing much you can do except scribble on it. Or, as dents in the tin and glassfibre cladding testify, take pot shots at it.

In this kind of wooded country the great pipeline is as innocuous a piece of hardware as a town water supply. It is utterly silent, with no vibration. You could walk within yards and not know it was there. For nearly half the distance between Prudhoe Bay and the tanker terminal at Valdez the pipeline is buried, and apart from its slowly

Zig-zagging southwards over the tundra on its 800-mile journey across the Alaskan wilderness to the Pacific coast at Valdez, the Alyeska pipeline leaves pumping station number one at Prudhoe Bay. BP photo.

healing scar the only sign of it is a well-built gravel road nearby, and the ugly pits from which the gravel came. Only in open country does the thing hit you in the eye, but then the sheer scale of the enterprise – a silver worm threading together vistas of great distance – can only be described as stunning. Crossing three mountain ranges, spanning eight hundred rivers and streams including the mighty Yukon, a focus for the eye in a 799·1-mile continuum of magnificent wilderness, the pipeline is unquestionably as much an engineering marvel as it is a terrible shame.

Flying over it in winter, the pipeline sems a hairline crack in the porcelain bowl of Alaska's ice-bound heartland; in summer it glints in the sunlight like the track of a purposeful snail. Wien-Alaska's 737 pilots point it out to passengers with the zeal of a home-owner showing off a new hi-fi. Its economics are equally beautiful. When running at full capacity, delivering 1,200,000 barrels of oil a day, the eight oil companies owning the pipeline will reap five thousand dollars every minute of every day.

This dream of an operation bringing urgently required energy to the nation – say the oil companies – is as insignificant in the environment as a chalk mark running the length of a football field. That's one point of view, with much to commend it. Another point of view, equally defensible, is that the trans-Alaska pipeline is as insignificant as a razor slash across the Mona Lisa.

The major environmental impact of the pipeline is not that it disturbs wildlife or drips oil, but that it exists. The pipeline is an insult because it deflowered and defiled the last truly virgin chunk of wilderness in the USA. The guts of environmentalist opposition to the pipeline is not fear of pollution and damage, although that plays a part and has been effectively wielded as a weapon to win public sympathy, but the certain knowledge of what the pipeline will bring. What it will bring is people.

Already the $30,000-a-mile gravel haul road paralleling the pipeline is busy with traffic – security men patrolling and inspecting the pipe, engineers doing maintenance, trucks hauling supplies and spare parts to the twelve pump stations along the route, and materials for the new pump stations which will increase the line's capacity. Overhead there is regular traffic of contrailing jets, buzzing light planes and thudding choppers. And this is just the beginning.

Before 1990, if the oil men find what they expect in other parts of the North Slope and offshore, at least two gas lines and one more oil line will be needed. The haul road will almost certainly be made accessible to the public and it is a good bet the pipeline corridor, fifteen miles wide, will become an Arctic arm of mobile America with accommodation lodges, gas stations and quick-food diners. From this trunk many branches are bound to grow, and even if the desires of environmentalists are fulfilled, and Congress decides that Alaska *can* be both oil barrel and national park to the nation, the precious wilderness will become nothing but a new Yellowstone. The pipeline has deprived Alaska of that one precious resource which no other part of the US could provide – true lonesomeness.

What makes environmentalists sick at heart is the idea that it might be all for nothing – that if the same huge sums were spent on insulating homes and developing solar energy the oil and gas from the Arctic would not be needed. They believe a change from today's high-energy lifestyle is inevitable, that we should make a start now to wean ourselves from oil, and exploiting Arctic resources only provides us with a false sense of security and delays the crunch.

There is no point in asking the engineer on the spot, or even his corporation president, whether our society should be governed by the profit motive. His job is devising a means of carrying hot oil through frozen ground, not setting himself up as an instrument of change, and when pitched this kind of question by indignant environmentalists is more likely to bat the pitcher over the head than strike out for a home run. No matter which way you question the morality of oil companies it is a simple fact that without oil and gas the industrial economy as we know it will collapse. In the southern states of USA and most of Europe a life without oil and gas would make many people physically uncomfortable and probably very angry, but in Canada and the northern tier states many people would die. Unlike the dancing Nugget Squares, the vast populations of northern city dwellers cannot trek out and cut their own firewood. And if oil companies do the job society expects of them and find more hydrocarbon reserves in the Arctic, pipelines like this will be the least expensive and least environmentally damaging means of transporting the stuff to where it is needed.

Worry over the impact of large numbers of Whites on small numbers of Indians and Eskimos living a gentle lifestyle on the banks and delta of the mighty Mackenzie River was also the root of resistance to the gas pipeline that gripped Canada from 1975–7. For the first time ever, multi-national corporations, with budgets greater than that of Canada herself, were stopped in their tracks – by a blind Eskimo, and an idealistic judge who made people see that the same northern territory considered to be the ultimate frontier of oil exploration was also the homeland of the people who lived there and should be treated as such. White society, the judge thought, should take this chance to do something right for the North American native. The judgement had many ironic results, as we shall see, not least of which was the immediate adoption of an alternative route through Fairbanks and the heart of Alaska. This line, carrying natural gas from Prudhoe Bay, will run alongside the Alyeska oil pipeline to Fairbanks then bend south-east to parallel the Alaska Highway through the Yukon and British Columbia; when sufficient gas is found in the Mackenzie Delta a 400-mile spur will follow the route of the Dempster Highway.

A third Arctic pipeline is being proposed, to bring the gas from Panarctic's Drake and Hecla fields in the islands to market in southern Ontario. While the Alyeska pipeline crosses only 250 miles of open tundra in the true Arctic (the remainder being in sub-Arctic

mountains and taiga, the stunted, marshy forest), the Polar Gas
Project plans to cut across 1,500 miles of fearsomely severe barren
lands and Arctic deserts west of Hudson Bay and north among the
Arctic islands, plus another 700 miles of boreal forest. It will also
make five sea crossings, one of ice-covered water nine hundred feet
deep. In theory it should be neither as environmentally sensitive as
Alyeska nor as socially detrimental as the Mackenzie Valley proposal, but it is delicately political because of pending Canadian
Eskimo land claims (see Chapter 14).

In any discussion of industrial development in the Arctic it is a
recognised tactic to formulate what is called a "worst case" scenario
as an example of the worst that *could* happen. The "black dawn"
described in the previous chapter is in this league. In other disaster-
prone activities such as air travel and oil-tanker operation there is a
wealth of previous experience from which accurate risk factors can
be computed. In the Arctic such calculations are guesswork based on
probabilities and limited records, but in the case of Arctic pipelines
many believe the "worst case" has already happened, in Alaska.

Engineers who came in from Houston and London from the start
equated the environmental challenges of the Arctic with those of
Arabia. "Hell, you just dig a big ditch and kick the pipe in – what's
the big deal?" The big deal was that in the first year a four-foot
pipeline filled with oil at a well-head temperature of 65 to 80 °F (18 to
26 °C) would melt out a trench in the permafrost twenty-six feet deep
and thirty feet wide. As most of the country's permafrost experts
lived not in Alaska, the only American state that has permafrost, but
in Menlo Park, California, or Hanover, New Hampshire, it took the
engineers some time to find this out. But the five years of delays,
caused first by the native land claims question then by an assortment
of opposition forces that collected under the environmentalist banner and successfully challenged the project on points of law, gave
engineers the time they needed to get to grips with the problems and
produce good solutions. In 1973 world-wide fuel shortages and the
price explosion following the OPEC oil embargo allowed the US
Congress to exempt the pipeline from further procedural delays "in
the national interest". The delay also enabled some realistic
environmental stipulations to be worked out, although monitoring
largely fell apart (see next chapter) due to the pressures of expediency. Today the pipeline's ultimate effect on the landscape in
terms of landslides, frost heave and drainage, and its engineering
integrity, including its ability to withstand severe earthquake, have
yet to be tested by time and event.

Construction of the whole thing cost $9 billion, nearly ten times more than was originally planned. The owning companies* were fortunate that during the same period the cost of oil rose so spectacularly. About seventy thousand people all over the world worked on design and construction at different times. Pipeliners on the site numbered 21,600 workers during the 1973–7 peak, earning a total $800,000 a day. They hit Fairbanks like a three-year pop festival. Labourers could pick up $1,000 a week, skilled men $1,600 or more.

The Teamsters Union became the largest and by far the most powerful special interest group in Alaska. Members of Teamsters Union Local 959 work in eighty crafts and trades, from surveyors and long-distance telephone operators to police officers, bakers, nurses, and drillers. Even by comparison with the oil giants its $100 million pension fund, invested almost entirely within the State, is a powerful financial force.

Fairbanks, hub of the pipeline activity, had been born on the site of a trade store supplying gold diggers in 1902 and took the boom more or less in its stride. The sad thing Fairbanks suffered most was sudden affluence at the cost of its soul. The style of life it enjoyed and wanted to keep was one of small businesses, diversity of interests, small population, and access to true wilderness. However, the arrival of big corporations and big government led to big crime, big unions and big problems. Overnight the place became a trailer town. Any tar-paper shack with a bed could be let for outrageous prices. The population increased by sixty per cent, as did incomes. Violent crime more than doubled while over half the town's police force, including its chief, went to work for the pipeline; Governor Jay Hammond wanted to send in State troopers to preserve law and order. Schools had to double shift, people waiting for pipeline work signed up for university courses so they could use cheap student accommodation. The number of divorces came within a hair's breadth of exceeding the number of marriages. Community planning went out of the window because so many people wanted to get rich, with the result that too many new homes tapped artesian water supplies and over-taxed the system which dried up so nobody could use it without sinking deeper, very expensive bores. Due to the lack of hydrants fire insurance premiums increased ten-fold.

Well over half the people of Fairbanks thought their town had changed for the worse and that their own quality of life had suffered. Intensity of work swept up women as well as men, demanding long periods away from home. Only a handful of people were smart

* Sohio 33·34 per cent, BP 15·84 per cent, ARCO 21 per cent, Exxon 20 per cent, Mobil 5 per cent, Union 1·66 per cent, Phillips 1·66 per cent, Amerada Hess 1·5 per cent.

enough to save money and, when it was all over, buy that dream-house or ranch. Most spent money as quickly as it was earned: every year one household in two bought a new car, truck or snow machine.

If the construction of a pipeline could have such a disruptive effect on Whites who were experienced practitioners and advocates of the cash and carry culture, what sort of economic neutron bomb would eventually fall on the tiny native communities scattered throughout the Arctic where a few hundred Indians and Eskimos made the best of a hunting and fishing lifestyle? This was the question that pre-occupied Canada, for a second pipeline was urgently needed to transport the natural gas produced as a by-product of Prudhoe Bay oil, and it was proposed that the gas pipeline should cut across the northern Yukon to the Mackenzie Delta where it could pick up the relatively small amounts of gas that had been discovered there then run parallel with the Mackenzie River to connect up with existing pipelines 1,500 miles to the south.

Millions of dollars were spent on environmental research and gearing up for the immense new project. The Canadian Cabinet declared the pipeline to be "in the national interest" and only one question remained to be settled: the native land claim. The fact that natives had a fundamental right to their lands had already been recognised by the government. Large cash settlements with rela-tively small pockets of special native land, on the lines of recent land settlements in Alaska and James Bay, were predicted. It was assumed the project would go ahead while these details were ham-mered out: the steam roller of government-backed big business would take a lot of stopping.

This proved to be a grave miscalculation. The Mackenzie natives did not want cash, they wanted to keep their land, all of it. When the pipeline was built they wanted a share of the action. Meanwhile, there would be no pipeline until the land claims issue was settled on their terms. For what they wanted most of all, according to the case subsequently put by their White advisers, was time – time to adjust to the increasing pace of what they termed acculturation, time for the land claim to be settled, time to work out how their own identities as Eskimos and Indians could be protected within the development context. In short, they pleaded for the fundamental right to decide their own futures.

This appeal touched a raw nerve in southern Canada, where the issue was seen as North America's last chance to deal fairly with the indigenous people – the last Indian war, and one which in the name of fair play it was Whites' turn to lose.

While Canada's National Energy Board conducted hearings to

decide formally whether a Mackenzie Valley pipeline was the nation's best answer to the energy crisis, the government commissioned Thomas R. Berger, a British Columbia judge, to decide what terms and conditions should be attached to the building of a pipeline. While the NEB decided in the national interest, Judge Berger considered what stipulations would best protect the environment and ecology and the well-being of local communities.

For twenty months Berger presided at hearings in forty-eight cities, towns and communities throughout Canada; some 1,800 people testified and the evidence amounted to 32,000 pages of transcript. The one-man inquiry became a forum for the discussion of national ideals, going far beyond the basic issues of how the impact of a pipeline could affect local interests.

An intense humanist and socialist, son of a RCMP sergeant, Berger had been briefly a Member of Parliament for the New Democratic Party and also the party's leader in BC. He was appointed to the job as a judge, but everyone conveniently overlooked the fact that he was first a politician of the left, and second one of the country's best-known Indian rights lawyers, having acted on behalf of BC's Indians in their eight-year fight for recognition of land claims. His victory there is the main basis for the assertion of all native rights in Canada today: three out of seven appeal judges in the Supreme Court found that the BC Indians not only had aboriginal title to the land before the white men arrived, but they still had it.

Berger made himself a folk hero by sheer patience. In corduroy jacket and construction boots, sometimes taking a break to bat a ball around with some local kids, Berger cut a friendly, low-key figure that anybody could talk to.

It was the first time the native voice had ever been formally and painstakingly listened to. Native advisers recognised that in the publicity spotlight simplicity and naïvety could be wielded like napalm on the jungle of public opinion. While industry men spoke of engineering detail, sophisticated biological studies, training schemes, employment opportunities, energy requirements and construction schedules, native men and their wives and children in front of Mr Berger's table spoke with eloquent directness of their lives in this land and how they wanted to preserve it for their children.

The evidence was deeply felt, and was a goldmine for the media circus travelling with Berger, but it involved a lot of posturing which Southern audiences were unable to recognise and put into perspective. In miles, the Mackenzie Delta is as distant from the great majority of Canadians as Central America, and the distance in understanding seems almost as great. Few Canadians were in a position to realise, for example, the level of social disruption that has already occurred without any kind of industrial development. They were too ready to accept at face value any native statement that everything new was to blame for social disruption, and that any form of development was all bad.

In the western Arctic the Eskimo native organisation was the Committee for Original People's Entitlement (COPE), headed by a local Eskimo called Sam Raddi who had been blinded a few years before. In Inuvik it was commonly believed he was blinded by drinking anti-freeze as a youth but Raddi himself refuses to talk about it. In the mud-slinging at Inuvik it was said that the team of Whites behind Raddi made him sign letters he could not see, and read aloud to him only those parts of newspaper reports that were favourable.

The native organisations were supported in their fight against the pipeline by two strong church groups. One was Project North, an amalgam of anti-development groups in the Roman Catholic, Lutheran, United and Presbyterean Churches. This powerful group roused Christian consciences on behalf of the natives and gave the impression of a huge groundswell of public opinion running against the pipeline.

While southern Whites were blind to the fact that natives had been needing a way out of social disruption since the turn of the century, and have been denied the kind of infrastructure which a pipeline could bring them, Whites in the north and working natives made the mistake of assuming the pipeline was inevitable, and that it was a waste of time stating the obvious in a courtroom.

There were other issues; the visual impact of a right-of-way 120 feet wide and 1,350 miles long (north of 60° lat.) with a pump station every fifty miles; the alteration of land drainage and turbidity of water affecting fish spawning and populations of small aquatic animals like the musk-rat, inevitable spillage from river traffic and construction vehicles. The pipeline had to cross the range of 100,000 barren ground caribou in the northern Yukon: a coastal route might interfere with calving grounds, an inland route with migration patterns. Development of gas-gathering systems and further wells in the delta region threatened beluga whales, which entered the warmer, turbid shallows to nurse their calves. Aircraft movements could disturb thousands of nesting wildfowl.

Unhappily for Arctic Gas, a consortium of twenty-eight oil and pipeline companies, the 214 days of NEB hearings were interrupted and delayed when the impartiality of its chairman was challenged. This allowed Berger to publish first. In May 1977 his report *Northern*

Frontier, Northern Homeland hit in a blizzard of publicity, and altered Canada's vision of the North from that of a frontier to be exploited to a homeland to be protected.

The Berger Report recommended a ten-year moratorium on the building of a Mackenzie Valley pipeline, completely ruled out any link across the northern Yukon, and proposed two wildlife reserves to protect the caribou and beluga. If Alaskan gas *had* to be brought down through Canada immediately, Berger recommended a pipeline should parallel the Alaska Highway where he thought environmental risks were smaller and there was already an established infrastructure. Influenced by southern Canada's warm and overwhelming support of Berger, the NEB opted for the Alaska Highway route.

The Canadian government might have been secretly appalled and astonished by the Berger Report but was able to live with it in view of the simple fact that 20 tcf of gas was needed to justify an all-Canadian pipeline but only 6 tcf had been found. There simply wasn't enough gas in the delta to get excited about.

Meanwhile, attention switched to the Alaska Highway. Canadian and US governments agreed the line would be built in Alaska by Northwest Energy Inc of Salt Lake City, which had joined forces in Canada with Alberta Gas Trunk Line Co Ltd (AGTL) and West Coast Transmission Co Ltd. The 2,400-mile pipeline would probably cost $14 billion at 1977 prices and carry 2·4 billion cubic feet of gas a day by the middle of 1983. A study of the 512-mile Yukon section of the route resulted in a recommendation that funds of $250 million be provided to compensate Yukon communities for the kinds of impact complained of by the residents of Fairbanks and that construction be delayed four years to permit implementation of land claims. AGTL intended applying immediately for permission to build the spur along the Dempster Highway between the Mackenzie Delta and Dawson.

Built piecemeal since 1958 and opened in 1979, the Dempster would be North America's first public highway to the Arctic. Ironically, scarcely any environmental information existed about either highway route. In the public mind, lack of information is generally equated with lack of problems, but this is not necessarily so. The range of the Porcupine caribou herd which Mr Berger was so anxious to protect in the northern Yukon is bisected by the Dempster Highway. Many experts believe this disturbance will have a far greater effect than the Arctic Gas proposal to build along the coastal fringe of the calving ground.

Meanwhile one company had been keeping a very low profile

throughout the pipeline argument in the western Arctic, for it was on the point of launching a battle of its own. Polar Gas Project, a consortium that includes Petro–Canada, the state oil company, and the Ontario Energy Board, wants to build a 2,338-mile pipeline between the Arctic Islands and southern Ontario. Ultimately the pipeline will be extended to other islands within 750 miles of the North Pole. The line will be 42 inches in diameter, carrying three billion cubic feet of gas a day (more than Canada's present total daily consumption), and will be buried along its entire length. If the logistics and technology of the Alyeska and Alaska Highway projects are stunning, those of Polar Gas are doubly so. More than 1500 miles of the route will lie in continuous permafrost. Five sea crossings totalling ninety miles have to be made, one of them nine hundred feet deep. These crossings will be made by lay-barge during the open-water season, by tunnelling, and by using platforms of artificially thickened ice like Panarctic's ice platforms as anchoring points for pulling the pipeline along the bottom.

At least, with a buried pipeline carrying chilled gas, neither the Alaska Highway pipeline operators nor Polar Gas faces the awful possibility haunting Alyeska, whose long mileages of raised pipeline carrying hot oil are more open to sabotage and accident. "We can only count on the goodwill of Mankind," a spokesman told me with tongue in cheek. "Really, there's no protection at all: we just have to hope it's left alone." Constant surveillance patrols were unable to prevent two sabotage incidents soon after the pipeline started flowing in 1977, and an industrial accident blew up a pumping station just outside Fairbanks. What would happen if technical trouble or sabotage caused a prolonged stoppage in the flow of oil through the pipe? It is only friction that keeps the oil warm, and it is so well insulated that if it stopped moving it would remain fluid for twenty-one days. But if it ever did stop long enough to freeze up the nine billion barrels of crude oil in the pipe would have to be chipped out – "What we'd have here in Alaska," said one engineer, "is the longest tube of Chapstick in the world."

8

ECO-WATCH

*Fact and fancy in the question of
preventing industrial damage to the
sensitive Arctic environment*

BP Flight One out of Anchorage for Deadhorse Airport was crowded
because the US Interstate Oil Compact Commission had taken a
day out from its annual conference to visit Prudhoe Bay. The
hundred-odd oil men also on board had made the trip scores of times
and groaned inwardly, but hardly looked up from their *Playboys*, as
the Boeing 727 banked steeply around the ten by twenty-mile patch
of flat gravel, boggy ponds and brown tussock so the VIP's could
view the silver-painted oilfield furniture sitting on top of a third of
US oil reserves and a tenth of her natural gas. The whole place
reminded me at once of a great estuary like The Wash, or Foulness
Sands at the mouth of the Thames, where you can see to the curve of
the earth but you keep looking over your shoulder in case the tide
gallops up muddy creeks between the sedge and cuts off your retreat.

Given a yellow hard-hat and cotton-wool ear plugs to wear in the
compressor stations, I joined the VIP's in an old schoolbus. Each of
the sixteen men in the party had been appointed to the Compact
Commission by the governor of his state to regulate oil and gas
production when prices were low. They were a mixed bunch of
middle-aged businessmen and it was their first time in the Arctic.
One wore a red-knitted cap, carried a transistor radio, and had a
toothpick behind each ear. Another wore a Russian hat and cowboy

boots. None was properly dressed for a Fall Arctic day and the way
they herded together for warmth during brief periods out in the wind
had its funny side. From the road built like a causeway on five-foot
embankments of gravel, we had a sweeping view of the tundra.

In a few minutes we learned a lot about Prudhoe Bay. The famous
pipeline was that silver thing coming out of the ground on the
horizon. If you were not the guest of an oil company the cost of
staying in Happy Horse camp was $238 a night. BP's power station
then was big enough to supply every Arctic village between Siberia
and Greenland. Due to permafrost there was no electrical ground, so
pylons had to carry extra cables. The white speck we could see in a
pond was a whistler swan, one of many reared here for Chesapeake
Bay, and on the left side we could see a small group of caribou.

The bus pulled up to a patter of Instamatic shutters and the silent
glide of zoom lenses. "We oughta send a picture of *that* to the goddam
environmentalists!" said a voice at the back.

"Yeah, those guys really fed us bullshit," said another.

On behalf of the various companies sharing the biggest oilfield in
USA, Prudhoe Bay operations are split almost equally between Arco
and BP. Atlantic Richfield (Arco) has close affiliations with Exxon,
and British Petroleum (BP) is majority shareholder in Sohio. The
scene is a picture of orderliness, a squeaky-clean operation with not a
dropped coffee cup in sight. The companies even have their own
traffic police. Arco's living complex is a series of interconnected
modules, like an underwater city stranded by low tide. There is a
handball court with a viewing gallery of which any middle America
town would be proud. The cinema, with two hundred thickly upholstered tiered seats, is probably the finest in Alaska. Films are shown at
8 am and 8 pm, so they can be seen by day shifts and night shifts.
Bronson and Eastwood films are packed; *The Maltese Falcon* had an
audience of ten. The BP complex is the ultimate in capsule living
offering a living experience halfway between a cruise in the *QEII* and
something out of *Star Wars*, there is even a sensation of weightlessness
after peeling off bulky protective clothes and sauntering in shirt-
sleeves and slippers around a "growth area" of birches, pines and
geraniums, known as the Prudhoe National Forest. Made of four
three-storey, 800-ton modules furnished and fitted out in Seattle
than barged to the Arctic, the complex stands on high pilings, its
edges bevelled so the wind sucks away snow drifts. Under a glass roof
is a large recreation area with an astro-turf running track (eleven
laps = one mile), volley ball court, judo mat and gymnasium. The
heated swimming pool serves as a water reservoir for fire fighting and
the fire truck is a second-hand milk tanker with "Support your local

Oil men dine in the shadow of an indoor garden (dubbed the Prudhoe Bay National Forest) in the British Petroleum Operations Centre on the Alaskan North Slope.

cow" written in large red letters on its tank. Dotted throughout the accommodation complex are snack stations, each one of them a schoolboy's delight with help-yourself ice cream and coffee machines, four-spout soda fountains, micro-wave cookers, fridges of juices, yoghurt, salads and frozen snacks. While exercising with weights or jogging to work off all that food you can look out through big windows and on a clear day see up the North Slope to the knotted muscles of the Brooks Range.

It happened that later, having split from the group, I was driven past the same caribou we had seen before and the driver stopped so I could get better pictures. The animals were much nearer the road, and as I focussed on the largest stag the 200 mm telephoto lens brought its heavily antlered head into sharp detail. Only then did I see that its antlers were thickly festooned with electrical wire.

Even as I pressed the shutter and tried to stalk nearer, until the stag trotted tamely away, I wondered how a journalist should use a picture like this. Like the pipeline argument, any discussion of the industrial threat to Arctic ecology is plagued by emotion and over-statement. Oil companies printed glossy pictures of flowers on the tundra and advertised, "We care too." Environmentalists countered with pictures of dead caribou entangled in seismic wire and said, "They don't care enough." In fact the number of animals killed by wire has been insignificant and the practice of abandoning it on the tundra was stopped (apparently with some lapses) years ago. But here was a case that proved the environmentalist case to the hilt. Or did it? That wire was the only bit of rubbish I noticed in the entire oilfield, and the animal was not dead: it seemed in good condition, in no way disturbed by what was happening all around it, and in a few weeks its antlers would drop off, solving the problem. So what was the fair point to make? One animal wearing a tangle of wire? Or the fact that a family of caribou – a stag, two does, one fawn – grazed within yards of a busy road, less than a mile from a noisy oil rig?

Responsible ecologists like Professor Bob Weeden of Fairbanks admit their case had to be over-blown to capture public attention and raise the consciousness required to exert quality control and impose regulations on industrial operators. Over-statement which wins public support is the ecologists' only real lever against the all-powerful, hugely rich, multi-national corporations accustomed (especially in frontier areas) to do what suits them. But over-blown statements are sensationalised even further by media. What ecologists really aimed at was halting the creeping cancer of urbanisation which would spread through the Alaskan wilderness as a result of the pipeline and oil exploration. The argument was about the *quality* of life in the Arctic, not whether it would survive.

Industry tends to take the stand that super-efficiency, intensive training, and large sums of money spent on ameliorative measures camouflages its impact on the environment, prevents accidents, and produces perfect systems and work practices. But their image is inevitably a hard one to protect in the long term because it takes only one bit of wire to make them look foolish.

At the other end of the rope many environmentalists take an overly precious attitude towards the Arctic, painting cameos of horror which may well be true in detail, and would make you weep, but which mean little in the magnitude of real scale.

Listening to them you might imagine the whole of the Arctic was littered with styrofoam, bulldozers and beer cans, which is not the case. There is much to care for in the Arctic, and much to regret in past actions, but industry men learned their lessons years ago and while it is generally true that mistakes have not been repeated, old images hang about like unexploded ammunition. In the general

English botanist Mark Hayward inspecting minor effects of thermokarst on the tundra of Cameron Island where Panarctic had drilled five wells in three years

climate of over-statement people working in the Arctic are divided into two camps – "goddam rabid eco-freaks" and "hard-hats hell-bent on industrial rape and pillage to profit a greedy and wasteful society."

The Arctic is fragile. *The Arctic is tough — it must be, to survive the winters.*

One footprint can permanently damage the landscape. *The landscape is a desert of ice, rock and bog extending thousands of miles.*

Tracks of a caterpillar tractor remain as long as a hundred years. *An entire drilling rig and camp shifted on a snow road hardly dents the moss.*

Damaged lichens take fifty years to recover. *Where men worked two or three years ago, plants are taller and greener.*

Buried refuse is frozen in the permafrost and preserved for thousands of years. *The greenest bits of the Arctic are found where prehistoric Eskimos chucked their garbage.*

Animals are spread thinly and the bare ground provides no cover; one man walking alone on the tundra alarms wildlife for miles around. *What wildlife? I've worked here ten years and never seen a living thing.*

Arctic ecology is so delicate that if one species is killed off all other species are endangered. *As long as you don't shoot them, or destroy their habitat, animals adapt to human presence; it is natural disasters, like freezing rain sheathing the ground in ice, that threaten survival.*

From the air, seismic lines cutting across the tundra for scores of miles are an aesthetic insult. *But at ground level, where it matters, they are practically invisible.*

The Arctic is part of our natural heritage and must be protected at all costs. *Who cares, nobody comes to see it?*

Arguments like these are unwinnable because each of these conflicting statements is basically true if you can qualify the time of year and the nature of the terrain. The Arctic is not just one environment but many, some areas more susceptible to damage than others. Most important to wildlife are the Arctic's lush spots and dry spots – its feeding and breeding areas. Less critical are the vast areas between and around them. Plants and marshy terrain are sensitive to damage only during the brief polar summer. When tundra is frozen solid and covered in snow, as it is most of the year, you can drive pretty much what you like over it. Vast areas of Arctic terrain are gravel desert, with few plants. Wheels make little impression on the hard, bare surface but do remain visible for many years, especially from the air; this is an aesthetic problem, not a biological one. With so many scientific and industrial parties working in remote regions of the Arctic the day has long since gone when you could confidently claim to be first on the spot – a discoverer. The sight of harmless wheel marks and caches of gas barrels for aircraft is something the modern pioneers must learn to accept, even if it does spoil romantic notions.

Nevertheless, in two unique ways the Arctic is hypersensitive to human activity – vehicle damage to soft terrain, and the small number of wildlife species (see next chapter). Also, low temperatures limit biological and chemical activity to a growing season as short as five or six weeks a year, and this adds significantly to the fragility of the Arctic because any damage to wildlife or environment takes so long to recover.

Permafrost is not a material, like gravel or silt, but the permanently frozen condition of the ground. It exists where the average annual air temperature is below freezing and occurs everywhere in the Arctic, in high latitudes extending beneath the surface for hundreds of feet. Gravel and other porous material are little affected, but silt and peat, which contain a lot of water, are frozen into a rock-solid "ice crete". The ground can also contain large chunks of ice, in the form of ice lenses which look like (and often are) frozen ponds that long ago became buried, and ice wedges which form when the ground is cracked by cold in winter and the crack fills with water in summer. The summer warmth melts only a few inches on the surface the boggy "active layer" where a thin layer of moss and plants takes root.

Machinery can be driven anywhere on tundra as long as the active layer is frozen. Lakes, ponds and swamps become as hard and smooth as highways, and if potholes occur they can be filled in with a bucket of water and allowed to freeze. When covered with a few inches of snow, soil and sedge-hummock terrain that in summer you would hesitate to walk over will take up to 180 thirty-ton truck-loads. But construction and industrial work is race against time and, if break-up should occur a little earlier than the work schedule allows, machinery is likely to be kept working while the snow road turns slushy. This is the danger point.

Once wheels begin to sink into the softening peat layer, so the snow road is sprinkled with black soil which absorbs the sun's warmth and hastens melting, the results can be horrifying. What happens is called thermokarst. The extra warmth deepens the active layer to form a trench, along which water begins to flow. The cutting effect of running water on ice is like a hot knife in butter. The steady trickle deepens the trench into a gully. As more soil and ice is exposed it attracts more heat which increases melt and creates faster run-off. In the worst case the track of a single caterpillar tractor crossing boggy tundra can develop in the space of a few months into a ravine wider than a man can jump and deep enough to be over his head; at best it becomes a chain of puddles that remains for decades.

Although I never saw it, I was told in the Mackenzie Delta of a man attending a coastal navigation beacon in the 1950s who became bored with his solitary life and bulldozed a four-letter work in the tundra; later it was amended but for generations to come the word BOOK will stare up at air travellers chancing on this remote spot in the polar wilderness.

In the first flush of the Prudhoe oil discovery and the exploration it stimulated in other parts of the Arctic, oil men and the government made mistakes. The Arctic tundra was regarded as a wasteland. No regulations covered its use and nobody cared much, least of all US and Canadian governments which allowed DEW-line stations to be abandoned with callous disregard for the environment, and permitted their own field officers to dump hundreds of thousands of empty fuel drums that were rolled far and wide over the level tundra by the wind.

At the moment, exploration crews are required to abide by strict stipulations. Tundra may not be bulldozed, camps must be on sand bars, vehicles must have low-pressure tyres, garbage must be burned or carried out, and kitchen and waste-water must be filtered before it is discharged. If oil is found in these areas an entirely new engineering technology will have to be developed. Now that land use regulations are catching up with industrial activity in the Arctic the companies are unable to get away with much, and in some circumstances even have to store their dishwater then fly it out, deep frozen in barrels.

As long as ice in the soil is not exposed wheel tracks can actually benefit the tundra. The weight of a vehicle compacts the soil which absorbs more energy from the sun and gets warmer, this allows more nitrogen fixation to occur so there is better plant growth. Where

Results of driving across the tundra in the Prudhoe Bay oil field – ten years ago the improperly constructed roads became so muddy that vehicles took to the tundra and these canals were the result; now, roads are built on causeways of gravel, five feet high, which protect and insulate the tundra

seismic trains have passed years before the tundra is often thick with cotton grass which migrating caribou sometimes turn and follow. Natural recovery of bald patches is swift as long as there is no erosion. This can be hastened by artificial seeding – "But then," a botanist explained with a sigh, "environmentalists complain of little green golf courses on the tundra." From this you might suppose that nitrogen applied in the form of fertiliser would turn the tundra into an Arctic prairie. Growth would certainly be spectacular at first, but after a few seasons the added shade reduces the depth of the active layer, allowing permafrost to creep nearer the surface and in the long term limit growth by lowering the soil temperature.

To study the natural recovery rate of High Arctic tundra after industrial disturbance three graduate students established a field camp on the site of Panarctic's Bent Horn oil field. After days of clammy drizzle the sun burst out and a plane could go in with supplies. As the Twin Otter circled I saw patterns of wheelmarks on the tundra but over a square mile the damage was not greater than that of a football field at the end of a season. Yet five oil wells had been drilled in this immediate locality and apart from the well-head "Christmas trees" sticking out of the ground there was not so much as a styrofoam chip to indicate that scores of men had worked here for three seasons.

The sleeping tents and a larger cook tent were pitched on the springy peat of a ridge overlooking a sea passage filled with chunks of floating ice. In the far distance, china white on a sea of Delft blue, was the hard edge of the permanent polar ice pack. The brisk breeze coming straight off it, billowing the tents into hard curves like galleon sails, was full of wintry promise. Hilary Mackenzie, the daughter of a Scottish diplomat, had been working in South America and taken a summer job with Ottawa University. She was working with Mark Hayward, just out from England, and as greenhorns they were being assisted by a French Canadian girl, Annick Le Henaff.

It might have been the tundra telegraph that signalled their presence to oil men in camps around about, it might have been Hilary's honeyed Scottish accent on the twice-daily radio sked. Within two days the first Panarctic plane dropped in to ask if they needed help and just happened to have on board some planks to make a floor for their cook-tent. Next day a helicopter came with a chocolate cake. Then a plane landed to take all three of them out to dinner at Rea Point, sixty miles away, where Hilary mentioned she loved apple juice and subsequently there were daily deliveries. One day a Twin Otter landed with twenty oil men who came visiting with a barbecue fireplace and a box of frozen T-bone steaks. A helicopter came in slinging a strange load which it lowered on the tundra a discreet distance from the tents. The pilot released the snap-hook and flew away. Curiously the three young people went to see what had been left – a portable outhouse, and on its door was painted "To Hilary, with love."

It would be pleasing to suppose that if all scientists studying the tracks of oil men on the tundra were charming, brainy and beautiful, the oil industry would be easily tamed. In fact, for all their hospitality and Albertan charm, and despite the very different policy adopted by their head office, oil men in hard hats – the men on the spot – tend to regard this kind of field research as a joke and a drain on themselves as tax-payers.

The current risks to the environment stem not only from cosmetic hazards like garbage disposal and thoughtless use of the tundra, but from new and untested operations like burying pipelines in permafrost and offshore drilling in sea-ice. This raises the question of the ability – and willingness – of government to devise and impose stipulations which adequately protect environment and wildlife without limiting engineers' scope for meeting the challenges of a technological adventure. But the monitoring of any stipulations, the exerting of regulatory influence designed to hold hazardous procedures in check, tends to fall on people who, by their nature, tend to be opposite in characters to the tough, hard-bitten, robust, worldly and usually older construction chiefs and drillers. You can impose almost any regulation and win any admission from a head office executive, but – as the Alyeska pipeline experience showed – it is the confrontation of personalities between men on the spot that counts on the day. One was by definition a capable and experienced leader of men, the other almost invariably young, unpractised at dealing with men, prickly because he was a lone watchdog in an alien world, unconfident because of the lack of true knowledge of the ecology he was attempting to protect. In Alaska the hard-hats called biological monitors "fuzzies" because so many were bearded and studious – the eco-fuzz.

Real knowledge of the Arctic is sparse. Training and experience may give biologists strong feelings for what is right and what could cause damage, but a case based on supposition and intuition requires a great deal of hard and personable salesmanship to convince an engineer trained to respond only to facts. For example, a crew installing a culvert might not have a pipe of the required diameter. To wait could cost a week so a smaller one is used. A biologist seeing the pipe going in might confront the site engineer. "The narrower diameter pipe could increase speed of water-flow and prevent fish swimming up to spawn."

"How many fish use this stream?"

"There's no fish count but..."

"Is there a spawning ground upstream?"

"We don't know, but..."

"But you seriously have the nerve to suggest I delay this project bringing urgently required energy to the nation by God knows how many days because a few fish *might* not reach a spawning ground that doesn't exist...?" In fact, biologists in Alaska didn't know how many streams had to be crossed until the pipeline reached them, let alone how many streams had fish in them. By the time the fuzz had argued his case the culvert was in place.

On the Alyeska project none of the different kinds of environmental monitors had real power. The company's own quality control inspectors reported to the construction manager whose priority was meeting deadlines. Engineers monitoring on behalf of the Alaska Pipeline Office (APO) of the Department of the Interior were concerned mainly with integrity of construction. They were also charged with preventing irreparable environmental damage, but among men with engineering stars in their eyes the definition of "damage" could be stretched many different ways. The first head of the APO was a retired general of Army engineers. The second was an engineer who liked to get things done and didn't have much sympathy for biologists whom he thought tended to cry wolf.

Federal and state fish and wildlife departments formed a special unit called the Joint Fish and Wildlife Advisory Team (JFWAT) which appointed biologists to monitor the construction activities, but no monitoring project was planned in advance. Problems had to be dealt with as they were found and argued on the spot. The more experienced, grizzled type of man was better at this than the anxious, red-faced, sensitive and touchy young biologist fresh out of school. Also, there was a basic conflict between biologists and their chiefs, who again were engineers. On all sides, engineers were caught up in the romance and magnitude of the project, and the need for "expediency". It was this word, used from Congress on down, that coloured every aspect of the pipeline construction: every day of delay was thought to put the State deeper in a hole, and sentence the Lower Forty-eight to continue suffering from gasoline shortages.

According to reports issued by the Fairbanks Environmental Centre virtually the whole spectrum of environmental stipulations was violated. River crossings were a "massacre" and "butcher jobs" that created excessive turbidities violating water quality standards "that for anyone else would have resulted in legal action". Untreated sewage was discharged on the tundra. There were numerous oil spills, including deliberately oiling the roads for dust control. Workers broke regulations against feeding wild animals which led to their destruction. Little effective control could be exerted over the workers because when it came to a show-down – as in the case of men caught illegally spearing fish – construction chiefs dared not face out the all-powerful unions. Lacking research data, backing from their chiefs, and the right kind of personality, it was a nearly impossible task for the eco-fuzz to swim against the wild rivers of expediency and public opinion.

The same kind of problem affects Canmar's offshore drilling in the Beaufort Sea. The federal government has placated public concern by placing two "experts" on each ship "to supervise drilling operations and insist on approved safety standards". Drillers on the job are men who have made international reputations: they are probably the best in the world. The short drilling season – the race against time as ice closes in around them – creates an intense feeling of pressure, although Canmar denies this has a bad influence on its men. The government inspectors tend to be comparatively young, highly trained in a formal way but lacking in practical experience. "After two weeks of living on board doing twelve-hour shifts it can be hard to beat the drum," one of them told me. "You are the one guy who can stop the whole $10,000-an-hour operation by forcing the driller to run additional tests. Having authority is not the problem – it's sticking to your guns and exerting authority in the face of hostility, impatience and huge costs. When you are face to face with an angry driller arguing a border-line case it can take a lot of guts to avoid being dominated and persuaded you're an old woman." In an exciting technological adventure like Beaufort Sea drilling it can be tough on the man expected to achieve maximum acceleration while putting the brakes on. It makes a lot of smoke.

Whether environmental monitors have been over-cautious, and whether the engineers and drillers have done a proper job despite the pressures of expediency, can only be tested by time. We won't know

Afloat on the ice-covered sea in Viscount Melville Sound, part of the Northwest Passage, a party of hydrographers watch a DC3 taxi back along a runway marked with snow-filled plastic bags to deliver a cargo of fuel. The heavy drums in the foreground will be manhandled aboard and flown back to the garbage dump at Resolute Bay; they contain frozen dishwater.

if the Alyeska pipeline will survive an earthquake of the severity that devastated Valdez and Anchorage in 1964 until another one occurs. We will never know the real environmental impact of the pipeline or a Beaufort Sea blowout if it occurs, because of the lack of baseline data for before and after comparisons. But this lack is changing.

Environmental impact analysis has become a major Arctic industry. Scores of firms which sprang up in western Canada made hay from the Mackenzie Valley pipeline proposal and are now turning their attention to the Alaska Highway and Polar Gas projects. Output of literature in the name of environmental study by government, industry, consultants and opposition interests seems to be proceeding rather faster than the discovery of oil and gas.

The first environmental impact statement prepared by the US Department of Interior for the trans-Alaska pipeline was only eight pages long. The second, drafted in January 1971 after protests from environmentalists, was 256 pages. The third and final version, published in March 1972, contained 3,736 pages in six volumes. The Canadian Arctic Gas application to build the Mackenzie pipeline and the Polar Gas environmental impact statement were equally verbose. Investigative work by industry has to be matched by government resulting in more paper. The various Mackenzie Valley reports occupy some five yards of shelf space, and the 202 volumes of the Berger Inquiry, plus index and supplementary volumes, fill another five yards.

Despite the avalanche of material – and most reports by consultants conclude with a recommendation for urgent further research – professional ecologists do not yet play a proper role in Arctic development. Ecology was the catchword of the 1970s but is little understood and is frequently misinterpreted to mean the destruction rather than the *study* of living things by Man. Ecology is the study of natural systems in relation to the whole spectrum of influences including such factors as climate, human activities and time. An ecologist is trained to think in terms of the total picture, in four dimensions. A biologist might determine that industrial activity will kill twenty per cent of a bird species in an area, but an ecologist would know whether this effect was significant in the context of a bad ice year that might kill off fifty per cent, and hunting activities on the migration fly-ways that killed ten per cent.

Typical of the emotional heat generated by self-professed ecologists in Canada was their reaction to the Ekofisk blowout in the North Sea, in summer 1977, when they were reported by the CBC to have branded it "an environmental disaster". Yet any marine scientist worth his salt would tell you that the danger to fish and marine life was minimal. Their reaction was emotional, not scientific.

It is urgent for the welfare of the Arctic that ecologists begin to concentrate on establishing a respected and secure professional reputation which is no longer confused with the banner-waving "eco-freaks". Only then will the right kinds of ecological questions be asked. As in the Beaufort Sea, where the real danger to the environment stems not from the unlikely event of spectacular oil blowout, but the *certainty* of persistent small-scale pollution from development of an oil field. Thousands of dollars are spent studying polar bears (see next chapter) but nothing is known about the polar cod, which is the lemming of the sea. If anything happened to the polar cod the whole ecological system would collapse: huge numbers of birds and seals feed on them, and polar bears feed on the seals, so they would all be in danger of being wiped out. Yet polar cod have never been studied and it is not known even where they breed or spend the winter.

The big decisions affecting the future of the Arctic are not made by ecologists but engineers, politicians and civil servants. For example, the route of the proposed Mackenzie Valley pipeline had to fall within laterally undefined limits of an energy corridor conceived to follow the line of a highway proposed as a political ploy then abandoned. Once there was a line on the map ecologists could argue only small-scale ameliorative measures and had no opportunity to examine the total picture. Ecologists with an understanding of engineering and political problems, in consultation with engineers and politicians with an understanding of ecological priorities, might well have decided from the very beginning that a pipeline following the Alaska and Dempster Highways would have been the best answer. Or that an *oil* pipeline along the Mackenzie would have been infinitely safer than the Alyeska pipeline which has resulted in great numbers of supertankers plying the north-west coast where pollution from a serious spill could affect many times more people, and many times more precious resources such as fish and recreation areas, than exist in the Mackenzie Valley.

Protection of the Arctic should be less a matter of day-to-day policing to prevent small-scale damage, and more the development of an overall policy of land use and management. The fifty-year beer can littering the tundra can be tidied up; the 1,500-mile pipeline buried in the wrong place for economic or political expediency will remain forever. Governments deserve much of the blame: lacking Arctic policies, they do not think positively but react, filtering the claims of private industry and deciding what should be permitted without considering the whole range of alternatives. Cynics suggest the federal government encourages it only because an ability to control oil and gas flowing out of the Arctic will put it on a par with powerful provincial governments like that of Alberta. Ottawa formed a Department of the Environment but gave responsibility for protecting the Arctic environment to the Department of Indian Affairs and Northern Development, which has the job of developing Arctic resources. As largest share-holder in Panarctic the government's motives are in any case highly questionable because in protecting the Arctic it is both burglar and policeman. Organisations like the Canadian Arctic Resources Committee (CARC) have also accused the government of concealing the true nature of risks involved in Beaufort Sea drilling, restricting the circulation of drilling reports showing what really happened, and acting primarily as industrial developer while disregarding its responsibilities to local people and the environment.

There are encouraging signs of change, however. The environmental study boom is consolidating more rationally. While the US is still to be tested, with the start of Arctic offshore drilling in 1980, Canada is adopting a cautious attitude towards development of its next most promising offshore drilling zone, in Lancaster Sound. This huge fault zone occurring where continental plates have pulled apart and filled with sediment is thought to be the place where Canada is most likely to find its Prudhoe Bay. Ecologically it could hardly be more precious. The sound is a highly important feeding area; up-welling waters provide food for masses of birds nesting in vertical, honeycombed cliffs rimming the nearby islands as well as for great numbers of sea mammals and polar bears. In effect it is the estuary of the eastern Arctic, a maritime polar oasis. Well-provided eating areas abound in the Sound's deep inlets, and as the ice breaks up in late spring marine mammals like harp seals (which pup off Newfoundland), walrus, beluga whale and narwhal can get closer and closer to the table. More than one million seabirds spend the summer breeding in the Sound and nearby waterways, occurring in densities as great as twenty thousand per square kilometre. The western side of Bylot Island is a critical nesting area for nearly one third of the world's greater snow geese. Among large colonies of cliff-nesters are about 400,000 thick-billed murres (Brunnich's guillemot), the black and white upright-walking birds that fill the same ecological niche in the Arctic as penguins in the Antarctic.

When they are sixteen days old and still flightless the young birds jump from their nests and flutter hundreds of feet down to the sea, their parents calling to them all the way down. Then, accompanied by the parent birds which become flightless as they moult, the young birds *swim* some four hundred miles to Greenland. Said ornithologist Dr David Nettleship: "It is appalling to imagine what an oil slick would do to one million flightless birds swimming across Baffin Bay." Already about half a million murres drown every year when they are entangled in salmon nets, and great numbers are shot for the pot by Greenlandic hunters in speedboats; the consequences of a serious oil slick would be disastrous.

Pollution, like beauty, is in the eye of the beholder. On one plane journey in the Arctic I found myself sitting next to a biologist who claimed that sky-diving down Alaska's Mount McKinley, highest mountain in the US, was pollution of the worst kind because it commercialised and desecrated the nobility of the mountain. Beechey Island, off the south-west tip of Devon Island, was the scene of two bizarre incidents representing yet other forms of pollution. It was here, in 1845–6, that the ill-fated Franklin expedition wintered before it vanished. The only relic of its passage had been found on the wide curving gravel beach at Beechey Island where carved head-boards marked the graves of three men. With another, where a member of one of the Franklin search expeditions was buried, the four graves are in a line at right angles to the beach. The place is bleakly picturesque: a vista of fjord-like bays rimmed by vertical cliffs above steep beaches. Where small islands like Beechey have formed, they have the appearance of mesas. It is the nearest thing to cowboy country in the Arctic, needing only a few cacti to look like a bleached-out version of Monument Valley, but only in a few damp spots does anything grow. Viewing the country from sea level, early explorers thought they were looking up at mountain ranges when in fact they were seeing only the edges of vast table lands extending in gently undulating plains for hundreds of miles.

With a party of archaeologists from the Arctic Institute of North America I flew along this coast to spy out sites of prehistoric Eskimo dwellings. At Beechey we circled low over a herd of walrus, sending them pounding into the sea, then settled bumpily on the sloping beach near the lonely graves. The wood of the headboards seemed silvered and desiccated with age, yet iron hard. The carved names and initials of the dead men had eroded, but to stare at the shallow knife marks made on this utterly remote polar island was like making contact with the doomed men themselves. Only as I began to walk away, a slight shiver playing up and down my spine, did I see a notice which said the original headboards had been removed for protection. The ones here were replicas – made of glassfibre.

A few days later another plane landed on Beechey Island bearing Commissioner of the Northwest Territories Stewart Hodgson,

Glassfibre headstone exactly simulating the original which was removed by Canada's National Museum to save it from vandalism at Beechey Island where the Franklin expedition wintered before sailing to its doom in 1846.

friends and officials. He had flown up from Yellowknife in his Grumman, changing planes at Resolute, to conduct a simple ceremony – the dedication of a cairn to the memory of one of his assistants who had died (of drink, it is commonly believed). The haunting beauty of this historic Arctic outpost is now enriched by a stone cairn bearing a heavy bronze plaque which states:

Within this cairn
rests the mortal remains
of
DESMOND HENRY FOGG
"Des"
Against the broad, black sky of night
For Des the stars will shine so bright,
The Northland's challenge he bravely met,
For Des, the glorious sun has set.

9

SURVIVORS IN A
LANDSCAPE

*Will polar bears, caribou, musk ox
and millions of birds share the oases
of polar deserts with Man?*

Three little black dots of its eyes and nose framed in a mask of fluff
caught my eye as the polar bear stood up on hind legs on the ice and
watched us fly overhead. The pilot banked the chopper and
descended low over the floes. A massive butterball, yellow against
the ice, the she-bear dropped on all fours and ambled through a pool
of peacock-green meltwater. With a great splash she belly-flopped
into a black lead that was scummy with grey new ice and struck out
powerfully towards the shore.

His lanky bushman's frame coiled like fencing wire amid the tiny
switches and dials of the cockpit, Bill set the machine gingerly on a
large floe while Hank, in the back seat, armed the ·32-gauge shotgun
with a six-inch dart attached to an alloy syringe. A Canadian Wildlife Service technician, Hank Kiliaan had tagged around nine
hundred bears and it was with a practised eye that he measured
amounts of knock-out drug and tranquilliser into the dart.

Before we drugged her the bear had to be ushered a long distance
from the water that was her natural element, because the drug was
designed to paralyse voluntary muscles and she could drown if she
reached water as it began to take effect. Hank explained the trick was
to hang well back and keep a low profile so the bear kept going in a
straight line. If she thought she could not out-run the helicopter she

would stand and fight. One swipe of those mighty paws making contact with our skids could flip the machine so the rotors brushed the ground – and the polar bear would have a cooked breakfast.

"Thwack!" The dart struck the bobbing rump just above its little tail. Instantly Bill sidled the orange Bell 206B sideways and perched on a vantage point. The bear had run four or five miles into a natural amphitheatre of bare rock, like a giant quarry. Snow flurried into the cabin through the open window as Hank poured coffee from a vacuum flask and passed around the cheese rolls. Now brilliantly white against the brown rock, the bear slowed to a walk. Wreathed in steam from her panting, she began to stagger. But she did not go down and we had to take off again to put another shot into her rump. At last the bear sat dizzily then flopped, like a cuddly toy that has lost its stuffing.

When Bill shut down the turbine the silence of the Arctic wilderness hit like a wave. We were on the north-west coast of Prince of Wales Island, its rocky tors inland hidden by low cloud, the ice-covered bay from which the bear had come partly obscured by a gauze of chill drizzle. Specks of bright lichen on the flat, sharp-edged rocks covering the landscape like a tide of axe-heads were the only colour in a scene of breathtaking desolation. Hank took a CO_2 pistol primed with another dart. Bill cradled a hunting rifle with the safety catch off and took a flanking route across the talus, so he had a clear line of fire if the bear charged. I carried the briefcase.

The bear's great head was rocking from side to side, her eyes watering as if from effort of will to make her muscles work. The drug appeared to have taken hold but her back legs were bunched beneath the barrel of her body and if she suddenly found the strength to attack there would be no warning. Once in five years of tagging had Hank had a bear killed, when a yearling charged, grabbed him by the foot, turned him upside down, and fell dead on top of him as Hank's Eskimo assistant put a bullet through its head. Now Hank bowled a wet rock down the slope towards the bear. Like a circus lion on a barrel, hissing from deep in her throat, she reared back. "Jesus-

Polar bear and cubs leap from floe to floe as a helicopter hovers overhead; top carnivores of the north, bears can reach eight feet in length, 1,600 pounds in weight, and are one of the few animals in the world that hunt Man for a meal.

stand by, Bill!" The only safe thing to do was return to the chopper and dart her again from the air. Then, lobbing more stones to skid under her black nose, Hank approached once more and suddenly was astride the polar bear, rumpling the fur between her ears as if patting a sheep-dog.

It's not every day you get a chance to shake hands with the great carnivore of the North, one that breathes gusts of hot, fishy air in your face as you force its stone-crusher jaws open with a stick of wood so a small pre-molar could be drawn; later it would be used to determine the bear's age. Man is meat to a polar bear: it is one of the few animals in the world that hunts you with the definite intention of eating you. The polar bear fears nothing, for it is king. One of the two oil-patch workers killed recently in the Mackenzie Delta was attacked and killed instantly as he got out of a pick-up to check lights on a drilling island. A front-end loader was driven at the bear repeatedly, but each time it dragged the corpse aside and batted the wheel with its massive paw.

To lie in your tent in the sunlit Arctic night expecting claws to slash through the nylon and drag you away is not an unreal fear. It happened to seismologist Tony Overton as he lay in his sleeping bag. The bear dragged him about thirty feet before his shouts woke a companion who grabbed the rifle; as the bear charged he coolly put a round up the spout and fired from the hip. The bear dropped dead on top of him. A third man woken by the shot raised himself on one elbow and asked blearily what was going on. "We just shot a bear."

"What bear?"

"The dead one on the pillow behind you."

Scientists make a habit of returning to camp circumspectly, half expecting to see the rear end of a polar bear sticking out of one of their tents. It happens often enough. In 1977 a pilot taking his morning constitutional in an outhouse made of packing-case lumber and anchored down with rocks watched through the upper half of the

"Sorry bear!" Biting on a wooden gag after having a convulsion, minus a small tooth removed for aging purposes, with red plastic tags in her ears, green tattooed numbers on her lip, and purple disinfectant on the tag wounds in her rump, bear H27 will be woozy for a couple of days but the cold sea will soon sterilise and repair her slight wounds.

stable door as a polar bear approached his helicopter, saw its reflection in the black perspex chin bubble, and shattered it with a blow. Later, ornithologists at the same camp on Prince Leopold Island watched helplessly from a cliff-top as a bear – perhaps the same one – methodically chewed up their inflatable boat on the beach.

In winter pregnant female bears seek areas where snow has remained from the previous year and burrow out dens in which to give birth. As snow drifts over the entrance and seals it up the bear claws a ventilation hole in the roof. If the interior ices up due to the warmth of its body the bear digs side chambers to allow stale air to seep out through the snow. By travelling around known denning areas biologists can count tracks and get an idea of population strength, but the job has its bad moments. One biologist on a denning survey suddenly disappeared from view when a bear reached up through the roof of her den and pulled him in. He was rescued only because the alert pilot jerked his machine into the air and hovered over the den so the bear cowered away while the man climbed out. Another who fell through the roof of a den was batted straight out again by a single swipe of a bear's paw and suffered nothing worse than a big bruise and a small fright. Two surveyors laying out a seismic line came to a steep snow-covered hillside and instead of walking down sat on their parkas and tobogganed, their impetus carrying them straight over the top of a polar bear den into which they would certainly have stumbled had they done the job properly; it was only when they reached the bottom and looked back that they saw an angry bear and two cubs looking at them.

If a bear doesn't take your head off with a single raking swipe it crunches the back of your skull, killing you like it would a seal. In snow it moves silently and is almost totally camouflaged; when hunting seals it sometimes covers its black nose with snow.

Polar bears grow up to eight feet long from nose to tail and weigh up to 1,600 lbs. Seals are their staple diet but they also take chicks and eggs from seabird nests, Canada geese, and as a last resort in summer scavenge for mushrooms, seaweed, berries and even lichens. Sometimes a bear might stampede a herd of walrus in the hope of getting a calf left behind in the rush, but a fully grown walrus is so heavily armoured with hide and blubber that a bear inevitably comes off second best in a fight. In most cases bears are merely curious about humans, but you can't help getting a prickly feeling in the back of your neck when your vision is restricted by a parka hood. One man walking down the snow-covered street in Churchill was stopped by a cruising Mountie and roughly ordered into the car.

"Why, what have . . .?"

Ear-tagged, tattooed, numbered and minus a small tooth, the polar bear will recover perfectly from its rendezvous with Arctic scientists, and the information collected about its movements will lead to a broader understanding of the territory it requires to survive.

"Don't argue – just get in!" Only when he looked out of the patrol-car window did he see the big polar bear that had been padding noiselessly behind him.

Despite such feelings your overwhelming first impression of the Arctic is one of emptiness. Nothing seems to move in this desert – barren rock and sticky bare soil in summer, a frozen sea of snow and ice covering land and water alike in winter and spring. No birds grubbing for insects. No scrub to provide cover in which you can sense the presence of wildlife. It's a landscape that seems to be waiting for its soul, like a new house before the furniture is moved in. Many oil men have worked here for years and never seen a living creature. During my own many hours of routine flying, often at low level, occasions when wildlife was encountered can be counted on the fingers – a herd of white whales off Fury Beach, walrus smashing into the sea as we circled them near Beechey Island, the musk ox being attacked by wolves near Eureka, a flick of white as a fox darted behind rock as we landed to check a navigation beacon at Bridport

Inlet. To find our first bear to tag we had flown a coastal search pattern of at least a hundred miles, and in a total five hours of low-altitude searching found bears in only three locations, caribou and musk ox in one valley, and seals lying on the ice floes in one bay. The apparent emptiness of the Arctic plays a significant part in fashioning the attitudes towards it of oil men and other developers. They tend to regard it not only as the desert it is, but as a useless and barren desert which it is not.

Once you develop an eye for it the Arctic is full of surprises. Life here is far from being a deep-frozen vacuum, but it *is* spread thinly, and tends to be concentrated into comparatively small areas that are easily missed unless you go looking for them.

Going north you find fewer species and more land required to support them. In the Arctic islands there are as few as twenty-eight flowering plants compared with about six hundred on the mainland coast. The North Slope has twenty-nine land mammals (polar bears count among seals, whales and walrus as marine mammals) but the islands only seven. Just south of the treeline there are ten thousand species of insects, but only five hundred just north of the treeline and twenty-eight in the northern islands. Every species must have adapted to survive the rigours of prolonged winter cold and darkness, a short but rapid growing season when light is continuous, and the drying and abrasive effect of constant summer winds. The forty species of Arctic moths, for example, have small eyes so they can see in constant daylight and broad wings that enable them to fly strongly against stiff breezes. The Arctic biological clock is slow. Insects take years to complete life cycles that in temperate zones take months. Fish, such as Arctic char, take up to twenty years to mature compared with two or three years in warmer waters. Some lichens grow only one inch in their first four hundred years, then increase by an inch every thousand years; the largest, found in Baffin Island, are eleven inches across and may be the world's oldest living organisms, having lived up to ten thousand years. It makes you rather thoughtful when choosing a place to pee.

Plant life, where it does exist, is tiny and hardy. Horizons in the Arctic are measured in scores of miles but beauty is in inches, and to appreciate it you have to get down on your hands and knees – cushions of moss campion with its tiny pink flowers; low and matted clusters of white or pink saxifrages; brilliant yellow poppies, in clumps only a few inches high, that turn their heads to face the sun as it goes round and round them; sunflowers bursting into bloom when they reach as high as your boots because if they spent time growing higher the winter would be on them before they seeded. When there are fewer than ten frost-free days a year the cold air temperature might suggest a growing environment as friendly as a combine harvester, but the local environment within the plant itself is often more favourable, like that of the delicate harebell which traps warm air rising from the ground, and other plants which crowd together for mutual shelter. In general, plants and animals in the Arctic do not compete with each other but are pitted together against the environment.

Like every desert, the Arctic does have oases. Suddenly the bare and barren landscape beneath the wing changes to a rolling prairie of golden-green meadows sequined with gleaming lakes and ponds. The hummocky sedge-moss glitters with a lacework of thin streams running out of heathland covering the surrounding higher country. It may look as bleak as a Scottish moor but compared with typical Arctic tundra it is a near thing to a polar paradise. In the Canadian archipelago such areas cover only about two per cent of the total land mass, but for wildlife it is the only two per cent that really matters. At the sound of your engines large brown boulders – or are they gasoline barrels? – suddenly gallop towards each other and form a circle: you have alarmed a herd of grazing musk ox. An iceberg on the edge of a pond suddenly takes the form of a polar bear, temporarily driven inland to forage for grass and berries until the sea-ice reforms and provides it with a platform for hunting seals. The glinting ponds and lakes are nesting grounds for thousands of waterfowl. For most of the year you would be lucky to find four or five species of birds here, but in summer there might be as many as eighty, not spread over a vast landscape but concentrated in the few favourable locations which ecologists term "critical habitats".

In establishing which habitats are critical in the Arctic, biologists are still essentially taking inventory. The main areas required for survival are small and widely scattered. In summer they can be identified easily by eye because they stand out as plainly as palm trees do in the Sahara. The degree of criticality still largely involves guesswork. The question is important because a Murphy's Law seems to be at work which makes the habitats supporting the most animals also the most desirable for industrial operations. Lancaster Sound, the marine oasis at the north end of Baffin Island, which was described in the previous chapter, is one example. Another is Cunningham Inlet, where I visited a party of scientists observing hundreds of beluga whales that brought their calves into shallow, warmer waters. A twenty-foot observation tower of aluminium scaffolding had been built in the shallows, and the scientists were photographing the whales using a radio-controlled model aeroplane carrying a camera in its bomb-bay. Like maggots twelve feet long, mottled pink, grey and brown, the white whales crowded into water, shallow enough to run aground, making "vocalisations" which the biologists catalogued thirty different ways (snort, burp, snarl, groan, moo, mew, gargle, trombone, fog-horn, ship's whistle, rusty door, terrier-yelp, geiger counter ...).

Nobody knows where these whales spend the winter, or why they enter the inlets, but there are probably 30,000 of them in the Canadian Arctic, including 4,500 in the Beaufort Sea. It was at Cunningham Inlet, a five miles by three bite out of the north coast of Somerset Island, where Polar Gas was planning to land thousands of tons of pipeline and construction equipment; when it was discovered that as many as 2,500 belugas visit Cunningham at one time, for just a few days sometime in August, the proposed dock was shifted to another bay eight miles west.

Given the great space of the Arctic it may seem easy to devise land-use regulations to keep industrial activity away from critical habitats, but no oasis can be considered in isolation for they are all part of a greater pattern. If man-made structures like roads or pipelines cross the barren areas between the lush spots, what will be the effect on nomadic species like caribou which migrate in herds from one prime area to another according to the seasons, and range over thousands of square miles? Due to lack of cover and sparseness of food, Arctic wildlife is hyper-sensitive to disturbance. Because "lush" Arctic vegetation is barely ankle-high – even willow trees spreadeagle themselves only a couple of inches above ground – animals are highly visible to hunters and are easily disturbed by their mere presence. Wherever man goes in the Arctic he makes big footprints in terms of noise and visibility, for in this bare land of far horizons nothing can be unobtrusive. The precise relationship between disturbance and survival is not known. Naturalists suspect the effects of disturbance may be biologically subtle and visible to none but a discerning eye especially as many species have a tenuous hold on longevity.

Caribou, for example, are constantly on the move in search of food. Vegetation available for grazing is less than one-thousandth that of an African savannah and the animals have to work hard for it, pawing through snow then foraging with fur-covered muzzles. It has been established that an adult caribou chased for ten minutes walks on rapidly for an hour and remains excited for a further hour; the energy expended requires nearly two pounds of extra forage. In the case of a large herd alarmed by an aircraft this could impose critical demands on vegetation. When extra food is not available, physical debilitation can result so that caribou and other mammals fail to become pregnant, fail to put on sufficient fat to survive the winter, or succumb within a few days to pneumonia. In this sense the Arctic is a big glassy pond in which one dropped pebble makes a lot of waves.

For the Eskimo the caribou is historically a staff of life; for those living inland from the coast it was the only certain source of meat, clothing and oil for light. More than any other Arctic animal, such as the seal or whale on which Eskimos also depended, the caribou has grown to be a symbol of the old and treasured ways of life, and the question of its survival as a food source has become complicated by taboos, nostalgia, politics, and heavy-handed management.

The North American caribou is the wild relative of the Eurasian reindeer which has long been domesticated. When reindeer return to the wild, as many did after unsuccessful farming experiments on the North Slope between the wars, they mingle and breed with caribou and revert.

The Peary caribou, shorter-legged and paler, lives in the Arctic islands in small bands of about five and does not migrate great distances. Numbers have dropped from about 24,000 in 1961 to 2,400 in 1977. There has been no calf production to speak of since the last good years in 1967–8 and for an unknown reason even pregnancy rates have dropped to zero while the severe 1973–4 winter caused fifty per cent mortality. The difference between a good year and a bad year for Arctic wildlife is ice-sliver thin. If snow stays on the ground until July, and frosts return by the middle of August, killing what little new grass has grown, the animals have little chance to fatten up. Freezing rain at the end of the season locks available forage in a glaze of ice, so animals expend more energy chipping it out than they gain from eating it.

The barren ground caribou, which lives on the mainland in ten principal herds between Alaska and Newfoundland, totalling more than one million animals, is heavier and darker with longer legs and big antlers. One of the largest herds is the 115,000-strong Porcupine herd which ranges across the border between Alaska and Canada and is threatened by the Dempster Highway, and the proposed pipeline which will run parallel to the Mackenzie Delta. When the early explorers and trappers saw these immense herds on the move they assumed the entire territory was as thick with them, and first estimates of total numbers of caribou were wildly exaggerated. Even with the benefit of aircraft and modern technology, subsequent estimates have also been inaccurate because the herds are constantly on the move and cover such vast areas. The Western Arctic herd, until recently by far the largest, winters south of the Brooks Range where the snow is soft and lichens are plentiful, then filters to the north side where the warmth strikes first; the animals head for the barren, windswept, cold coastal areas where they find relief from insects and calve all at once, most females in the herd dropping their calves within the same five days. Then the animals swing west, sometimes in huge masses, sometimes in small groups, grazing on the tundra and returning through the passes late in the year.

The trouble with aerial surveying of caribou is that you never know when you are right: basic assumptions of random distribution have no validity. The animals seem to appear from nowhere and go nowhere; in fact, locating caribou poses the same problem it did in prehistoric times. Recently a 50,000 herd in northern Manitoba simply vanished, and didn't appear again until the following spring. However, when the animals appear, they can be counted easily from an aerial photograph.

The ripples-in-a-pond effect of heavy-handed wildlife management is reflected in the current plight of the Western Arctic herd. Decimated by hunters supplying the whalers and later the gold rush at Nome in 1901–3, it reached an all-time high of 250,000 animals in 1970, considerably higher than the estimated maximum "normal" peak of 160,000. This might have been due to a succession of mild winters but the cause was more likely to have been an artificial one: large numbers of wolves hunted from ski-equipped aircraft for the $100 value of their skins and a $50 State bounty, so reduced predation that the herd boomed – then crashed. By 1976 the herd was reduced to only 52,000. Alaskan Eskimos blamed the decline on industrial activity and the oil pipeline, but this herd did not come within three or four hundred miles of such activity. The most likely reason was over-crowding – over-grazing accentuated by bad weather seasons reduced food supply, a higher incidence of disease and crippling due to population stress, an increased number of wolves when the aerial hunting was stopped, and increased harvest and waste due to natives using snow machines. The ten thousand natives of north and west Alaska were *taking* 30,000 caribou a year and possibly wasting a great many more. The wolf kill (one wolf needs about twenty-three caribou a year to survive) could be controlled by licensing hunters to resume aerial shooting, but biologists believe if the herd is to survive the human harvest must be reduced to 1,500. As the range is so depleted due to low stocks of vegetation from the previous boom years, the surviving animals go nearer the coast where people live, and Eskimos asked by the State Department of Fish and Game not to shoot caribou are seeing more than they have ever seen in the past fifteen years. Eskimos want subsistence hunting to continue at all costs, are distrustful of scientists and win much support from the Lower Forty-eight.

Most research material concerning caribou is either theoretical or based on the domesticated reindeer. There is a desperate need to define the agents of mortality and determine the reality of a natural disaster – does a bad winter wipe out ten or fifty per cent of a herd, and how quickly does it recover? Until more is known about their ecology, potential threats of industrial development cannot be put into perspective. The greatest threat is not development at all but hunting from Skidoos when herds winter near communities. "It would not be so bad if hunters stalked and shot carefully," says biologist George Calef, "but they roar up, get dozens of animals running in panic, and shoot wildly leaving scores of wounded lying around."

The Alyeska pipeline did not interrupt a major migration route of caribou but it did run parallel with the annual movement of a small herd of five thousand. Oil men have pointed with pride – and some scorn directed towards environmentalists – at the caribou they see finding shade, a cool breeze and relief from insects beneath the pipeline itself. But those animals are nearly always young bulls, caribou cows and calves, and old bulls, avoid the pipeline and Prudhoe Bay as do most waterfowl which formerly nested in great numbers on the lakes.

The total effects of industrial activity on animals like caribou can only be guessed at. For example, they are known to be spooked by objects on the skyline and this was exploited by prehistoric Eskimos who built man-like figures of rocks called *inukshuks* along ridges to funnel caribou into valleys where they could be more easily ambushed with spears or bows and arrows. But the Arctic landscape is one big skyline: nothing can happen within ten miles without an animal knowing about it. A buried gas pipeline of the kind proposed by Polar Gas is thought to be relatively harmless once it is in place. Biologists are in no doubt that some impact of industrial activity can be absorbed. As long as important habitats like calving grounds are protected, and animals are not shot by hunters, they will survive as a species. But the question for Eskimos is whether the animals will survive as a harvestable *resource*. Like the North American buffalo, will they exist only in a small number of reserves, or will they continue to see them across thousands of square miles of tundra as they have done for thousands of years as one of the greatest wildlife spectacles Man has ever witnessed?

It can be difficult for the hard-hat industry men to believe in any threat to ecology when foxes play among aerials on snow-covered

Salvage archeologist Caroline Parmentier of the Canadian National Museum, inspects rusty food cans and barrel hoops, cached on Fury Beach, Somerset Island, after the wreck of HMS Fury *in 1825.*

roofs of their huts in winter, caribou sometimes have to be chased off airstrips before planes can land, and wolves eat out of their hands and bring pups into camps. One man told me how, alone on the tundra one bitterly cold night, he had to change a wheel of his pick-up; sensing something looking over his shoulder, he turned and looked into the face of a wolf – "I flung the wheel wrench at it but the bastard just picked it up and trotted off with it!"

A factor of increasing concern is the activity of biologists themselves. Nearly every scientific report about Arctic animals contains photographs of them – invariably running. Three times I happened to be in aircraft flying over the walrus haul-out near Beechey Island and each time we circled to give scientists on board (not always zoologists, but archaeologists, geologists, botanists, and myself) an opportunity to see the beasts avalanching into the sea. In two weeks I heard of at least half a dozen other planes that had done the same thing, including helicopters chartered by CWS naturalists who had landed for a look. Individual scientists act responsibly and refrain from chasing animals for more than a few moments, but it is the cumulative effect of stress from constant disturbance, especially at a period which is critical for calves and building of weight for the coming winter, which is a danger.

Some stress is inevitable and necessary if a correct assessment of wildlife reaction to disturbance is to be gained. Hank Kiliaan and CWS zoologists could not determine the population dynamics of polar bears, for example, without tagging them. But industry men, prevented from carrying out surveys or construction operations because of the stress they may cause, observe with ever-growing astonishment the antics of naturalists chasing wildlife. Like Don Connolly, a grizzled Arctic hand who looks big and tough enough to spread his toast with lumberjacks and is Panarctic's construction foreman at Rea Point, who told me they had been stopped from doing a seismic survey on Prince Patrick Island because it might interfere with caribou. "Then I saw a black and yellow Helio Courier diving down on a small group of caribou. They pounded across the tundra with rolling eyes, and the plane dive-bombed them with a cloud of red paint. It turned out to be CWS naturalists who said later they spotted the same red-painted caribou three hundred miles away on Melville Island. They said it was the first time they had been able to verify inter-island movement of caribou – in my opinion it was because the poor little bastards never stopped running!"

But the oil man's scathing assessment was the biologist's solution to a mystery. "We didn't know why caribou just disappeared from certain islands without leaving carcasses," said Dr Frank Miller, of the CWS. "Spray-dying small groups of caribou – they stood out like traffic lights on the tundra – enabled us to get the first documentation of caribou migration over sea-ice." This means that from an ecological point of view, the whole group of islands on which the oil men are working must be treated as a single caribou habitat, and although some animals were harassed the knowledge gained is of great significance.

Ecological questions are difficult to resolve in any discussions with Eskimos who depend on hunting and trapping for subsistence and who distrust both industry men and scientists. They claim to have inherited generations of true understanding of Arctic animals from the necessity to depend on them, and to be the world's finest conservationists. But this is easily shown to be patent nonsense. In former days Eskimos killed everything they could lay their hands on, and were conservationists only because their primitive weapons did not allow them to make a significant dent in wildlife populations; it is true they lived in harmony with wildlife, but this was not done consciously. Today, they wish to have the same freedom to hunt with rifle, snow-machine, and fast motorboat as they enjoyed in the days of spear, dog-team and kayak, and the threat of over-hunting is as great as that of industrial development.

On Banks Island, where the whole community of Sachs Harbour lives off the land successfully by trapping foxes, Eskimos complained foxes were being driven away be seismic activity and simply did not believe it when survey crews said foxes followed them and were pests because they chewed plastic insulation from cables and gnawed at hydrophones. When two trappers at a time were permitted to travel with the seismic crews as "observers" they caught more foxes than ever before. The seismic work thus opened up new hunting territory, relieving pressure nearer the settlement, fox numbers increased and trappers caught more of them.

One dreads to think what Eskimos and oil men alike would have said about Frank Miller's experiments on Prince of Wales Island, where he was deliberately harassing animals with helicopters to determine responses. Such work is easy to justify, on the grounds that some stress suffered by a few animals could prevent ultimate extinction of all. When I dropped in on the harassment-study camp I was greeted by the wary stares of twenty-five musk ox browsing like big four-legged blankets, their shaggy brown hair streaming in the wind, as we flew in high so as not to disturb them. The camp was inland: half a dozen orange Parcol tents clustered on a gravel flat in a wide, rolling valley of tawny tussock. The terrain was spotted with white snowy owls sitting on their nests. Half a dozen caribou sprang away at a tip-toe trot as the chopper landed.

Over coffee and a slice of Dr Miller's camp-made bread, the pilot of the second machine was astonished that so much money could be spent flying back and forth over groups of animals. "To me it makes no difference, some days they run like hell and some days they stay in their beds," he said. But for biologists it is the differences that are interesting.

The overall aim was to determine a threshold altitude above which passing aircraft would not affect the animals' well-being. Observers were sent out to watch a particular group of animals then the helicopter made several passes at predetermined heights. The animals' reactions and subsequent behaviour were noted. "If we're causing them any real grief it's not detectable," Dr Miller said. He pointed out that caribou are on the move all the time in any case, merging, circulating, or just walking through the country. Reactions to aircraft seem to depend on the state of their nerves, which in turn are affected by such things as changing barometric pressure, humidity, and whether wolves are near enough to make them edgy.

During the previous year the team had made ninety-two separate helicopter flights totalling eighty-three hours, simulating pipeline construction flights on musk ox. The biologists observed no splintering of the herd, no abandonment of calves, no injuries, and only one group galloped more than a thousand metres during any harassment, but they found that any flight nearer than a thousand feet up and two miles away did impose some kind of stress. During the flights – made at different altitudes to simulate pipeline inspection, cargo slinging, and landing construction workers – thirty-four per cent of musk ox galloped off, twenty-seven per cent walked, thirty-nine per cent stayed. However, those which stayed were not necessarily taking it all equably.

Incidentally the musk ox does not produce musk and does not belong to any cattle family, but is a kind of goat-antelope which survives in its natural state only a long way north of the Arctic Circle. The odour secreted by a rutting bull is not related to musk, but may account for its name. Up to the First World War, when hunting was banned until it was resumed by quota in 1969, thousands had been killed by whalers, gold-miners, explorers and trappers: in 1917 they had become extinct in Alaska and were reduced to less than ten thousand in Canada. Compared with the harried caribou, which snatches food on the run, the musk ox is fly-proof, largely wolf-proof, its range is comparatively small and it moves less than a mile a day, although from time to time it does seek out new ranges.

Musk ox have been reintroduced from the Arctic Islands to Alaska, where they have been domesticated for the beautifully fine underwool they shed in summer, and Arctic Quebec where they were released into the wild to restock the range. The twenty-seven introduced to Søndre Strømfjord in Greenland in 1968 are now a herd of about one hundred fat, fine animals. Growing up to 900 pounds in weight, its great head seemingly bowed beneath the weight of immense horns twisting downwards and outwards from the heavy boss worn on the forehead like a bronze helmet, the musk ox is agile, fast, inquisitive and playful. Calves caught in the wild can be domesticated with ease, and on a farm young bulls race back and forth or jump on a sled towed by a tractor and go for a ride. The musk ox is particularly sensitive to disturbance because it has sweat glands only in its feet and can quickly become overheated, so it enjoys winter more than summer. Foraging on slopes and ridges as well as lowlands, it can dig through more than four feet of snow to get its food, but one shower of freezing rain laying down a porcelain-hard crust of ice can be devastating.

In the mid-1960s there was worldwide concern at the alarming increase in hunting of polar bears with the mobility brought by snow machines. Bear hides, for years worth something between fifteen and fifty dollars, suddenly fetched as much as $300 and in 1966 the bear kill nearly doubled to seven hundred. Five countries belonging to the International Union for the Conservation of Nature (USA, Canada, Denmark, Norway, USSR) formed a polar bear group. Norway and USSR banned bear hunting completely and Greenland severely restricted it. In Alaska, pilot guides specialised in flying trophy hunters to shoot bears but aerial hunting was stopped in June 1972 with the idea that Eskimos using dog teams and skidoos could take over as guides and the local economy would benefit, but within a few weeks the Marine Mammals Protection Act placed a moratorium of unspecified length on the hunting of all marine mammals. Now no polar bear hide, no matter where it was obtained or how old it is, may be imported to the US. Eskimos were exempted from the Act as long as the animal products were used only for subsistence; skins could not be sold or given to non-natives unless they were manufactured into handicrafts using "traditional" methods (sewing machines, for example, are not permitted). The Act scotched an economic opportunity for Eskimos and now most hides taken from polar bears in Alaska – which meant three new pairs of trousers to the traditional Eskimo – are wasted.

The habitat of polar bears is the floating ice-pack, but the animals are driven ashore in summer when the ice melts and usually find the most suitable denning areas on land. The extent of their trans-polar movements is only just becoming known. Canadian experts have identified at least fifteen distinct local populations but it is not known how much they intermingle. Bears that den in Svalbard (Spitzbergen) hunt on the ice and frequently become trapped when it drifts away to the south-west and they come ashore in southern Greenland. Alaskan polar bears drift with the ice to USSR. As bears on the sea-ice are so hard to identify from the air scientists have been experimenting with infra-red scanners. A bear is so well insulated by its thick blubber that it has only three hot spots – nose, eyes, and the soles of its feet – but these do not show up. What does show up on the heat sensitive film is the trail made by a bear on snow-covered ice. Each footprint contains a small degree of residual heat left by the bear; also, a footprint is warmer than the surrounding snow because the bottom of the indentation is nearer to comparatively warm sea water underlying the ice.

One polar bear in the Chukchi Sea has been "talking" to a satellite, an experiment which stopped only when the bear headed into Soviet territory and the batteries of the transmitter encapsulated in a ten-pound collar around its neck faded out. US Fish and Wildlife biologist Jack Lentfer had released the bear near Barrow in June 1977. For one second every minute, for eight hours every fourth day, the tiny transmitter sent signals to the Nimbus 6 Satellite in polar orbit, and Jack Lentfer received a printout of the bear's latitude and longitude from NASA. In three months the bear travelled 650 miles west of Barrow and was thought to be denning near Wrangell Island. Soviet scientists had agreed to try to retrieve the collar during the summer of 1978, and the polar bear group of IUCN was planning an international bear-watch by satellite, fitting several bears in different countries with collar transmitters.

The piecing together of the Arctic's ecological jigsaw to determine which areas are critical, which are borderline and which can be used by industry without risk, is an enormously long and expensive undertaking. Musk ox might well survive in totally protected areas of tussocky upland, like polar ranches, if reservations were big enough. Caribou might survive if industrial activities were carefully phased to avoid critical areas at certain times of year and care was taken to avoid building objects on the skyline and harassing animals with aircraft. And there are many other species – lemmings, on which foxes and snowy owls depend, wolves, gyrfalcons, ptarmigan, seals and walrus, narwhal and bowhead whales, ermine, wolverine, barren ground grizzly bears, and a host of others – all of them balanced on an ecological see-saw which the weight of Man's activities is bound to tilt. For Arctic ecology is not fragile so much as unstable. It is easily affected by outside influences and takes a long time to recover. As the experience with the Western Arctic caribou herd has shown, even beneficial effects can turn out to be disastrous in the long term: once the see-saw starts going it can be a hard thing to stop.

Meanwhile, our bear spreadeagled on a talus slope in the rain on Prince of Wales Island was suffering the indignity of being manhandled in a good cause. By the time Hank had finished she was not a pretty sight. Streaks of scarlet blood dribbled from her ears and the dart marks on her rump. Green tattoo ink mingled with frothy saliva and bubbled down her chin. The darts had been removed and the small wounds they made dressed with blobs of gentian violet. Then Hank had used an aerosol can of Lady Clairol hair dye to spray a large black number on her back so her location could be recorded if she were spotted during subsequent surveys. In short, bear H29 looked a Technicolor disaster area. But she would feel woozy only a couple of days, and sea water would cleanse her wounds and disperse the colouring. Hank had worked with deft precision and a compassion that was demonstrated when the bear went into convulsions.

*As near (I hope) to being a hearth rug as she will ever be, the drugged 900-pound
sow polar bear is rolled over for girth measuring by helicopter pilot and wildlife
technician on the barren slopes of Prince of Wales Island in the Canadian Arctic.*

Instantly Hank leapt astride the bear and with both hands lifted
the wooden gag in her mouth so she did not break her jaw on the
rocks: it took strength, and both Hank and the bear were gasping
almost equally as the shudders subsided and the big creature finally
relaxed, exhausted. Convulsions are brought on by the immobilising
drug and are meant to be checked by the tranquiliser, but the
balance between these ingredients is delicate and sometimes the
condition is exacerbated by the business of being manhandled and
the unfamiliar noise of instruments, cameras, and conversation.

Hank hefted his briefcase and scratched the thick, short hair
between the bear's ears. "Sorry bear!" he said. A few minutes later
Bill fired up and we took off, leaving bear H29 spreadeagled on the
rocks, as near to being a hearth rug I hoped as she would ever be.

10

BREAKING THE ICE BARRIER

How the new generation of super-ships opening up Arctic sea routes could shift the focus of world power

When it is two inches thick the ice bends like a bow wave in front of a moving dog sled. The back ends of the runners might break through, so the driver's feet drag in the sea, but the paws of an eight-dog team acting as thirty-two powerful friction pads keep him going as long as he doesn't stop yelling and whipping. When it is five or six inches thick the ice rises higher in the water, grey rather than black, and you can camp on it. At three feet thick it is blinding white with a covering of snow, so level and solid that even Eskimos had to dig down to check whether they were on land or sea, but you can safely land a DC3 or drive a truck on it. Five feet of ice will bear the seventy-five tons of a loaded Hercules, and six feet a Boeing 727 filled with passengers and cargo.

The sea begins to make ice when its temperature drops to 29 °F (-2 °C) and it can grow at a rate of four or five inches a night. The first twelve inches form rapidly because its whiteness reflects the incoming radiation so much better than the dark-coloured sea, and water temperature drops rapidly. As the ice thickens it begins to have an insulating effect and the process slows, but by the end of November the continents and islands that face each other across the top of the world are sealed together by a virtually solid sheet of ice.

In early May, when it is six to eight feet thick, the ice stops growing

A geographic realm unlike any other – rotten pack ice in summer. Sea ice gains a metre in winter, loses a metre in summer, and is very hard if hit with a ship because all the salt has drained from it. Average thickness in winter is about ten feet but pressure ridges can be a hundred feet thick.

and begins to rot, becoming a mushy, pot-holed, hummocky scum on the summer sea. Meltwater collects on the ice sheet in brilliant turquoise pools shaped like a mass of individual ink blots. Where the warm ocean has attacked from beneath and made drain holes it shows through in lustreless black patterns. The first of October is the birthday of ice, and the floes which have survived the summer's melt freeze together again in gnarled and weathered "multi-year" ice that thickens to as much as fifteen feet. During its first year the brine in the frozen sea water collects in pockets which dissipate downwards, so old or polar ice is made of water fresh enough to drink. This hummocky ice is hard enough to be avoided by icebreakers that can smash through the smooth, salty, first-year ice without much trouble.

Arctic sea ice – the polar pack – is a geographic realm quite unlike any other. One moment still as a grave, solid from one horizon to the other, then imperceptibly moving in the grip of hugely powerful forces, growling into mountain ridges in front of your eyes, splitting into long and erratic fractures that widen to expose the dark sea beneath. Tropically warm compared with the bitter cold of the air, the sea "smokes" like a prairie grass-fire when it is exposed, laying trails of long, low cirrus that can be detected from far beyond the horizon. This "water sky" indicated a way out for trapped ships, and showed areas to be avoided by dog-sled travellers. When the mirror-calm water of newly opened leads freezes hard it makes smooth aprons, ideal highways for sleds and snow machines. Until, without warning, the edges of the leads steadily grind together, squeezing the thinner new ice into larva-like eruptions that pile great chunks of ice into "pressure ridges" fifteen or twenty feet high and about eighty feet deep. In the polar pack, which in winter covers ten per cent of northern seas, there are typically eight pressure ridges to the mile.

Seals beneath the ice scratch out breathing holes which become covered in snow and serve to insulate their "windows" from the cold air and prevent their freezing over. Polar bears hunt over the ice for seals, sneaking up with snow camouflaging their black muzzles while seals sleep on the ice, or snatching them out of their breathing holes with massive paws. In their traditional way of life Eskimos spent at least a quarter of their year living or hunting seals on the ice, a rigorous and hazardous existence for which they developed a unique awareness of the subtle changes of colouring and pattern in snow, ice and cloud which served as the only landmarks and indicators of direction in their spinning, jolting environment. Even these minimal visual clues were easily obscured by fog, snow, wind, glare, darkness and that eerily disconcerting condition of shadowlessness called whiteout. In the bland whiteness around him the Eskimo hunter recognised textures and shades as significant to him as the colours of grass and autumn leaves: he had twenty-five words to describe different kinds of ice and one hundred words for snow, but no collective terms for ice or snow as such.

Over sea ice on a sunny day the blue of a clear sky is bleached out by reflected dazzle, and you sense how a moth feels when crawling over the lens of a spot-light; mariners know this white sky, like a transparent pearly smog, as "ice blink" because it indicates pack ice lying beneath it over the horizon. In fog or overcast, ice and atmosphere seem to merge in a disorienting void, a white hole in space. People and objects look like cut-outs on white paper. Unless you are

born Eskimo it is an alien world. The vastness of it jolts your bump of location; your mental compass, like any other compass near the North Pole, goes haywire. Distances are impossible to judge. The flatness and infinity of the sea ice seems to rub your retina against the knap, and it is a relief to get inside a vehicle or tent where the eye has near objects on which to focus. And always there is that sense of uncertainty when you can never be quite sure a crack won't suddenly appear between your feet and the two halves drift steadily but remorselessly apart.

Although it is rated the fourth largest ocean in the world and is five times bigger than the Mediterranean, the Arctic Ocean is really an inland sea lying between the great nations of the world. Its waters are calm because waves are damped by the great lid of ice. In summer its five million square miles of drifting ice shrinks to about three million square miles and the ice becomes half as thick. The shorefast ice breaks up and ships are able to penetrate the perimeter of the ocean, moving in icebreaker-escorted convoys between the river-mouth ports along the north coast of USSR, and around Point Barrow into the Beaufort Sea. Ice in the sea passages between the Arctic Islands usually disperses sufficiently to allow barges and ships to run in with a year's fuel and bulk supplies, and to lay out caches for scientific camps planned a year ahead. For four months the shallow and wide Mackenzie River becomes a super-highway for thousands of tons of supplies and new houses barged to remote Arctic beach-heads; in the first couple of weeks after break-up a fleet of twenty-eight tugs hauling 170 loaded barges heads northwards. Supported by ice-breakers in case they are trapped, other convoys run to Barrow and Prudhoe Bay by way of Bering Strait, and to the eastern Arctic and Hudson Bay from Montreal.

Fused into weathered hummocks, blown clean of snow because the ice contains no salt to make it moist and sticky, polar ice diminishes in summer but never disappears and was known by Alaskan Eskimos as "mother ice". In 1975 the mother ice capriciously did not release its grip of the land and a convoy of twenty-three

Greenland passenger ship Disko *weaves through the glacial ice crowding Disko Bay; most icebergs survive for about three years, melting 1,800 miles farther south when they strike the warmer waters of the Grand Banks off Newfoundland.*

tugs and forty-seven barges taking tons of urgently required construction equipment and supplies to the Prudhoe Bay oilfield were trapped. In conditions described as ten times worse than normal the barges reached Barrow and waited for the ice to retreat from the tip of the point, but it did not do so and possibly the greatest maritime mass movement of cargo since wartime was delayed two months. Finally, only twenty-fives barges got through and the remainder had to return to Valdez, their cargo trucked north at great additional cost.

The polar pack rotates clockwise around the Arctic Ocean about once every ten years, finding an outlet only between Greenland and Svalbard. The centre of the gyre is not the North Pole but a point – "the pole of inaccessibility" – four hundred miles nearer to eastern Siberia. For many miles along the north-west shore of Ellesmere and Axel Heiberg Islands the freezing and thawing of the sea over hundreds of years has created a massive shelf of ice two hundred feet thick. Occasionally segments are snapped off by tidal rise and fall, to drift away with the pack ice as floating ice "islands". Dirty because of the dust they have collected over the years, the ice islands are often so large and land-like that explorers mistook them for real islands. Their table-flat surfaces are marked in summer by parallel strips of water between ridges of ice, so they are easily identifiable from the air, but despite their great thickness their top surface is only twenty feet above sea level.

Drifting ice islands are quite distinct from the icebergs sculpted by melting processes into fantastic cathedral, dry-dock and town hall shapes. These spectacular and picturesque floating mountains, two hundred feet high, originate from great glaciers creeping downward from the immense ice cap covering all but the coastal perimeter of Greenland. Every year thousands of icebergs calve into the sea from the coast of Greenland. Some from the east coast are carried by currents around Greenland's southern tip and northwards along the west coast into Davis Strait. There they meet icebergs from north-west Greenland and drift down the coast of Labrador, dotting the ocean at eight to the square mile. Aircraft of the International Ice Patrol, run by the US Coast Guard, monitor icebergs as they drift into the shipping lanes in the vicinity of the Grand Banks and melt away in warmer waters. For identification some are bombed with paint. Every year about five hundred drift south of 48 °N but in 1972, a bad ice year, as many as 1,500 came south of this latitude.

Solid enough to sail through the polar pack without fracturing, and level enough to provide landing strips, ice islands are sought by scientists for use as drifting research stations. One of them, first sighted as a radar target off Barrow in 1950, was four by nine miles in extent and first occupied by US oceanographers and meteorologists when it was near the North Pole in 1952, but had to be abandoned when it ran aground off Ellesmere Island. After three years it drifted free again and was reoccupied by a big scientific team as part of International Geophysical Year in 1957. Known as Drift Station Alpha, it was visited by the submarine *USS Skate* which homed in on the scientists' camp by listening to the sound of an outboard motor. It is still on the move around the Arctic, currently off Ellef Ringnes Island carrying an electronic beacon which automatically reports its position to a satellite.

Another project was the US-Canadian Arctic Ice Dynamics Joint Experiment (AIDJEX) which culminated in fifty men established on four drift stations far out in the pack ice north of Alaska, for fourteen months during 1975–6. The $20 million project was mounted to study the mechanical properties of sea ice and the stresses and strains that make it behave the way it does, with the aim of ultimately being able to predict its movements. But the stresses and strains of science were too much for the ice platform supporting the main camp, which suddenly split from end to end, dividing camp and runway in two. Powerlines connecting huts and tents had to be hurriedly unplugged as the two halves drifted apart. One side slid out from beneath the mess hut, leaving half of it cantilevered over the water so it had to be hauled aboard the floe by bulldozer. The runway cracked into several pieces. The split was never very wide but before the pieces came together again they moved laterally by a quarter of a mile. Then another crack appeared, at right angles to the first, and the camp had to be abandoned.

Soviet scientists have occupied drift stations regularly since the early 1950s. Some of their men from a Soviet ice island designated North Pole 19 caused bureaucratic consternation when they visited the AIDJEX camp and passed through Barrow without visas. Another camp was established in 1969 on NP-22, an ice island two by three and a half miles and ninety-seven feet thick, which created rather more than consternation because it drifted within the Canadian 200-mile economic zone. Manned by up to one hundred people from the Arctic and Antarctic Scientific Institute of Leningrad, the island broke free from Siberian waters in 1973 and drifted into the Canadian sector in 1977, when the CBC reported it on newscasts as "a Russian base that keeps getting closer and closer". Canadian jet F5 Freedom Fighters flew in convoy with a tanker aircraft and buzzed the camp periodically to take photographs and show that Canada was alive and well. A CBC TV crew chartered a

Twin Otter from Resolute and found the ice island 330 miles north-west of Isachsen. The films made for television by reporter Jim Bitterman ("The Russians say it's a scientific station investigating ocean, ice and air – that's what they *say*") made a spy-ship mystery of the whole thing, and was a rather different story from that of pilot Pat Doyle who was captain of the aircraft. "The fact was," he told me, "we landed while everybody was asleep because they were working on a different time frame to us. They were unbelievably friendly, showed us everything we wanted to see, and laid out a tremendous five-course supper." A Maple Leaf flag, given to the Russians to hoist alongside their own Hammer and Sickle "to remind you you're in Canada" was no longer evident when the Freedom Fighters buzzed over again later.

Asserting her sovereignty over land where at most only a handful of people live has always been difficult for Canada. Her biggest threat has been the de facto presence of the US. During the Second World War the fifteen thousand US troops in the Yukon and NWT, building airfields and the Alaska Highway, amounted almost to an army of occupation. In 1946, as US ships loaded up to establish a string of new weather stations in the Arctic Islands, it was only when officials in Ottawa noticed newspaper advertisement s for personnel, and asked what was going on, that the US realised nobody had asked Canada's permission; the project was postponed a year and became a joint one between the two countries. When the Cold War required an Arctic defence system to protect the North American heartland, Canadians were too thin on the ground to build it or even to carry out effective supervision of American activities. In the Eastern Arctic, an area as large as the US east of the Mississippi, there were six Anglican missionaries, fifteen Catholic missionaries, fifteen Hudson's Bay traders and clerks, fifteen Mounties, all nomi-nally Canadians looking after the few scattered Eskimos – and two thousand US construction workers. When voices in Congress began to suggest the US had "special rights" in the Canadian Arctic, Canada became alarmed and purchased outright all military assets in her North. When the first large-scale Canadian scientific effort in the Arctic was started in 1954 it was as much to get men up there doing a job, to show the world that the territories were being occupied and used, as to discover what Canada actually owned in her Arctic. The first task of the Polar Continental Shelf Project was to produce accurate maps and plot geological and geophysical informa-tion. Since then it has grown into the government umbrella organisa-tion that provides logistical support for more than one hundred scientific projects in the Arctic every year, nurse-maiding eight hundred scientists scattered in small camps over an area as big as Europe.

In international law the contiguous sea-ice defies definition. Should sea be considered as land when you can walk and drive over it? Should ice be treated as an open waterway when it is perpetually frozen and (until the present) virtually closed to shipping? The issue is confused by the sector theory, by which countries with Arctic coastline claim the segment of ocean that lies between the North Pole and their extreme east and west meridians. In other words, the Arctic Ocean is divided into triangular slices, like a cake, with the North Pole at the centre. Canada claims her Arctic sector, as the USSR does, but does not assert it. Says Canada's Foreign Ministry: "It is a policy of constructive ambiguity." All official Canadian maps except those of the RCMP show the sector. Canada reckons to exercise certain jurisdictions, such as protection of wildlife and air-sea rescue responsibilities, but in the House of Commons there have been as many statements "disaffirming" the polar sector as there have been affirming it. The US adopts a less proprietary policy for two reasons. One is that its own share of the polar cake is so much smaller than that of Canada and USSR. The second is commercially and strategically important because the US has always insisted that the Northwest Passage is not an internal waterway but is an international strait. Canada *asserts* the Northwest Passage is internal, but has never formally *declared* it (the nuances of diplomatic language being legally significant), so its status is confused even in the Canadian mind. The Northwest Passage has never been an international strait, says Canada. But it will become one, says the US.

The pressure of polar ice against the western edge of the Arctic archipelago never slackens at any time of year, so ships must take one of the two inside passages between Baffin Bay and the Beaufort Sea. The southern route, by way of the Coronation Gulf, is unquestionably internal because the straits through the maze of islands are so narrow. But the northern route, through Lancaster Sound, Barrow Strait, Viscount Melville Sound, and M'Clure Strait – the Northwest Passage – narrows to twenty miles at one point between small islands, but is thirty to ninety miles broad over the rest of its 800-mile length. Of the handful of ships to have sailed the passage only one or two managed to push through M'Clure Strait, the others turning south through narrow Prince of Wales Strait. However, the whole route may be easily navigated by submarines and there is no telling how often it has been used by them.

The question was academic until 1968 when oil was discovered in Prudhoe Bay and the Humble Oil Company spent $56 million sending America's largest oil tanker through the Northwest Passage to test whether North Slope Oil could be exported by sea. Permission from the Canadian government was not sought, but Canada side-stepped direct confrontation with the US by giving permission any-way, and sending the icebreaker *John A. Macdonald* to "help" the ice-strengthened supertanker *Manhattan* through the ice with her load of Pennsylvania harbour water and, on the return journey, one symbolic barrel of oil. When Canada did formally declare a measure of control, by means of a 100-mile Arctic coastal pollution prevention zone in which she declared the right to regulate classes and types of ships, President Nixon retaliated by cutting US oil imports from Canada. The heat went out of the issue when the North Slope oil companies opted for a pipeline but the status of the Northwest Passage as an international strait was still not resolved. With the building of powerful new icebreakers, and development of ice-breaking supertankers, this uncertainty is unlikely to remain for much longer.

Industry has been prevented from tearing the Arctic apart (so far) by only one obstacle – the lack of transport. The sea ice which has become the exciting new frontier of oil and gas exploration and scientific understanding, has been a frontier as solid as the Iron Curtain as far as shipping is concerned. But if the sea-ice barriers were to be broken, the potential impact of the Northwest Passage is blazed on every globe. From Resolute, hub of the High Arctic, a 4,000-mile radius embraces practically every industrial nation in the world. By ship, the English Channel is only one day's steaming farther than Montreal. From the North Slope, Japan is as close as California. If ships could sail direct between Japan and Europe by way of the Northwest Passage the voyage could be reduced by two-thirds. In addition to oil and gas, the North Slope has massive reserves of coal, Baffin Island has millions of tons of iron ore, and throughout the Canadian Arctic and Greenland there are valuable resources of asbestos, copper, zinc, lead, gold, silver, and uranium which lack only a transport system to make them economically viable. During the 1980's, for the first time in history, the barriers of sea ice which have locked up the Arctic will be broken.

One proposal for unlocking Arctic resources has come from Boeing, using a fleet of giant aircraft flying twenty hours a day. Each one would carry more than one thousand tons of oil or ore in quickly removable cargo pods slotted into its wings. Each pod would be as big as the fuselage of a jumbo jet, and the aircraft would be powered by twelve jet engines. General Dynamics has drawn plans of a 250,000-ton bulk-cargo submarine which could operate throughout

Canadian icebreakers like this one were built mainly for the Gulf of St Lawrence and can enter Arctic waters only in late summer; the largest Soviet ice breaker, by comparison, has forged her way to the North Pole and back in only two weeks

the Arctic Ocean year-round, whatever the ice conditions on the surface, although its survival equipment would have to include a means of making a skylight in the ice if the crew ever had to abandon ship. A submarine could not carry liquefied gas because it is buoyant, and in many waters such as Davis Strait there would barely be room to navigate its immense bulk between the deepest keels of icebergs and the seabed. But both these ideas have been made to look economically and technically fanciful by plans to build a new generation of very large ships sufficiently powerful and robust to break through any ice.

The *Manhattan* voyage proved that power to keep it going at a steady rate, combined with mass that provides the momentum with which it smashes through thick pressure ridges, is a ship's most effective weapon against ice. The 150,000-ton *Manhattan* was herself only a half-scale model of the ultimate polar cargo carrier. With a new down-breaker bow that forced the ice downwards, and a strengthened belt of steel nine feet thick along each side, the ship was strong enough to cope with the ice but only one-fifth of her 43,000 horsepower was available in reverse, when it was also prone to over-heat. Had the ship been fitted with powerful engines like an icebreaker it would have been able to go astern quickly and accelerate more rapidly. The voyage also showed the greatest danger to the Arctic stemmed not from pollution but the risk of running aground in uncharted waters. Captain Tom Pullen, former captain of Canada's only naval icebreaker, and the only Canadian observer on board the supertanker, reported that besetments in ice were often due to inept ship handling by the three conning officers. There were seven captains on the ship's bridge, plus three mates with master's certificates, yet the ship was often manoeuvred by eye with no fixes on the chart. Nor did the ship take advantage of two parallel tracks of soundings on the chart but steamed between them. Once a pinnacle came within four fathoms of the keel and nobody aboard the *Manhattan* saw it until the icebreaker following astern called up and there was a rush to the depth recorder.

At the moment the ship blundered into a heavy floe five miles across, and stalled on a weathered ridge fifteen feet thick in its centre, the master was below being interviewed by US Press about how it felt to be the first man in history to take a ship through M'Clure Strait (to which he replied that he was "underwhelmed"), and open water was in sight, but four hours of battering produced less than a mile of progress and the ship had to be freed by the icebreaker then retreat and sail by way of Prince of Wales Strait. According to Captain Pullen the large floe that stopped the *Manhattan* could have been avoided if the ship's officers had used their binoculars, and made proper use of their ice-reconnaissance helicopters which were flying press photographers around the ship.

The lessons learned on this adventure are now to be applied by Melville Shipping Ltd, a study group comprising shipping and pipeline companies, and the Canadian government. It is planning to build two ice-breaking gas tankers which should be delivering Panarctic's natural gas in liquefied form to eastern seaboard ports by 1983. The huge ships will be able to call up 180,000 shaft horsepower, more than four times that of the *Manhattan*, and move at a steady three knots through ice seven feet thick, averaging sixteen days a round trip between New Brunswick and Bridport Inlet, a deep bay protected by a long natural breakwater on the south coast of Melville Island. Gas reserves proven on Melville Island alone could keep a fleet of ten such ships busy for twenty years with no necessity to build the Polar Gas pipeline. If new discoveries mean the pipeline is built the ships will be able to tap reserves on other islands, or run to Cape Parry to collect gas from the Mackenzie Delta. If the gas pipeline proved to be as expensive as Alyeska, it would equal the cost of an ice-breaking gas tanker every sixteen miles.

Tanker operations of this kind are logical for Canada because her energy field can be tapped as required. When more gas is required she builds more ships. Once a pipeline is built it will bring four million cubic feet of gas a day to a country that consumes only 2·5 mcf, and the surplus must be exported to pay for the pipeline. Ten ships could meet Canada's total gas needs and ensure that all her reserves are retained for her own use, although the oil companies would not receive such a quick return on their exploration investment. Getting gas moving out of the Arctic will encourage exploration: so far only about 250 holes have been drilled in the entire area, compared with 1,700 a *month* in Alberta. The flexibility of shipping means that small fields can be tapped as they are discovered, and this could provide the necessary cash flow on which to base finance for accelerated exploration. The energy crisis is as much a transportation crisis as a shortage of resources. The Alyeska pipeline has succeeded only in delivering oil to the west coast of USA where there is already a glut, while shortages continue in the northern tier and eastern states. Once the northern ice barrier is broken, oil could be shipped by icebreaking tankers direct from Alaska to New York for just half the cost of bringing it by pipeline to Valdez and by tanker via Panama to the Gulf of Mexico. If Alaska's offshore potential is realised and it continues to be the major US energy source, as many as fifty-two icebreaking supertankers could be shuttling through the Northwest Passage by the year 2000.

Until now, a number of companies have been sitting on the fence waiting for somebody else to jump so they can profit from their experience. Now that Melville Shipping is taking the plunge, the 1980s are likely to see spectacular developments. Dome Petroleum signed up Bengt Johansson, designer of Finland's largest icebreakers, and from his drawing board are springing a variety of new projects, including a massive barge-like icebreaker artfully called an Arctic Marine Locomotive (AML) to support Beaufort Sea drilling operations, moored drill ships that could operate year-round in ice-covered seas, and supertankers to ship oil and gas through the Northwest Passage. The imaginative AML concept may well be the first of the new generation of superships – with 150,000 shaft horsepower it will be twice as powerful as the largest Russian icebreakers, currently the biggest in the world.

By 1985 Trans Canada Pipelines plans to be running two ice-breaking gas tankers between King Christian Island and New Brunswick. American interests are considering mining the vast lead-zinc deposits in western Alaska for which the market is Europe; an Arctic sea route would save forty-three per cent of the shipping distance via Panama. The Canadian Coast Guard is responding to these commercial ventures by finalising the details of a nuclear-powered Class Ten icebreaker of about 180,000 shaft horsepower which could be operational by 1987.

Meanwhile a joint effort between shipping companies and the Canadian government in 1978 put the world's first heavy icebreaking bulk carrier in operation, the 35,000-ton *Arctic*. The ship is designed to operate in the eastern Arctic independently of icebreakers for six months a year, and farther west in summer, and at a stroke has doubled the Hudson Bay shipping season. Ice in Hudson Bay is no worse than in the northern Baltic, which has been open year-round since 1974, so it will be only a matter of time before ships can sail anywhere in Arctic seas that are coloured white on the map as well as those coloured blue.

The "glamour" ships of the 1980s, these vast and powerful new icebreakers and icebreaking tankers driving through ice-covered seas will open a new chapter in maritime history. There will be nothing delicate about them. They will be large brutes whose only enemies will be large bergs, ice islands, and other ships. Bulkheads in tanks will have to be exceedingly strong to withstand the sloshing of jerky motion through the ice. There are no repair yards in the Arctic so propellers prone to ice damage will have to be replaceable on the spot. All windows will have to be specially heated. Survival gear will probably include snow machines as well as lifeboats and ships may have escape chutes like those in jet aircraft. The new "Seasat" satellites will enable the ship to receive instant photographs of icefields ahead, but individual large icebergs will be a danger because they do not always show up on radar. Captain Pullen once nosed his ship right up to a 150-foot iceberg before it showed on the radar screen. Small "growlers" lying low in the water are especially dangerous and extensive use will be made of infra-red and image-intensified television. The ships will encounter continuous darkness two months a year, fog one day in four during the summer, not to mention blowing snow and whiteouts. In Bridport Inlet a cold-air bubbling system will keep the docking area free of ice. The liquefication and pumping plants, and accommodation, will be constructed on barges towed into position. Tugs may not be required because the ice acts as a brake – "Once you've cut a channel through shorefast ice," says Captain Pullen, "reversing out would be like running on a railway line."

Regular traffic will create continuously open leads which may change the habits of wildlife: seals will be attracted to the open water, polar bears will be attracted by the seals; seabirds and whales will also be affected. Risk of pollution by a gas tanker stems only from its own fuel supply: gas might go bang, but it will not pollute.

Conventional icebreakers are also undergoing a long overdue quantum leap in development. At present the USSR has a fleet of forty-one icebreakers. The Canadian Coast Guard has nine (some small, most of them old) of which the largest is the 13,000-ton *Louis St Laurent* which can muster 28,000 horsepower. The US Coast Guard has six old vessels plus two dashing new ones, *Polar Sea* and *Polar Star*, which were being recommissioned in 1979 after more than two years' teething troubles with hydraulic linkages to the variable-pitch propellers that will enable them to change quickly between forward and reverse thrust. These pretty 12,000-ton ships, officially rated at 60,000 horsepower, will move continuously through six feet of ice and dynamite their way through the big pressure ridges they cannot defeat by ramming in order to move through the polar pack. In a dramatic demonstration of Soviet icebreaking ability, the first surface ship to reach the North Pole was the 25,000-ton *Arktika* in 1977; one of Russia's two largest icebreakers (the other is the *Sibir*), its nuclear-powered engines can provide 75,000 horsepower.

Apart from ambitious commercial enterprises, all still on the drawing board or under construction, Canada has no icebreaker capable of entering any part of her own Arctic "internal" waters at any time of year. No naval fighting ship is capable of operating north of the Arctic Circle, ever. When its only icebreaker *HMCS Labrador* was sold twenty years ago the Canadian Navy cut itself off from effective Arctic participation. The pollution prevention acts which angered the US divided ships into nine classes and partitioned waters of the Canadian Arctic sector into sixteen shipping zones. The higher the number of zone the thinner its ice cover. Classified according to their ability to deal with ice, ships of different types may enter certain zones only at designated times of year. But Canada has no way of enforcing what has been described as "this sneaky way of exerting sovereignty" and until her super-icebreaker is built may be forced to sit back and watch the new US Coast Guard vessels, or even Soviet icebreakers, navigate the Northwest Passage freely and establish its vality as an international strait.

In fact, Canada can exert nothing in her Arctic. The coastline of the Arctic Islands alone is greater than the circumference of the earth. You could say it is the longest undefended frontier in the world – and her principal enemy could walk there.

This is not as unimportant as it may sound for if Canada succeeds in her objective to be self-sufficient in energy much of her oil will come from Arctic fields. Prudhoe Bay already represents a third of US oil reserves. In the event of hostilities between NATO and the USSR these hydrocarbon and mineral resources, and icebreaker shipping routes, will transform the North American Arctic into something it has never been before – a strategic and tactical target area. On these grounds alone the Arctic can no longer be considered North America's strategic desert – a no-man's-land of "scorched ice" that acts as its own best defence because any attacker advancing over it can be seen coming. There are also other pressing reasons for military defence of the Arctic.

NATO has capability to hit the Soviet Union from the Mediterranean, Atlantic and Pacific with Poseidon missiles fired from submarines, and has lots of friendly ocean to hide them in. The USSR has only the Arctic Ocean to call her own, so why should her ships leave the only sea area in the northern hemisphere which can be neither mined nor observed? NATO expects Soviet submarines to surge through the Greenland–Iceland–UK gap to attack Atlantic shipping, but a Soviet submarine does not have to surface in Hudson Bay in order to hit Detroit: the new Delta nuclear submarines, armed with SSN-8 missiles having a 5,000-mile range, would not have to leave the Barents Sea. However, only part of the Barents Sea is deep enough for submarines to hide in, and to protect her fleet as NATO forces counter-attacked round the north of Norway the USSR would have to disperse them. The handiest hiding place is beneath the ice of the polar pack, where the noise of grinding floes jams the sonar equipment of anti-submarine aircraft and hunter-killer submarines.

In terms of nuclear deterrent, for the foreseeable future the move is towards the sea. If Canada developed the capability to operate in ice-infested waters she would make an important contribution to the NATO flank by depriving Soviet submarines of a certain hiding place. At present North America's only protection from enemy submarines using ice as cover for launching a missile attack is USSR's apparent lack of navigation technology. Before firing a warhead a submarine would have to surface long enough to pinpoint exactly its position, and its tremendous heat output would be detectable by satellite. It is widely believed that US and Soviet submarines already use the Northwest Passage, and Canada is experimenting with ways of separating out the ice noise and is setting out self-contained "listening buoys" which detect submarine engine noise and transmit the information ashore. Sound carries a long way because waves are reflected upward by the seabed and downward by the ice cover. Small explosions have been "heard" electronically as far away as 1,500 miles. Theoretically, if ice noise could be filtered out, every ship in or under the Arctic ice could be detected from a listening post like that at Alert. In spring 1977 there was an alarm when an Eskimo trapper reported seeing the periscope of a wrecked submarine in the ice near Cambridge Bay. Mounties immediately flew out to investigate and found it was an experimental listening buoy that had broken loose, although it was announced as a navigation buoy.

Apart from the DEW-line and the top secret listening posts at Alert and Inuvik, the Canadian military has no defence task in the Arctic. Its Northern Region Headquarters, established only recently in Yellowknife, 360 miles from the northern coastline, coordinates exercises and provides support for such things as search and rescue, fire-fighting and medical evacuations from remote settlements. Its two Twin Otters are Canada's only military aircraft stationed permanently north of 60° lat., and there are only seventy men. In the office of Major David Sproule, senior operations officer, I admired the mass of yellow pins on the map. "You've got a lot to look after," I said.

"Yes, but it's nothing to do with the map: the pins show where I have been."

The chief permanent military presence is supplied by three hundred Eskimos armed with Lee Enfield ·303 rifles – the Arctic Rangers. The force was started in the Cold War days when it seemed the archipelago would be a valid place for an enemy to do something. It was modelled on the Pacific Rangers established to watch for Japanese during the Second World War. Rifles are provided to enable rangers to kill themselves a seal for survival. "It was never intended that they should dig in and defend themselves," said staff officer Major Bob Lemaire. "The force is really a cheap corps of eyes and ears which can act as guides, coast watchers, aircraft spotters, rescue parties, and assist the Mounties in discovering, reporting, and apprehending enemy agents and saboteurs." Formal training was not started until 1971, when it was thought a good idea to have a more organised ground surveillance force in the Arctic, but the total budget is only $44,500 a year.

The Rangers' only operational tasking since 1948 was an alert for a Polish schooner which in 1975 sailed through Barrow Strait and anchored in Resolute Bay. Nobody had seen it coming and it had no permission to be there, so it was told to leave. Despite prolonged searches Canadian Forces lost track of it, and did not find the ship again until it turned up in Greenland. Whether it had been an innocent adventure or a deliberate test of Canadian capability is unknown but Canada was shown stumbling around her geographic attic like a man without a torch.

In Alaska, where the USAF provides "top cover for North America" the picture could not be more different. Described by a USAF general as "the most central place in the world for aircraft", Fairbanks is two hours' flying closer to Frankfurt than Miami is. Alaska is an important midway staging point on the great circle route between US west coast bases and the Far East, and is as near to the world's largest military base – on the Kola Peninsula of USSR, near Murmansk – as Spain is. Besides this strategic and commanding position on top of the world Alaska shares a maritime frontier with the USSR and for this reason looks west rather than north. The Bering Strait is only about fifty miles wide. Two islands, Big Diomede and Little Diomede, belonging respectively to USSR and USA, are two and half miles apart and in winter are joined together by sea ice on which Yupik Eskimo families from each island, who are related to each other, sometimes meet while fishing.

With three bases and 12,000 personnel, Alaska Air Command operates two squadrons of F4 Phantoms, thirteen aircraft control and warning sites dotted along the coast, and missile batteries for defence. It is supported by a Strategic Air Command wing of KC135s (Boeing 707 tanker aircraft) which would rendezvous with any flights of bombers flying overhead from the nearest bases in Spokane, Washington, to refuel them. SAC also operates electronic reconnaissance aircraft from a base at Shemya, a tiny island 1,500 miles away at the eastern end of the Aleutians; the island has only eight or ten clear and "unblustery" days a year, and the edges of the short runway are so precipitous that pilots rumour it is not dry land at all but a grounded aircraft carrier. These listening flights patrolling the Siberian seaboard are highly secret and technical, different from the usual SAC mission profile described on the pilots' briefing room notice-board: "Taxi on the yellow line, take off at the white line, fly on the black line, turn at the circles, refuel at the squares, bomb the triangles..." This has an element of truth because in winter coloured dye is used to mark out runways and taxiways covered in snow and ice. Confrontations in Alaskan air space are few. About once every ten days Soviet aircraft come close to US air space and are watched by the radar stations which draw their flight paths on a huge screen in the "battle room" at Elmendorf Air Force Base in Anchorage. Occasionally these are Soviet TU16 Badgers flying down the line to test US wakefulness but more often they are Soviet ice reconnaissance aircraft, one of which made an emergency landing on St Lawrence Island in 1975 and after days of paperwork was refuelled and sent home.

A major US military presence is also maintained at Thule, an air base in the north-west corner of Greenland. So strange is the converging geography on the roof of the world that Thule is no further distant from Fairbanks than Seattle is. An advance post commanding the whole of the Arctic Ocean and northern Soviet coastline, Thule has been important since the Cold War because it is an excellent place from which to threaten. Built in the early 1950s by agreement with Denmark, Thule has had nearly ten thousand personnel and construction men on the base at one time. Now it is virtually a staging post kept open in case of need. Its interceptor squadrons were withdrawn in 1966, and although bombers refuel there they do not use it as a base. This has been a sensitive issue since January 1968 when a B-52 bomber taking off from Thule on a 24-hour alert mission caught fire, crashed, and scattered four nuclear bombs over the sea ice. At first the ice was not thick enough to support vehicles and the first rescuers had to go out to the wreckage by dog-team. Helicopters could not land because their rotor wash created too much of a snow cloud. It was so cold that flashlight batteries lasted only ten minutes. A colony of a hundred igloos was built to provide shelter for up to 565 people cleaning up and filling six hundred containers with contaminated snow shipped to South Carolina for disposal. Plutonium levels increased for twelve miles around the crash site, although not to an extent that it endangered life, but it might have been different had the crash occurred on the ice cap where radioactivity would have been trapped in the ice, ultimately washing out into the sea with the icebergs over a period of centuries.

You can't travel far north of the Arctic Circle without encountering those eerie, silent, barracks-like buildings topped with giant white domes that could be igloos or golf balls – the DEW-line. The reason they are so evident is that the airstrips built for them during the early 1950s have, in some places, served as the infrastructure by which aircraft have made the rest of the Arctic accessible. The Distant Early Warning system is a chain of radar stations, roughly along the seventieth parallel at the top of the North American continent, stretching from the far west coast of Alaska to the east coast of Greenland. Originally there were sixty-one sites, averaging one every fifty miles. Now there are thirty-one – six in Alaska, twenty-one in Canada and four in Greenland – tied into the North

Atlantic radio system via Iceland, and the North American air defence system in Colorado. Now being made redundant by satellite surveillance, the system was intended to give warning of bomber attack from across the Arctic Ocean. In 1969 it was supplemented by the Ballistic Missile Early Warning system (BMEWS) which uses massive antennae at Clear (Alaska), Thule (Greenland) and Fylingdales (Yorkshire, UK) to give at least fifteen minutes' warning of missile attack.

DEW-line stations on the Greenland ice-cap occupy one of the most bizarre geographic environments on earth. Steel boxes built on legs, like offshore oil rigs, they shake so much in 200-knot winds screaming over the ice-cap in winter that water slops out of a glass, and the fifteen men inside can seldom go out. Snow for drinking water is collected from the platform by dragline. As the ice on which they rest is gradually sinking, and the snow builds up around them, every four or five years the platforms have to be jacked up twenty or thirty feet on extended legs. At station Dye 3, on the ice-cap, the footings have become twisted so the whole thing has had to be skidded sideways and erected on new foundations.

In the Canadian Arctic the larger DEW-line stations house up to a hundred men who are seldom seen out of doors. The stations are serviced by their own chartered airliners. Men hardly ever leave the base to hunt, visit the settlements, or get some fresh air, even in summer. Yet most of them spend nine months a year on the job. At Hall Beach I visited a big station called Fox Main. The grey buildings banked up with snowdrifts, and steel-lattice antennae, were wreathed in convection fog caused by the exhausts of a departing Hercules aircraft. Indoors, the atmosphere was hot and stale, with a strong smell of socks.

The station supervisor was at first unhelpful and brisk, though later he thawed and took me to lunch in a canteen-style dining room where the food was on a par with that served in oil camps. "You can come on the base and see how we shovel snow, how we do our washing..."

"How many men here?"

"Can't say."

"Where are the other bases?"

"Spread along the top, but if you say how many, or where, you'll be in trouble."

"How many bars are there on the base?"

"You can't print that. We don't have any problems here. Only toothache."

"How many Americans?"

Drillers of a wildcat rig afloat in the Arctic on an artificially made raft of ice fight −40° cold.

Little snow falls in the Arctic because the air is so cold, but the same snow blows round and round; noon at Prudhoe Bay, Alaska (BP photo).

Chocolate cake, a 'port-a-loo' and daily deliveries of apple juice — the young botanists' camp on Cameron Island, Canada.

Frozen-over sea fjord at Pangnirtung, Baffin Island, is airstrip and hockey rink in cold, bright days of spring.

Fishermen in Greenland can earn big money in summer but prefer to sit in the midnight sunshine.

Ears tagged, lip tattooed, minus a tooth, this polar bear will recover rapidly and add to scientific knowledge.

Yellow against the ice, a sow polar bear and two cubs leap from floe to floe then round on the helicopter hovering just out of their reach.

In traditional style an Eskimo family butchers a pair of walrus on the beach at Barrow, Alaska.

With rifle as protection against polar bears, a biologist examines the carcass of a beluga (white) whale at Cunningham Inlet where, for a few days every summer, thousands of whales congregate.

Halibut fisherman, Disko Bay

April Brower, Barrow

A new Greenlander and Disko

Refuelling: Hank Kiliaan

Young girl at Narssa

Eskimo baseballer, Chesterfield Inlet

Pitsiulalaaq Kelly of Frobisher

A smiling face in Holsteinsborg

Nylon fur and sunglasses: the new Eskimo

...landic lady in national dress

Street-corner teenagers, Godhavn

Girl at a water tap, Narssaq

...Top of the World schoolgirl, Resolute

School principal Metro Solomon, Chesterfield Inle...

(Overleaf) *Rotten ice adrift in the Northwest Passage in August.*

Electronic sentinels of the 70th parallel, the eerie radar stations of the DEW-line scattered along the Arctic coast of the North American mainland and across central Greenland are stockades from which men seldom venture, even in summer. The construction of these stations in the mid-1950s did more than anything else to bring civilisation to the Arctic, and in the process Eskimo people saw the wasteful consumer-oriented society at its worst. This station is at Tuktoyaktuk, in north-west Canada.

"A few, it's a Canadian base. I'm from Winnipeg."

"Run by Americans?"

"Well, it's an American company, an American trade union, American vehicles, USAF charter flights..." The DEW-line stations are run under contract by FELEC, an American subsidiary of ITT. The trade union is the International Brotherhood of Electrical Workers.

Like the supervisor, who had been fourteen years in the job, the medic who had greeted me had never been more than a few yards from the buildings of the base unless it was to go to the airstrip or, once in a blue moon, by truck to the Hudson's Bay store in the Eskimo settlement three miles away. I already knew there were three bars on the base. One of them, the Golden Ussuk Club, was the domain of the small contingent of military personnel. The bar was decorated with *ussuks* – walrus penis bones – and the largest, painted gold, was reckoned to be the staff of office of the senior of the four Canadian and two US officers. "Toothache? It's a bit of a problem, I guess," the medic told me later. "Guys line up in the mornings and say they're sick so I give 'em a couple of aspirins and they go back to work: hangovers are the problem. It's tough on guys who don't drink, being up here. Fuck all else to do."

If the Arctic sea ice presented no barrier to maritime activities – suggesting a coastline that would look like something between that of the Red Sea and the Shetland Islands – the Northwest Passage would be one of the principal sea lanes of the world. Instead of the Alyeska pipeline, Prudhoe Bay oil would almost certainly be carried direct to the eastern states by supertanker. At least one of the deep natural harbours of Melville Island would be a major Naval base while the Beaufort Sea and the northern coastline of the Arctic Islands and Greenland would be the scene of frequent naval exercises and manoeuvres. Instead, apart from submarines, not a single NATO warship is capable of operating in ice-infested waters. As the new generation of super-ships breaks down the ice barrier during the next decade the strategic picture will be likely to change radically, as will that of commercial trade routes. As this development is matched by that of northern Siberia it is possible that a whole new generation of over-ice military amphibious vehicles will evolve, which in turn may have a spin-off in terms of civilian transport for the Arctic.

The ultimate consequences of the great opening up of Arctic sea routes during the 1980s are exciting, and more than any other influence could result in the shifting of the world's power centre away from the Persian Gulf and Europe, and focussing it on the frozen arena of the Arctic Ocean.

Part III

SPACE-AGE ESKIMO

11

POINT OF ORIGIN

*How an Arctic time bomb was
created when Eskimos were pushed
into the deep end of modern life*

Point Hope is at the end of a tapering shingle spit jutting into the Chukchi Sea towards Siberia, on the map a little curl springing from the broad forehead of Alaska. We landed in a spatter of fine stones on the rutted strip, and in the buzzing silence that follows switch-off I crunched around the heaped-up gas barrels taking in a view that was majestic only in its dismalness. Almost hull down on the horizon of shingle, the houses of the village lay a mile and a half away and the mainland proper was thirty miles beyond. The swash of road-grey waves scouring away the gravel on one side of the spit and replacing it on the other made a mournful hiss. The shoreline was littered with plastic bags, bottles, pop cans, and whale vertebrae on which seabirds pecked at streamers of gristle. Early autumn, and although it was cold as yet there was no sign of the great ice-floes which, November to June, jostle round the point opening up leads where the Eskimos of Point Hope have hunted bowhead whales for at least four thousand years.

The high-pitched whine of an engine penetrated the distance like an electric drill. Bug-like, a small black dot detached itself from the far village and bounded towards us over the shallow ridges and hollows of gravel: a red Honda three-wheeler with fat low-pressure tyres driven by a young Eskimo who stood on the footrests and slalomed the machine as if he were on skis. Dressed for a Marlboro

Country poster with a wool tea-cosy hat instead of a stetson, he reined up with a skidding turn that showered the plane with stones. "Hi, you fellas want somethin'?"

"What about a ride into town?"

He lit a Marlboro with a gas lighter, shrugged, and kicked the engine up. "I thought you was my brother bringing his new rifle," he said. Then he revved to a scream and tore away as if the cops were after him. A fine, cold rain started.

Inhabited continuously longer than any other part of North America, this unrelentingly barren and unwelcoming outpost has seen a unique way of life persist little known and unchanged throughout the entire span of known history. Until, within the memory of a teenager like the one we had seen, the culture jumped from dog-team to 50 cc Honda. Before the night was out we would find ourselves on the receiving end of a vivid demonstration of the social stress caused by the speed of this transition from stone age to space age. Meanwhile, in the traditional Eskimo way, we refined our gear to barest essentials, hefted it on our backs, and set out on a hard slog through soft gravel. For two Whites who had just flown six hundred miles in four hours it was a short but earnest lesson in the realities of what it must have been like, on a *good* day, to have been born Eskimo.

It was through country like this – low-lying gravel ridges and swampy tundra dotted with lagoons – that the first small bands of migrating Eskimos pushed eastwards out of Asia into northern Alaska and later, as the glaciers of the last Ice Age retreated, fanned out across the top of the world. There are theories that Eskimos were a Canadian invention, a people driven north by more aggressive Indians, but it is more likely they evolved in central Asia and, like the original wild horses and many species of North American wildlife, crossed Bering Strait when it was still a marsh, frozen in winter, which bridged the continents. The Eskimos' straight black hair, brown eyes, high cheekbones and broad face suggest an almost certain Mongolian origin; these features are sometimes so exaggerated that you can put a ruler across both cheeks without touching the nose. Though deeply burned by sun-glare and wind, the skin is the pale yellow-brown of Asia. Those who turned south, inhabiting the western and southern coasts of Alaska, and the Aleutian Islands, came to lead a less mobile lifestyle and spawned their own languages and cultures. Those who moved north along the Arctic coast were forced by the seasonal migration of game and the constant coming and going of sea-ice to be nomadic. They became the true polar Eskimos, calling themselves Inuit (*the* people), and until the First World War some groups in the remoter parts of the Canadian Arctic islands believed they were the world's sole inhabitants.

The polar Eskimos ranged over six million square miles of land and frozen sea, occupying the longest linear distance of any single racial and linguistic group in the world. They are the only native people to have inhabited both Asia and America and have never been conquered or subdued by Whites or any other race. Although they developed regional dialects polar Eskimos were linked by common language just as they were by the highway afforded by the frozen sea, and to this day the Greenland Eskimo can make himself understood, although with some difficulty, in Canada and northern Alaska. Yet their numbers were probably never greater than today's population of about 65,000 (Alaska 8,000, Canada 17,000, Greenland 40,000). Counting in the 17,000 Yupik Eskimos of south and west Alaska, their 1,600 cousins in Siberia, and 2,000 Aleuts, the total number of all Eskimos is no greater than the new births brought into the world daily.

Despite the great spaciousness of their environment polar Eskimos crowded for warmth and convenience into very small living spaces where they developed a keen sensibility of each others' needs. Their way of life was that of a collective: a perfect communism, without bureaucrats, imposed only by the necessity to survive. Material possessions were reduced to what could be carried over long distances. Food was shared more or less equally until it was gone. Prestige was counted in terms of hunting ability and qualities of leadership. Living on top of each other in a small family group there was intense pressure towards self control, and to this day Eskimos try to please you by telling you what they think you want to hear, on the grounds that everybody should be kind to everybody. Curiosity was impertinent because only in his thoughts could a person obtain privacy. Children were explicitly taught to substitute feelings of amusement for those of annoyance. Like species of Arctic wildlife, which do not compete against each other for survival but support each other in the struggle against the environment, Eskimos decided long ago that living on the top shelf of the world was difficult enough without making life unpleasant for each other.

Hardy, inventive, technically skilled, they developed a technology for survival that is a stark contrast to that of wasteful, volatile Whites. The caribou, seals, walruses and whales they hunted fulfilled all material needs, providing food, clothing, heat, light, tools, transport and building materials. The Eskimo way of life was the supreme example of today's developing "small is beautiful" philosophy. A sled, for example, could be made from a polar bear skin that was frozen solid, its slippery hairs providing good friction-less runners. Runners could also be made from split fish glued together with frozen blood, whalebones, walrus tusks, or caribou hides soaked in water, rolled tightly, bent into the right shape then frozen, the hair inside acting as reinforcement as straw does in a mud brick. To make the runners slide smoothly they were iced with water. The water was boiled to remove the oxygen and make the ice harder, then sprayed on by mouth because water at body temperature freezes at just the correct rate to be neither too hard nor too soft. On the trail you could give the runners a new surface with urine. Danish explorer Knud Rasmussen went one better and made runners of frozen oatmeal which later served its intended purpose and was fed to the dogs. When driving a dog team you had to avoid their defaecations or the runners would melt and become rough, and you had to be careful that the dogs did not eat the sealskin harnesses.

One of the most remarkable features of the Eskimo culture has been its continuity. When ancient Egyptians first smelted lead, producing enough smoke for pollution to drift into the upper atmos-phere and fall with the snow to be recorded in the layers of the Arctic ice caps, small bands of Eskimos were already moving seasonally across the tundra-top, wresting a meagre living from the most hostile physical environment Man has ever mastered. When Jesus Christ was born the Eskimo culture had been established many centuries and was to change only in detail through the entire span of Christianity. During the rise and fall of successive European powers, and the discovery of the New World, the Eskimo hunter stood with rock-like patience and poised spear beside seal-holes on the Arctic ice as he had always done, and as he continued to do long after the sky above him became striped by the jet contrails of Boeing 707s carrying passengers over the Pole.

In the land where biological processes are so slow that a piece of musk ox dung takes ten years to be broken down and vegetation cover is less than one per cent that of temperate areas, archaeologists can look for tent-rings by air. Artifacts perfectly preserved in the top few inches of frozen ground have enabled the chronology of changing lifestyles over five thousand years to be pieced together. During this time the Arctic topography changed around the Eskimos, the land rising one hundred and fifty feet because it had been relieved of its great weight of ice; today it still rebounds at the rate of three feet a century and archaeologists must search for early Eskimo habitations near old beaches that may be many miles inland. On the way to Point Hope we had flown over Cape Krusenstern, where 114 different beaches step down to meet the sea in front of dwelling sites fifty centuries old.

The most recent thin wave of migration, known from archaeological finds in north-west Greenland as the Thule culture, came from northern Alaska one thousand years ago, during a period of warmer climate. The newcomers brought their own rich technology and rapidly displaced or absorbed the Dorset culture that had reached the central Arctic about 800 BC. The Dorset people did not use dogs or bows and arrows, and did not hunt the bowhead whale, but are believed to have taught the Thule people how to make the snow house, or igloo. The Thule culture remained more or less unchanged in northern Alaska until recent times, but in Greenland and the central Arctic it entered a new phase in the seventeenth century when the "little ice age" increased ice cover and limited the range of the bowhead whale so the people had to rely more heavily on seals hunted from igloo camps on the sea ice. It was this modified way of life that British navigators encountered on their quest for a north-west passage when the Royal Navy, idle after the long wars with France, entered a period known as its "white madness", and despatched one expedition after another to find a northern short cut between the Atlantic and Pacific. Detailed drawings of igloos, kayaks, and sleds constructed of ice, made by Lt Edward Parry during his two winters in Foxe Basin in 1821–3, made a deep impression in Britain for many years and still form the basis of what we think of as the "classic" Eskimo. In fact, fewer than fifteen per cent of Eskimos made extensive use of igloos, most of them living in skin tents, and sod or rock houses banked up with snow and roofed with skins on rafters of whale ribs.

With the explorers came a warming climate and the whalers. As today, the civilised world then looked North for its oil, in the form of barrels of rendered blubber from the hugely fat and docile bowhead whale. Since 1610 it had been hunted in northern seas, first from Spitsbergen then Davis Strait. The Dutch alone had nearly six thousand whaling ships between 1675 and 1721, and it is said that whale oil – because it fuelled the first streetlamps – made a bigger contribution to safety on the streets of London than the invention of the policeman. One whale provided twenty-five tons of oil plus a ton of baleen. Before the invention of plastic it was baleen that provided materials for such things as stuffing for chairs, umbrella ribs, and fishing rods. Tough, flexible and springy, the baleen plates used by the whale to filter out tiny organisms from the sea were what made the Victorian figure possible because they made ideal corset stays, and were worth up to six dollars a pound. As rich new whaling

grounds were found in Lancaster Sound, Foxe Basin and Hudson
Bay, the isolation of nearly fifty centuries of Arctic lifestyle came to
an end. Eskimos greeted the whalers warily but welcomed the tools
that made their own lives easier – first small things like needles, steel
knives and bits of cloth, and by 1880 a brisk trade in rifles. Imagine
what it meant, when food, clothing and warmth depended entirely
on hunting animals with spears and bows and arrows, to be given a
rifle! The price paid by Eskimos was ultimately a dear one, as
epidemics of measels, influenza and mumps swept through them,
but the benefit of contact with Whites was irresistable. In the central
and eastern Arctic the consequences were not disastrous because
communities were scattered and contact with whalers was not prolonged. Greenland was by then a closed country. But in the west, in
the Eskimo communities on the shores of the Beaufort Sea, it was a
different story.

When the American whaling fleet revived after its ruin in the Civil
War and pushed north, beyond Point Hope, it brought news to
Alaskan Eskimos that their land had been bought from Russia by the
US in 1867 for seven million dollars; the Eskimos had never been
aware that they were "owned" by anyone. In 1880 steam whalers
reaching the Beaufort Sea, found all the whales they could handle,
and a new rush was on. Due to ice conditions it was necessary for
every ship to spend at least one winter in the Arctic and most chose
the harbour at Herschel Island, off the Mackenzie Delta. In this part
of the Arctic Eskimos were more concentrated and lived close to the
tree-line where muskrat trapping offered an alternative economy.
Now, with at least six hundred rough and ready whalers requiring
food, Eskimos flocked to Herschel Island to exchange meat and fur
clothing for trade goods. Contact with Whites was sudden and
intense. In the eastern Arctic whalers had carried small amounts of
liquor for their own use, but here they made it readily available to
Eskimos and taught them how to distil it from molasses or potatoes.
The Eskimos were virtually wiped out. Four out of five fell to raging
epidemics. One RCMP census, made soon after the bottom dropped
out of the baleen market in 1908, found only forty of the area's
original inhabitants still alive. The gap had been filled by migrations
from Alaska where caribou had been hunted out during the gold
rushes.

In the remote and unexplored islands north of the mainland some
Eskimo bands still did not know the White man existed. At this time
the old way of life might have been reasserted had not a profitable
new market been found for furs. During the First World War and
1920s high prices were paid for the beautiful soft white fur of Arctic

fox: a single skin was worth up to seventy dollars, and one silver fox could be exchanged for a whaleboat. With the collapse of whaling many whalers stayed on to become traders and trappers, earning good livings alongside the Eskimos. Consumer goods abounded. Eskimo families living in crude lumber houses ate canned food and yeast bread, and became owners of iron beds, lino, canned food, sewing machines, cameras, hair clippers, vacuum flasks, and type-writers. The average outfit purchased by Eskimo family going off to trap white fox on the Banks Island in the 1920s cost between five and six thousand dollars, and it was considered that some Eskimos had a higher standard of living than working class families in eastern Canada.

The pace was more restrained over the rest of the Arctic. As the Hudson's Bay Company extended its network of trading posts north of the tree-line Eskimos were encouraged to bring in fox pelts in exchange for staple trade goods like rifles, ammunition, tea, sugar, needles and pressure stoves. Missionaries followed the traders and from 1914 the RCMP extended its influence, ruling remote Arctic communities with the free hand of Sanders of the River. On the North Slope of Alaska Eskimos divided their time between hunting whales and seals on the sea ice and caribou on the tundra, but had a longer tradition of trade. On the way to summer hunting and fishing camps they cut oil-saturated peat into blocks, later collecting the bricks of congealed pitch to keep their sod houses warm through the winter, little realising how these oil seeps would transform their lives in the future.

The dream-time of the Arctic persisted through the Second World War. American forces constructed the infrastructure of airfields which is still in use. One chain of airfields across the eastern Arctic – Le Pas, Churchill, Coral Harbour, Frobisher Bay, Søndre Strømfiord and Iceland – was known as the Crimson Staging Route because it was designed for the evacuation of casualties after the Normandy landings, but casualties were lighter than expected. Another chain built westwards for delivering US-built aircraft to the Russian front had its mirror image in Siberia. Apart from a sudden drop in fur prices and occasional contact with construction men, Eskimos were largely unaffected by war. Canvas had by then replaced skins for making tents, and nets were used for catching fish rather than the old-style stone traps in which milling fish were speared. After the war weather stations were established and con-verted Lancaster bombers photographed the Arctic for mapping purposes but Canada and USA were too busy changing into peacetime gear to worry about the Arctic. A minor social revolution came when Canada introduced pensions and child allowances; Eskimo families who seldom saw so much cash in a year were suddenly handed twenty dollars or more a month, and the age-old practices of letting unwanted children die at birth, and helping old people to die when times were hard, were ended. But Mounties still communicated with each other by valve radios that hummed with the static of northern skies, and brought the mail in by dog team twice a year.

Civilisation came to the Eskimos in the mid-1950s, not as an awakening sunrise following naturally on the White dawn that had stolen over the Arctic during decades, but as a thunderstorm breaking violently out of the South. It washed the Eskimos straight out of the Stone Age into the gutters of the modern world. The dimunition of native ways had been trickling on steadily for nearly a century and eaten into the foundations of Eskimo life. At the very moment when the rot became evident on the surface, the trickle became a flash flood.

The rot had grown like cheese-mould in the lungs of a native race no longer protected by its robust carnivorous diet, excellent fur clothing and traditional style of tent or snow-house. Store-bought food, clothes made from textiles, poorly insulated huts built of scrap lumber, were inadequate for Arctic survival and brought squalid living conditions. Due to the lack of insulation every hole in a shack had to be plugged, often with chewing gum, and the resulting dampness from cooking and heating with kerosene (which produces its own volume in water vapour when it burns) nurtured tuberculosis. Eskimos were a dying race. Deaths from TB alone exceeded the birth rate. Every Eskimo older than six, and many younger, was infected. On the barrens west of Hudson Bay, where the inland Eskimos depended on caribou for everything, over-hunting and other factors made the migrating herds scarce and in 1953, the year of Elizabeth II's coronation, scores of her Eskimo subjects in one of her richest dominions simply froze or starved to death.

The storm broke over this weakened social fabric in two surges. In 1955 the Cold War with Russia prompted the construction of seventy manned Distant Early Warning radar stations – the DEW-line – across the top of North America and through the middle of Greenland. With wonder, the Eskimos watched great white radar domes rise beside their igloos. The invasion of White technology came as if in answer to the prayers of a cargo cult, but unlike the Papuan natives who made model airstrips with hopes of luring flying treasure ships out of the sky, Eskimos never had to build decoys. The aeroplanes came uninvited, disgorging thousands of tons of food, tools and materials. Eskimos whose material possessions had been limited to what they could carry saw the wastefulness of White society at its worst – scores of bulldozers and trucks simply abandoned on the tundra, or set on fire, because it was uneconomic to fly them out again; their land littered with thousands of empty gas barrels scattered far and wide across the level wastes by the wind; mountains of food thrown out because it had "spoiled" due to freezing. They were also exposed to White people at their worst – construction gangs with hard liquor. Eskimos took temporary jobs which disrupted seasonal hunting and fishing: cash was no help when it came to surviving the long winter.

Meanwhile Canada woke up to the potential of the northern territories she had administered so long in a state of almost continued absence of mind. Parliament now spoke of Arctic territories as "our great northern treasure chest" and serious exploration was initiated to find out what Canada owned up there. A new government department called Northern Affairs and Natural Resources was formed with the twin aims of exploiting the Arctic, and giving Eskimos "the same rights, privileges, opportunities and responsibilities as all other Canadians – in short, to enable them to share fully in the life of Canada". Nobody asked Eskimos if the White lifestyle was suitable for their unique environment. Prompted solely by good intentions Whites told the Eskimos: "We're going to do a good thing for you." As aircraft patrols extended the influence of burgeoning administrations the state of the Eskimo people had come as a shock. By 1956 one in seven was either in a sanitorium with TB or in transit to one. Life expectancy of an Eskimo was only twenty-five years, compared with seventy-five in the South. Infant mortality was many times higher in the Arctic: only one Eskimo baby in four lived. Health services were not the only urgent need. Patchy education that had been available here and there was taken out of the hands of missionaries, and government boarding schools were set up. Matchbox houses were provided on a welfare basis and cash handouts were increased. Teachers, nurses and administrators placed increasing demands on the government to do more. The Eskimos were never consulted for it was obvious what they needed.

In Canada, when the federal government took over the reins of Arctic education, Eskimo children were sent to boarding schools where they were punished for speaking their own language and forced into curricula imported from the provinces – "You're Canadian now, so if you learn fast you'll be like us, which is a good way to be." The aim to equip every Eskimo with an education that would

However bright, white children in Eskimo schools are invariably top of the heap and very seldom learn a word of Inuktitut; all games involving Whites and Eskimos are invariably White in origin — like these Resolute youngsters waiting to be selected for a softball side.

enable them to achieve anything in Canada was well-intended enough, and it is interesting that today's Eskimo leaders are all products of that stern regime, but it was forgotten that Eskimos were human and that children might not take kindly to a raw-meat diet in a skin tent after spending ten months in a centrally heated hostel with cornflakes for breakfast, or that if children were punished quite severely for chattering in their mother tongue they might not be able to communicate with their mothers when they met up with them again. Most parents regarded children sent out to school as "lost" and many chose not to declare at least some of their children whom they taught the traditional way of life as insurance for their old age.

Even if Eskimos were now trappers rather than hunters, used motorboats to reach summer camps and collected other bits and pieces of modern hardware, in most areas the old way of life continued to stay afloat. They still came into the trading posts by dog team or boat two or three times a year to trade furs for an increasing variety of trade goods, to have a party, and to pick up children from school or relatives from hospital. Traditional values of life on the land still obtained: the skilled hunter walked tall, elderly people commanded a natural respect, harmony with the environment was the continuing keynote of their lifestyle. It could not last much longer.

The storm of civilisation became overwhelming when White-style suburbs came to the Arctic. In theory it was the government's new low-rental housing programme designed to improve living conditions for native people in the Arctic, but Eskimos knew little of the economic or political context from which the gesture sprang. They saw houses with regular windows and doors and insulated walls, ready fitted with central heating, running water and power, unloaded from ships and barges and set out in neat rows joined up with telephone and electricity cables. In the centre of each community rose a beautiful new school so children could now live at home with their parents, and gleaming new health centres run by dedicated young nurses. Trading posts became the equal of supermarkets offering dazzling arrays of consumer goods – pop, frozen TV dinners, chocolate bars, comics, tinned fruit, record players, and snow machines. The same hurricane of change hit Greenland and Alaska, although it was handled in different ways. For any person who worked anywhere in the Arctic fifteen or twenty years before, only the familiar shape of the land and sea would suggest it was the same place: the transformation was sudden and total, but whether it had also been successful and worthwhile for the Eskimos themselves was less certain. From a health point of view the change from sod hut to modern suburb was clearly desirable: TB is now negligible, Eskimos live as long as Whites, better care and improved living conditions have made the Eskimo birth rate one of the highest in the world. The Eskimo asked for nothing and was given everything. He has been "modernised" by outside influences – lured away from his old way of life, set up for a new one, then left in the lurch. Eskimos have been given the rights and most of the privileges enjoyed by Whites, but not the opportunities.

The scale of the disaster brewing for the Eskimos is evident in any school, like one I visited in Igloolik. A long row of scores of pairs of little snow-boots faced the wall beneath pegs hung with fur-trimmed

How the Eskimos "got slummed": one in three Greenlanders lives in apartments, many of them like these ugly and crowded blocks in the capital, Godthåb. People were settled into the apartments direct from the out-ports with no training in urban living. Provided with heat and flushing lavatories, but no furniture, many of them settled with their chickens on the hardwood floor and butchered their seals in the bath. A typical example of White policy in the Arctic — "We're doing a good thing for you . . ."

parkas. As I kicked off my own boots, seven-leaguers compared with these, I realised they were a symbol of the pace of change in the Arctic. All the boots were made of rubber or plastic and imported from the South by The Bay or the Co-op. Fewer than half the parkas hanging on hooks – beneath names like Manasie, Lino, Judah, Geronimo and Davidee – were trimmed with natural fur and only a small number were home-made: the majority were fleeced with nylon, quilted with dacron, and bought at the cheap end of the clothing rack at the store. Padding down the long hot corridor in my socks, looking over the top of my spectacles which had misted up the instant I stepped in from the bright $-30\,°F$ $(-34\,°C)$ air, I looked at the framed photographs on the wall which showed life in Igloolik little more than a decade ago, when the hamlet was merely a trading post, mission station, and half a dozen sod houses and igloos serving as a centre of hunting camps in the vicinity. One of the old faces framed in the hood of caribou-fur parka, her tattooed lips grinning widely like a canoe in a storm of wrinkles, was Attagutaluk, a folk-hero about whom there are conflicting accounts of how, stranded on the ice without food, she saved herself from starvation by eating her husband, her three children, and most of her clothes. The school, built in 1969, was named after her.

In a Southern suburb an elementary school of this size would serve a fair-sized community. Attagutaluk School serves barely one hundred homes, nearly all of them built in the last decade. Thirteen new houses, some with five bedrooms, were under construction. Chained out on the sea ice at the foot of the hamlet, howling for their rations of seal-meat or fish, were eight or ten of the last working dog-teams in the Canadian Arctic. Geographically, figuratively and literally Igloolik is exactly on the point of balance between the old and new ways of the Eskimo – a microcosm of what is happening across the great breadth of the Arctic from Point Hope in the west to Angmagssalik in the east. The school, by far the largest building in the place, was the catalyst that has made it all happen. And it was in its hot, bright, clean and well-equipped classrooms filled with glowing and grinning young faces that the school was nurturing the time-bomb of the Arctic.

The walls of the classrooms were hung with crayon pictures of snow machines, Twin Otters, dog teams, rifles, churches and carpentry tools. Evidently Mrs Tiggy-Winkle the hedgehog and Squirrel Nutkin do not figure in a world of caribou, polar bears, whales, and seals. Today, one-third of all Eskimos in the world can be found within the four walls of classrooms like these. Of the 680 people now living in Igloolik, all but a handful of them Eskimos, 465 are either at school or coming up to school; three in every five are under the age of sixteen. So far, only two pupils have graduated to the residential high school at Frobisher, five hundred miles away, and resisted pressures to drop out. But in this hamlet there are only about fifty wage-paying jobs, some of them seasonal and nearly all provided in one form or another by the government. Few of these jobs offer much prospect of advancement; most are menial and most are filled by young adults unlikely to vacate their posts for a long time to come. So what are the scores of Eskimo kids leaving this school every year going to *do?*

On the large scale, Greenland has to find 1,400 new jobs every year for those leaving school and is expecting unemployment of around thirty-five per cent. On the small scale, the tiny and remote community of Igloolik has to find at least 250 new jobs over the next ten years for its ill-equipped youngsters.

Education has been the most potent force of change and now it is shaping a course for disaster. Eskimos regard it as a failure because it forces them to lose their culture. They cannot understand why, if going to school is a ticket to the new cash-and-carry culture, it does not entitle them to jobs. Whites think of it as a failure in their terms because it has not become a production line of blueprint Canadians like themselves, and cannot understand why Eskimo parents are upset that their kids are brought up in a different world and able to communicate over their heads in another language. As NWT education minister Arnold McCallum told me: "When a child asks what is in it for him, we ought to be able to say it's good for him; in fact, we have given him the *right* to education, but what is the *use?*"

To make matters worse, the next generation of Eskimos is in the grip of a backlash. In the mid-1970s White teachers saw that children were not being trained in traditional skills because their parents had lost interest and no longer took them out on the land. Using parts of the school budget intended to pay local people to do small maintenance jobs they commissioned retired hunters to tell stories in the classrooms. Instead of repairing windows, Eskimo elders spent a few hours a week telling boys how to hunt and showing girls how to sew. Then, dissatisfied with token payments of two or three dollars a session, they claimed they were fully fledged teachers and the phrase "cultural inclusion" crept into the Arctic vocabulary. Demand for cultural inclusion snowballed and was pressed for by the native political organisations like ITC (see chapter 13). Educators agreed to modify their aims and now, on the grounds that any education is good, school buildings and funds are provided by the NWT and curriculum decisions are made by a local committee. Schools are trending towards a philosophy of "training in life skills" in which

This crowd greeting a ship on the quay at Frederikshåb is almost a living histogram of the population explosion: few old people, few babies, masses of teenagers.

hunting and sewing are given equal weight with reading, writing and arithmetic. But the simple reality of the world is that if you want to be a hunter every day spent in a classroom is wasted, and for academic success every day in a classroom must be spent over books. There is no middle way, so children are graduating into a cultural vacuum. Those who want to be hunters find the land devoid of wildlife. Those who study find there are no jobs, as will be explained. They are the redundant generation: their future is utterly blank.

This dichotomy of purpose was evident within Attagutaluk School itself. In one classroom two plump Eskimo women sat on a floor scraping caribou skin and chewing it with their teeth while half a dozen girls aged between twelve and fifteen, wearing faded denims and sneakers, stood around with nothing in their hands and looking bored to tears. In the library a tall rack of books – *Lord Jim, Tom Sawyer,*

Great Expectations – showed hardly a thumb mark. When I located the headmaster, showing older pupils (for the third time) a television-cassette film about diving for treasure in the Aegean, he explained that although Eskimo children could cope with the words they simply could not understand the concepts of such books. The cultural inclusion problem was a harassing one. "The kids dip out because they aren't interested," he said. "Boys are taught to make harpoons but all they want to know is how to clean a gun or repair a Skidoo. Girls don't want to know about chewing caribou to make it soft when they can buy printed cotton at the store. Tutors are impatient and don't let kids make their own mistakes. We're supposed to teach them how to make an igloo, but the tutors won't do it because it's too cold, and when the weather gets warm there's no snow."

Handicapped by a lack of trained Eskimo colleagues, White teachers fall back on their own resources. One of the cultural-inclusion programmes provided for teachers from the NWT capital in Yellowknife is a book that describes the use of traditional tools. One tool is the *sambgut*, a wooden or steel shaft with a handle of ivory or antler, like a rapier with a knob on the end, used for testing the texture of snow for igloo building. Prodding with this tool you can feel how much hard, wind-impacted snow lies beneath the soft upper layer. Teachers are told how to demonstrate this to pupils – by burying a single layer of Kleenex in sand and prodding it with a pencil.

The Eskimo language is the only thing in the Arctic that does not come from somewhere else and in the struggle to retain it Eskimo leaders may be striking a blow for culture but at the same time are hampering development, particularly when they insist on retaining the "traditional" syllabic system of writing, like a boxy kind of shorthand, which was invented by a missionary at the turn of the century. The western Arctic has in any case always used Roman lexicography, as have Alaska and Greenland. Learning the language suffers the same indifference as cultural inclusion. The attitude of older kids is "why should I learn *Inuktitut* – to freeze my ass in an igloo when I could be watching TV?" The language is polysyllabic, words being chained together to make long single words which in English would be a whole sentence:

Tuktoo: a caribou
Tuktoojuak: a big caribou
Tuktoojuakseok: hunt a big caribou
Tuktoojuakseokniak: will hunt a big caribou
Tuktoojuakseokniakpunga: I will hunt a big caribou.

History and language teacher Mary Cousins (right) has collected scores of tape recordings from people who knew the old way of life on the land, like 65-year-old Pitsiulalaaq Kelly (left) of Frobisher.

While North American Eskimos can boast of practically nothing written in their language but prayers and politics, Greenlanders have a literature of nearly one thousand titles and a newspaper published weekly since 1861. To a White person's eye the syllables dance like palings of a picket fence. When I asked Greenlandic teacher Abia Abelsen for a typical phrase this is what he wrote (and even he had to stop to think how to spell it): *Nalunaarasuartastilio-qatigiiffissualiulersaalersluallaraminngooraasiinngooq* – they are going to build a big transmitting station one day.

Lay catechist teachers have worked in Greenland communities for two hundred years. The system was not designed to prepare Eskimos for life elsewhere, or for jobs which might not exist, but everyone was taught to read and write. When the big wheel of education started to turn, at the same time as in Canada, the main effort went into graduating and training native teachers and now Greenland can look forward to the day when the last White teacher will leave. Already one school principal in three is Greenlandic, and the first few native doctors, lawyers, architects and psychologists are graduating from Danish universities, although, as in Canada and Alaska, the drop-out rate has been almost total. Now big training centres for nursing, teaching, building and ship-wrighting, and metalwork have opened in Greenland. Of 40,000 people born in Greenland 12,000 are children attending one hundred schools, while the 12,000 children in a Copenhagen district of 150,000 people attend fourteen schools.

In Alaska English was enforced in government schools until recently; now only two-thirds of North Slope Eskimos can speak their language, *Inupiat*, and fewer can write it. The average education level of Alaska natives is only 2·6 years (compared with 12·5 years in the US). For high school education Eskimos had to go to Indian schools as far away as Oklahoma, which is like asking a New Yorker to send his kids as far as Peru, or a Londoner to Nigeria. In 1971–2 twenty-three Alaskan native teenagers, most of them Eskimos, were boarded in private homes at the small town of Bethel to attend high school. In two years seventeen of them developed emotional and social problems. Of the eight who did not drop out none wanted to stay, six wanted to attend a high school at home if one existed, and in their two years the average gain in reading achievement was zero.

When Eskimos go South, which is rare, it may be for a good time but it is never for a long time. Much of the drop-out rate of Eskimos at high schools, technical colleges and universities, which runs at very nearly one hundred per cent, might be attributed to alcoholism, drug abuse or loneliness, but these are only the symptoms of a disease which is no more complicated than profound homesickness. Eskimos say it is something in their blood, Whites have told me it is something to do with humidity that makes Eskimos "sick". It is a mystery which suggests that although Eskimos have been modernised, and have adapted well to a new mode of life, a large part of their souls still reside in the shadows of the past. In Canada only a few dozen Eskimos live in southern cities. Most of the community of about one thousand Greenlanders living in Copenhagen have Danish blood and are retired folk with a long history of association, or marriage, with Danes. In Alaska, Eskimos might go to Hawaii for holidays but seldom stay long.

This homesickness might be a blessing for it stops Eskimos being lured to the bright lights. Poorly educated and competing against the mass of unemployed Whites, they would end up with other natives on Skid Row. Yet the overwhelming irony is that any Eskimo who does get a Grade Ten education, and who is willing to leave home, can get almost any job he wants and could make himself the super-Eskimo of tomorrow.

It is strange how even the Eskimos working as translators or social workers alongside Whites as equal colleagues go to extreme lengths to avoid going South, and, if persuaded to attend a conference in a city like Montreal, will spend free time in their room watching TV. This noticeable lack of curiosity among Eskimos seems to go far deeper than the old-time distaste for inquisitiveness. Teachers and sociologists with experience abroad in organisations like the Peace Corps are puzzled by the bland lack of interest they encounter in the Arctic. In places like Ethiopia and Nigeria they are practically knocked down by the clamour for education; in Singapore the race for knowledge is so intense that schools run triple shifts. Arctic children do not spark in the same way. School attendance is barely half, parents letting children decide for themselves whether to attend just as they decide when to go to bed, and the momentum for education seems to require regenerating every day. Teachers are surprised at how difficult it is to impress an Eskimo. You never hear a class expressing a loud "Ooh!" when shown something special, be it beautiful or horrible. Adults react the same way. There is a story about Pierre Trudeau who wanted to buy a carving from an Eskimo but didn't have the cash in his pocket and neither did his aides. The Eskimo wouldn't take a cheque, not even from the Prime Minister of Canada.

In the seeds of today, Whites are creating the monsters of tomorrow. Within a decade, unless the Arctic time-bomb is defused, the semi-educated who have completed school but have no jobs to go to will comprise the majority of the Arctic population. The Arctic will be populated by what Whites are already terming "a load of half-educated bums". If the Eskimo won't go to Skid Row then Skid Row will come to the Eskimo.

Schooling, which promised so much and for which the old way of life was sacrificed, is proving to be a mirage, qualifying new generations of Eskimos for nothing but a plunge into delinquency.

It is in Alaska where the pressures of modernisation are most extreme, and it is commonly said that what happens here will happen five years later in Greenland and ten years later in the Canadian Arctic. It is not a reassuring picture, as I discovered when at last we struggled through the soft gravel into the village of Point Hope.

Due to coastal erosion the sixty houses of the village had just been moved a mile and a half to a cheerless new site where there was not a

Point Hope mayor John Oktollik, a whaling captain, following the night's vandalism when teenagers went on the rampage breaking machinery and windows – "People come to me with problems, but I have nothing to tell them ..."

thing growing. The pilot, Terry McFadden, was a Fairbanks engineer who had flown to Point Hope in his private plane to inspect a snow-collecting experiment. He led me to a dilapidated clapboard building that served as a health centre, and here we unrolled our sleeping bags on a fold-out chesterfield, warmed a can of stew on the single-ring cooker, and stirred our coffee with sterile tongue sticks. Long after dark, as we played backgammon under the bare electric bulb, we heard the crunching of footsteps all around us. Then we lay wakefully in our bags listening to the catcalls of groups of teenagers whistling to each other across the village, an unsettling sound.

The first stone came through the window around midnight, showering our clothes and beds with shards of glass. We waited quietly, hearts racing, forcing calmness. Then we heard a giggle and footsteps crunching away. We cleaned up and went back to bed. Then the electric wires were pulled out so we had no power and the only light came in from a weak aurora. Crash! Another stone burst through the window, then another. Stones came from all sides and there was nowhere to hide except under the bed.

In the morning we found the trouble had not been the anti-White hostility we feared but an urban rampage by teenagers who had broken windows all over the village and smashed eight Honda three-wheelers with hammers. We found the experimental snow fence in ruins, broken up at cost of a great deal of effort. The village mayor, John Oktollik, a whaling captain, was sitting with broken glass all around him in his office in a new bungalow that served as the all-purpose village "safety building". "It's difficult being mayor when people come here with problems and I have nothing to tell them," he said. "We have no work here, only the income derived from moving the village and building thirty new federal-subsidised houses. There's nothing else."

Later, at the site of the old village, I ran into four teenagers sunning themselves in long grass growing on the top of a whalebone-roofed sod house that had been inhabited (with electricity supplied) until a couple of years ago. Nearby an *umiak* (skin boat used for whaling) was turned upside down on a high rack to keep it out of reach of dogs which no longer existed, and a large polar bear skin had been spread out to dry on top of it. The boys, wearing jeans and T-shirts, as good-looking and long-limbed as any other American teenager, knew nothing of the vandalism, did not want to live away from Point Hope ("I get sick when I go South," said one), saw no point in further education or training because there were no jobs, did not read books, and were bored with everything they were doing. Whale-hunting in spring wasn't bad fun – "But, you know, it's kinda miserable freezing your butt out there on the ice when you can buy food at the store." What they really wanted, to fill the achingly empty days, was television. So far Point Hope had only one modern facility, a telephone which had been smashed during the night.

The sound of a plane drew us down to the airstrip where a Cessna unloaded a Point Hope teenager, his mother, and a gleaming new 150 cc Suzuki cross-country motorcycle, its tyres so narrow that it had to go at forty miles an hour to avoid sinking into the gravel. A few minutes later a Piper Aztec landed to take the mayor three hundred miles to a conference being held in Barrow to discuss how North Slope Eskimos could fend off the International Whaling Commission's efforts to stop them hunting bowhead whales on the grounds that whales were no longer essential to their style of life and livelihood. Carrying a briefcase and dressed in a suit, the mayor arrived to board the plane on a trailer towed by a caterpillar tractor. The plane had brought a small parcel of engine spares for the village garage and the foreman drove out in a $150,000 balloon-tyred, Texas-made Rolligon, about four times larger than a tank, to pick it up. Moments later another village official came out, driving a $160,000 six-wheel, twenty -ton Forward dump-truck. Six members of John Oktollik's family came out on some of the surviving Hondas to see him off.

After watching this parade of technology we took off in Terry's tin-and-fabric Bellanca, which fortunately had escaped the vandalism of the night. The boys were no longer sitting on the grassy mound dreaming at the sky but methodically throwing stones at the *umiak*. Then we flew over posts made of whalebones where hunters and trappers once tied their dogs: now the gaunt ribs stood like withered monuments to a forgotten way of life. The graveyard, fenced entirely with whale ribs weathered dark silver, came into view and I was reminded of the way buried objects rise upwards due to frost-heave. Formerly the Eskimos lived virtually under the ground and put their dead on the surface. "We were warm and the dead were happy", they said. "Then the Whites came and we had to live above the ground and bury our dead – since then, we haven't been warm and the dead haven't been happy."

12

BACK TO THE LAND?

*Not even their land offers a retreat
from the nothing life to which
Eskimos have been sentenced*

Icebergs littering the fjord fizzed with a rustly tinkle as they were
struck by the ship's bow wave, then lurched soggily and sometimes
rolled over and over as they were caught by the larger stern wave. A
toy passenger liner with a bright red hull, *Kununguak* steamed
through the horizontal slot between sagging grey cloud and mirror-
ing sea. Vivid in the neutral light, purple-black screes and mossy
fields dropped like tweedy curtains almost vertically out of the cloud,
meeting their reflections along a beach of glistening black granite.
The slab-sided mountains rising straight above them on either side
were sensed rather than seen because the day before, with dry
mouths and wet palms, we had watched them slide by the wingtips of
the Boeing 727. Flying with landing gear down and full flap, it had
made a gripping, ten-minute, low-level approach – driving up the
winding fjord with dandelions and waterfalls brushing the wingtips,
and touching down on a runway that ended at the face of a wide
glacier snaking down from the ice cap.

After this sensational, nerve-tingling end to a four-hour flight from
Copenhagen and Iceland, I had been puzzled by the crowd standing
in the light rain outside the shack that served as an air terminal.
Long after the gangway was pushed up they continued to wave. Even
those who disembarked first and had already greeted their friends

and families continued to wave in an off-hand, irritated way. Three paces into Greenland I discovered why. The long runway at Narssarssuaq, near Greenland's southern tip, had been built for the US Air Force as a transatlantic staging post during the Second World War and now it served squadrons of mosquitoes so large that they cast shadows on the ground and so dense that your hands had to move as steadily as windscreen wipers to ward then off. I soon found they could bite through tough denim jeans and thick socks. While waiting for the luggage to come I watched mothers spraying their kids with aerosol cans of insect repellant. It smelled like Anti-mate. Now, as the 2,200-ton *Kununguak* turned between low-lying mossy skerries and headed towards the village of Narssaq, the droning hordes returned and the crowds of teenagers lining the rails for first glimpses of home after half a year away at technical colleges in Denmark began waving long before anything was in sight.

Then, with the suddenness that characterises summer weather in Greenland, the clouds seemed to be torn upwards. Sunshine burst through and the village that came into view could have been a stage set for a Grimms' fairy tale: a hillside of Hansel and Gretel cottages wreathed in filmy steam and grouped around a cove of crimson-hulled fishing boats and wedding-cake icebergs. As the watery sun gained intensity a light-bulb seemed to be switched on inside each of the hundreds of icebergs packing the bay. Some were smooth, opaquely white and very grand, like cruise ships. Others, no larger than grand pianos, were jagged and diamond clear. The little ship slowed almost to a halt then picked a determined, zig-zag course between them, the bridge officers making the best of the strange combination of weather conditions by wearing shinily wet raincoats and Polaroids.

On its summertime beat up and down the west coast the ship came this far south only once in two or three weeks and stayed no more than a couple of hours, so her arrival was an event. The whole village of about 1,800 was converging on the dock in a tide of brightly coloured ski jackets and slickers. A motor launch snubbed an iceberg clear of the berth, and the throng cheered as the gangway was jiggled into position by fork-lift. They were a handsome lot: hearty-looking young people with quick smiles and clear complexions, dressed in jeans, T-shirts with adverts for Adidas and Merc Power, and brightly coloured jackets or jumpers. Kids rode bicycles at breakneck speed through the crowd, skidding deliberately in the puddles.

"They look happy," I said to a Danish officer standing beside me at the rail.

A veteran of three years' navigating this ill-lit and dangerous coast, he turned down the corners of his mouth and said drily, "What do you expect? It's pay day!"

I walked the steep streets between quaint, brightly coloured wooden houses with steeply pitched roofs, racks of fish drying in the sun and plastic shopping bags of cheese hung out of the windows to keep cool. Honey-coloured Icelandic ponies were grazing on buttercups against a fabulous background of heaped-up icebergs, and I kidded with doll-like children sucking Kojak lollies, then sat in the sun on the fish dock watching glass-fibre runabouts zooming in with plastic buckets of big cod and halibut. It was hard not to be impressed by the garden-of-Eden of it all. But Greenlanders have vast reserves of the traditional Eskimo talent for stoic cheerfulness and when this quality in the people is matched by a flash of sunshine the eye of a new visitor is easily deceived. Everywhere you look there are clues to the neuroses of the nothing life which loom in this country as large as its drifting icebergs. At first your eye skips over them, making allowances, but in a short time you notice nothing else. The name itself was a con-trick of Erik the Red: exiled from Iceland a thousand years ago, the Norseman sailed to this very fjord and settled down to farm sheep, recruiting more settlers with glowing pictures of his "green" land. Today the name is even more cynically appropriate because the twenty-five thousand adult Greenlanders drink twenty-seven *million* tins of lager a year, and everywhere you look heaped-up moraines of green-labelled Carlsberg and Tuborg beer cans form unlikely Arctic greenbelts around the communities.

Unlike their Eskimo cousins in Canada and Alaska, who in government terms were hardly known to exist before the early 1950s, Greenlanders lived under White control for two and a half centuries. In 1720 Greenland was colonised by Danes and in 1780 the whole country, as large as Mexico and inhabited by only a few thousand hunters, was deliberately closed to the outside world. The number of Danes in Greenland until the end of the Second World War never exceeded 402, the average being nearer 250. Outsiders were kept out and trade was monopolised by the KGH (Royal Greenland Trade Department) which filled much the same role as the Hudson's Bay Company. Eskimos were kept in isolated groups and lived as they had always done. Trade in sealskins, and one small cryolite mine, balanced the books and the country was administered as a handful of tiny, independent colonies. Only when Hitler invaded Denmark and new communications links were forged westwards to the US was the door opened a chink, and people living in sod houses and fishing from kayaks glimpsed a different world. In 1948 Danish Premier Hans Hedtoft made a long tour through Greenland and was charmed, as I was in Narssaq, by a good summer and smiling faces: he became convinced that Greenlanders wanted and needed to enter the swim of the modern world. One of the first principles established by the Royal Commission he set up to plot the modernisation of Greenland was that Denmark would help her to float and the country no longer had to be self-sufficient. Nobody could have foreseen that within a short time the cod fishing would fail, the population would double on half its income, and – as in Canada – it might ultimately have proved cheaper to lodge every Eskimo in a Holiday Inn.

In order to provide the health and education services Greenland sorely needed, Denmark decided to concentrate all 4,500 new houses and apartments in eighteen villages. Some apartments, like those in Godthåb, were in five-storey blocks four hundred feet long. As remote outposts were abandoned the density of living changed from something like six square miles per person to twenty-eight square yards. There were heart-rending scenes on the beaches as families of hunters and fishermen walked away from their primitive wooden shacks with heaps of garbage at the side and kayaks resting on wooden frames, and were rowed out to motor boats which conveyed them to apartment buildings with central heating and flushing toilets, but no furniture. There they settled on the hardwood floor. No home economist or welfare counsellor came to show them how to live in such a place. Nobody came to say that kitchen cabinets were not for keeping chickens, or the bath for flensing seals. None of the close neighbours they had known all their lives were on hand to share the strangeness or offer moral support. Instead of raw fish and raw meat their diet was often reduced to beer and potato chips. Similar kinds of cultural deluge struck the Eskimos of Canada and Alaska at the same time. No pilot projects were run, and administrators in places like Copenhagen, Ottawa and Washington, reviewing programmes which on paper appeared unarguably successful, knew little of how, in the process, the Eskimos they were trying to help effectively "got slummed."

It was not considered that Eskimos who for thousands of years had survived the harshest wilderness on this planet might not have the attitudes and values which were essential for success in a White-style suburban society. The Eskimo was a hunter as well educated for his way of life as the White for his, but because he now lived in a house with electric light, and wore plaid shirts and woollen socks instead of caribou fur and sealskin *kamiks*, he was expected to have the same interests in formal education and the same ambition to accumulate wealth and achieve material success. But the hunting mentality lingered, and feet that had walked unhesitatingly over shifting Arctic ice-floes now faltered on warm polished floors. The complexity of urban living demanded a totally different type of excellence. Self-esteem began to erode because every quality that made the Eskimo supremely well adapted for his old way of life on the land made him ill-suited for his new life in a suburb. Formerly, the necessity to survive meant that everything was shared; now there was a crime called theft. The man who conserved resources so painstakingly he would split a match four ways with a needle now propped his door open wastefully when the furnace made his house too hot. When work needed doing in a hunting camp a man kept at it until the job was done, but a wage-earning job demanded only that he attend and actual out-put was a low priority. In the old days he made every tool with his own hands and when it broke he made a new one; suddenly he was expected to have a concept of maintenance, but what was the point when the store was full of new tools?

In the old days practically all garbage was edible and could be scavenged by dogs; now an Eskimo was constantly accosted by Whites demanding that he keep his yard tidy. Ever an optimist, the Eskimo was a model consumer because he ate what he had and let the next day take care of itself; now he was expected to handle money and plan for the future. All the old standards by which self-esteem was judged became irrelevant. People were given roles that were incompatible with their traditional values and the cost of being made "equal" to Whites in terms of rights, privileges and lifestyle became a slide into frustration, despair and a feeling of worthlessness. Increasingly the clever and resourceful hunter who had been admired for the way he provided for his family by his wits, courage and the strength in his arms, woke every morning only to wonder what the hell he was supposed to do with his day.

The slippery slope into hopelessness and depression was further polished and greased by other results of the White ("We're going to do a good thing for you") cash-and-carry lifestyle, such as changes in diet and the components of the family itself.

Eskimos living off the land consumed up to six times as much protein in a meal as Whites, and were unique in eating neither cereals nor sugar. The name Eskimo is an Algonquin Indian word for "raw meat eater" adapted to French in the seventeenth century and picked up by the English. Over the centuries Eskimos have adapted to handle iron-rich blood in their systems, but they still lack certain enzymes that would enable them to drink milk without throwing up. The wild meat and fish on which they lived contained nearly twice as much protein as an equivalent amount of imported

White Society blames itself for modernising Eskimos too quickly, but how many of these children using the Coral Harbour recreation hall as a seat-of-the-pants toboggan run would have died at birth, or would be in a TB sanatorium, when every single person was infected and life expectancy was about twenty-five years?

pork or grain-fed beef but less than one-tenth as much fat. Now half those living in White-style settlements for longer than ten years show visible calcification of arteries, compared with only one in fifty of those still in camps. Sugar intake has increased by about six hundred per cent in twenty years and many show a distinct glucose intolerance which makes them prone to diabetes and other disorders. Eskimos might have been cured of TB but, living on store-bought food advertised on their television sets, many have been afflicted by problems of affluence such as acne, increased blood pressure, heart problems, gallstones, myopia and obesity. Once the roly-poly Eskimo appearance was due to their bulky clothes, and hunters led such hard physical lives that anthropologists often had trouble getting skin-folds for measurements (Eskimos were generally only two to four per cent fat compared with the twelve per cent of the average White male young adult); now, sadly, Eskimos lead sedentary lives and are usually as fat as they look.

Teeth show the same ratio of ruin. Despite the money poured into Arctic health services there is a one-year wait for routine dentistry in Greenland, and on the North Slope of Alaska the state of peoples' teeth is such a disaster that the one dentist can do nothing but extract teeth that hurt and concentrate on preserving teeth in young children. This is an up-hill battle when it is easier and safer, due to the risk of hepatitis in sewer-less Arctic communities, to drink pop. One-third of Eskimo children suffer from Otitis media, or "running ears", which takes up more nursing time than any other health-care problem and has led to partial deafness due to perforated eardrums in many young people. Dr Otto Schaefer, chief of the Northern Medical Research Unit in Canada, who started his Arctic work in Aklavik in 1952 when not a single native child in the school was free of TB, has discovered that tinned and powdered milk is much to blame. Bottle-feeding has increased the chance of ear problems in children by five times.

The milk bottle replaced breast feeding at the same time that TB was controlled, living conditions were greatly improved and life expectancy doubled. Formerly, an Eskimo woman's fertility was partly controlled by lactation. She breast-fed a baby until it was two or three years old, then the next one came along. Now she could have a baby every year. The combination of circumstances had a profound effect. From being a dying race in 1955 Eskimos became in ten years the fastest growing race on earth. The birth-rate rocketed, Greenland achieved a population growth in twenty-five years that had taken Denmark 150 years.

The Danish mania for statistics, which presents a detailed picture of every development in Greenland since 1780, down to the last sealskin, shows that ten thousand packets of condoms were shipped there in 1956 and 66,000 in 1966. But it was the 18,000 courses of birth control pills shipped during the same year that did the trick, and by 1974 the birth rate declined abruptly from the biggest in the world to nearly zero. In Canada the Eskimo birth rate peaked at fifty per thousand in 1964 and ten years later was down to twenty-eight, still nearly three times that of the rest of Canada. The effects of this great birth bulge were clearly observable from the upper deck of the *Kununguak* as a long blast of her siren brought the people of Narssaq streaming once more down to the dock.

Whatever the effects of diet deficiencies on Greenlanders they seemed to have been born waterproof. Clouds swept in raggedly and a steady rain started but there were few raincoats and only one umbrella. Now, perceiving the reality behind the vivid first impressions of sunny quaintness, I noticed how many people had beer in their hands. As the ship hauled her bow out from the dock an iceberg that slid in under her counter became the target for a rain of cans and bottles.

Wherever you look, not only in Igloolik or Point Hope, the stresses of so-called civilisation are tearing the Eskimos apart. These are merely the headlines of destruction:

Greenlanders, per capita, drink more alcohol and use more penicillin than anyone else in the world. Every person over fourteen drinks an average 412 litres a year, forty per cent more than in Denmark which has one of the highest consumption rates in the West. In 1979 alcohol rationing was being introduced in Greenland, every person over eighteen being limited to the equivalent of seventy-two cans of beer or three bottles of spirits per month. Gonorrhoea and syphilis comprise one-third of all notifiable diseases and are four times more prevalent than influenza. One in every four Greenlanders has a venereal disease, and the incidence is concentrated among the majority of teenagers and young unmarried adults. Illegitimacy, practically unheard of before the Second World War, was running at fifty-six per cent in 1974 and was four times higher than in Denmark, in this respect also one of the most "liberal" of Western nations. Alcohol-related accidents, mostly drownings, account for one in three deaths and are the main cause of all deaths. One death in twenty is a suicide and the average age of suicide victims is twenty-three.

In the Northwest Territories cases of VD among people in the Inuvik area, most of them Eskimo, increased by fifty-eight per cent in one year and one person in six is infected; over the whole of the NWT venereal disease is spreading twenty times faster than in the rest of Canada. Liquor is one of the principal sources of income for the Government of NWT and consumption (3·4 gallons of pure alcohol per person over fifteen per year) is more than forty per cent higher than the national average. Violent deaths – accident, homicide, suicide, poisoning – have been the main cause of death among Eskimos and NWT Indians since 1967, rising from 14·1 per cent of all deaths in 1966 to 23·4 per cent in 1974 (compared with 10·2 per cent in the rest of Canada). Violent deaths due to alcohol have doubled to about forty per cent among natives in Alaska. In Barrow, in 1975, every single death was linked to heavy use of alcohol. Assaults causing injury rose from 162 (123 alcohol related) in 1973 to 231 (180) in 1975. During the same period suicides increased from two to eight, and suicide attempts from seven to twenty-three. Among the four thousand Eskimos in the Kotzebue region of Northwest Alaska there were seventeen suicides of teenagers and young adults in one recent winter. Among all Alaskan natives suicide has increased threefold in the last ten years. Charlotte Brower, a young mother of four children who is the judge in Barrow, told me that between January and August in 1977 she registered twenty-six marriages, fifty-nine births – and twenty-four deaths of which only three were due to old age or cancer and the remainder resulted from accidents, mostly alcohol related.

One of the most sinister and less frequently recorded symptoms of social stress has been the break-up of family life. The destruction of Eskimo society has been so great in some areas that in the process of curing diseases like TB worse effects have taken their place. They may be symptomatic of boredom, a sense of hopelessness, or overcrowding, but they show that authorities, having done something about birth control, need to turn their attention to death control. A part of the problem is the listlessness and apathy with which an Eskimo now greets each new day.

The Eskimo family as a whole, once close, complete, and with unquestioned interdependence, drifts apart because members no longer need each other. Even if the pitfalls of alcohol are avoided and they enter the wage-earning economy, families suffer tremendous strains: young people have to choose between ways of life that offer very little, husbands and fathers have to decide whether to leave their communities to find work.

In accepting a new lifestyle in sub-zero suburbs Eskimos had to allow for the rapid erosion of their culture and, with it, their identity as Eskimos. The whole basis of their being was their knowledge of the land and, by implication, the sea-ice and the harvest of bears, caribou, seals, walrus and fish on which they all depended. All skills, traditions, and instincts were harmonised around this one particular gift of Creation. When the Eskimo hunter opened his new curtains and looked out through his double-glazed glass window he saw that his land was still there. Continued use of it, applying old skills together with new equipment, allowed him to retain some vestiges of former dignity and pride. Ability to survive and make use of the fierce polar landscapes that everyone else regards as a barren, hostile and unbelievably unpleasant desert has always been the Eskimo's unique accomplishment, and there was no reason why that should change. The concentration of people into a small number of settlements with modern facilities had been counteracted with a new kind of super-mobility provided by the snow machine and (especially in Greenland) the outboard motor or "kicker". Eskimos did not have to fight for their survival in the same harsh way as before, but they might still live off the land, harvesting furs which could be sold for cash and living simply off caribou, seals, dried fish and waterfowl as they had always done. But could an Eskimo claim to be a traditional hunter if he used modern technological devices like outboard motors and high-powered rifles, and drank coffee from a Thermos? Was it possible to call yourself a hunter and trapper and spend five days a week driving a bulldozer? Could you follow the seasonal migrations of game as before, and live in a house equipped with a deep-freeze? Eskimos answered these questions for themselves years ago. It was only human to desire an easier life, with facilities and entertainments that Whites were so anxious to provide for them. But the more they took advantage of it. the tighter they kept hold of their sense of *right* to use the land in the old way.

Resources of the land, hunted and brought home on a *komatik* pulled by a snow machine, play a fundamental role in modern Eskimo life. Haunches of frozen caribou meat might be stored on the roof, black and bloody seal meat might be kept in the bath, but without it, according to Jose Kusujak, a director of the Inuit Cultural Institute at Eskimo Point, a person goes into a decline. "It's something in your blood, you must have it," he says. "You can see the effects in old people: if they don't get wild meat for a while they get edgy and sit and sulk." Eskimos are happy to buy potato crisps rather than potatoes because neither of these items are traditional, but caribou has always been available for the cost of a bullet, and they resent having to purchase steak or frozen hamburger. In the mid-1970s about sixty per cent of Eskimos counted "native food" as half their diet, and the proportion was similar on the North Slope and parts of Greenland; only one in five lived mainly on store food, and an equal number on mainly native food. The importance of wild meat, for spiritual as well as economic reasons, is recognised by the Government of NWT. For Eskimo communities unable to obtain caribou the government charters a DC3 to take two or three hunters and snow machines to kill about sixty animals which are distributed to the whole community; the enterprise is some times combined with biological research.

Living off the land is seen as the only alternative to the nothing life that Whites have brought the Eskimo. The right to hunt, for food or otherwise, is the Eskimo's single remaining link with his past. There is a certain security in believing he can simply go back to the land to secure a livelihood if the pressures and complications of modern life become overwhelming, but will the land continue to support a hunting culture in which a greatly increased population uses equipment undreamed of in the days of the kayak and the bow and arrow? Eskimos are educated enough to taunt Whites with their record in slaughtering buffalo and bowhead whales to the point of extinction, but are neither wise nor strong-minded enough to act on the evidence that the number of hunters is growing faster than the rate at which the ecology can provide food. Native organisations know their image as simple and gallant hunters wins much sympathy among the powerful White pressure groups who support them in the South, and find a ready scapegoat in any sort of industrial activity such as exploration for oil.

In places like Igloolik, where there is little employment, a considerable proportion of men born and reared on the land continue to hunt and trap full-time. Unless they work for the school, the power plant or the council they *must* depend on caribou to a certain extent. As in every other community, those with full-time wage-paying jobs also hunt and trap, spending weekends and vacations out on the land supplementing their incomes with free meat and living the lives of their ancestors. Conflict occurs because those in jobs have cash to buy the best equipment: full-time hunters might have prestige and dignity as true Eskimos, but this counts little when they enter a store alongside the garbage collector who has a week's pay in his pocket. When those on good wages claim the right to subsistence use of natural resources there is a case for counting it as recreation with emotional and cultural overtones, and the White recreation hunter can claim exactly the same right.

Subsistence that once meant survival is now being turned into a business. Hunters are not always shooting for the pot, but collecting such things as walrus ivory which is sold for cash to buy store food while carcasses of good wild meat are left to rot. In the past, the land has always provided. If the Eskimo did not kill when the opportunity arose he risked going hungry for a very long time, but his weapons were primitive and Nature worked her own magic of conservation by inflicting starvation to ensure that numbers of people were always in balance with the resources of the land. Now there are not only more Eskimos, but modern equipment allows them to use the land more intensively than before: a hunter has the weapons and machinery to kill a hundred animals in an afternoon. When this fire power is in the hands of a young, semi-educated generation untrained in the ways of the land, wasteful over-hunting and wholesale slaughter are common. A hunter's reputation traditionally depended on his ability to kill animals of the right sex and age, and these were the only ones selected to take home. Today's inexperienced hunters often kill indiscriminately, shooting many more animals than they need, and leaving carcasses behind to rot.

Over-hunting affects more than caribou. Under existing NWT regulations any Eskimo can kill up to seven walrus for his family and dogs as long as they are used for food. Now, with walrus ivory worth twenty dollars a pound and many Eskimos equipped with bigger rifles and faster boats capable of carrying more people, walrus are shot in large numbers and left with only their tusks removed. Game officers see two or three hunters with about twenty dead walrus and know that none of them have any dogs to feed, but are stymied when the hunters say they plan to distribute the meat among their families which they might do in merely a token sort of way.

In some communities there is a growing awareness of the need for restraint. Canadian Eskimos long ago agreed to quotas for narwhal and polar bears, and do not shoot female bears with cubs, but political leaders are militantly hostile to any further control over what they regard as inalienable and historic rights. Some quotas are already set in Alaska, but are usually ignored for the same political reasons. Greenlanders, however, are protecting the future potential of partly traditional life-styles by regulating hunting methods: whales must be harpooned, not shot (Canadian Eskimos say it can't be done, despite the fact that biologists use harpoons for tagging whales); when going after caribou snow machines are not permitted and hunters must use dog teams; new regulations in the pipeline will limit the size of outboard motors to ten horsepower when boats are used in the hunting of murres.

Even living from the land as a trapper is suffering from over-use and other pressures. For example, the public outcry over the clubbing of baby seals in Newfoundland has virtually wiped out the market for all sealskins, ending a modest but steady source of income

Polar bear hides were worth up to $3,000 until the Sea Mammals Protection Act of 1972 prohibited their import into the U.S. A hide in good condition, like this one drying on a line in Chesterfield Inlet, is worth about $700.

for scores of Eskimos in Greenland and Canada. Trapping Arctic foxes for their fur provides enough for a family to live on but to buy his traps and snow machine a trapper must take a summer job. Those who can't work, or who spend their money, have to get a grubstake from the game officer and the money is supposed to be repaid from earnings. But because trappers now live centrally in communities, and nearby land is trapped out by wage-earning people going out only at weekends, they have to travel anything up to three hundred miles before laying out their own traps in a line that may be two or three hundred miles long. The leg-hold traps used by Eskimos are already banned by eleven countries and some Canadian provinces such as British Columbia, and humane societies have forced them to be sold with short chains (so animals will be more restricted and cannot fight the trap). Eskimos use a different method of securing the trap from that of bush trappers and have to buy extra lengths of chain so they can be frozen into the ground. The so-called "humane" traps devised in the South do not work so well in hard snow and deep cold. When two parallel lines of traps were set at Coral Harbour the leg-hold traps caught thirty foxes and the new "humane" ones, heavier and more expensive, only three.

It is one thing hunting occasionally for the pot, with a ready supply of frozen hamburger available in the store if you come home empty handed. It is quite different being self-sufficient on the land. This requires a lifetime of training and hardening, but the young generation either does not know how to do it or does not have the stamina. Those who make the loudest noises about the purity of their traditional life on the land, and their right to live it, are young political leaders in the South. The older generations who do have the ability to be self-sufficient on the land have no intention of leaving their warm houses because they *know* how hard and testing it was; many people camp temporarily on the land, perhaps for two or three months at a time, but I was reliably informed that there is no family head under the age of thirty-five *living* on the land.

This is being put to the test in Canada where the NWT government subsidises an increasingly popular "back to the land" movement. Eskimos can apply for funds to establish an outpost camp. Grants are available for building cabins, heating fuel, transport of materials and supplies, and – once a year – transport of people. Cash with which to buy supplies and trapping equipment can be borrowed, but repayment terms have to be flexible when borrowers are living outside the cash economy in the frozen wilderness. There is nothing wrong with a self-help programme which enables Eskimos to maintain dignity and independence. It was available "for any part of the year . . . for people who wish to improve their quality of life by establishing camps in isolated areas where there are adequate supplies of fish and wildlife" but so many people were using the programme to finance hunting vacations that a minimum period of six months had to be imposed. In its second year the programme financed eighty families in twenty-eight outpost camps with an average $3,600 each. One of the biggest camps, of fifty-nine people on Allen Island, near Frobisher, chartered Twin Otters to fly supplies in and furs out. Another camp requested its fuel to be flown in but when things did not happen quickly enough the hunters did the job themselves by snow machine and were paid $7,000 in wages and equipment costs for transporting their own fuel.

Despite what many administrators believe, the outpost camp is proving to be anything but an Eskimo renaissance. It is successful in taking some of the steam out of pressure to return to old ways

Steam rising from their mouths, blood from the carcass making a frozen gumbo on the snow, two hunters from Repulse Bay skin a caribou on a bitterly raw March morning. Eskimos require lots of land to maintain their lifestyle, and even more to sustain the wildlife on which they depend.

because it shows just how hard life really is on the land, yet it also smacks of moral sabotage because the basic life skills on which survival depended – keeping warm, building shelter, travelling – are provided by government grant. This illusion that nostalgia for old ways offers a viable alternative may ultimately prove to be unkind. Although they are healthier and less neurotic than people in settlements, Eskimos in camps lead a basically false way of life in the sense that they are no more in harmony with their environment than a White family going on a camping holiday with a trailer home.

In the long term not even the land offers Eskimos an escape from the stresses and strains of the modern age. To protect their land, and continue to make use of it as they have always done and thereby preserve their links with their past and identity as Eskimos, their attitudes must catch up with the new technology. This is hard, if not impossible, when everything around them is changing so rapidly and the only apparently stable factor – a kind of lifeline in the storm of change – is the land itself. When even the lifeline begins to fail the sense of hopelessness becomes profound.

It was in Barrow, Alaska, that I saw the most vivid example of how old ways are combined with new.

Two walrus carcasses lay belly up on the high-water mark where they had been beached during the night and dry-docked by the tide. A couple of tons apiece, their tough leathery hides folded and wrinkled, they looked like a pair of deflated dirigibles. Tourists had wandered down from the hotel to photograph this real slice of Arctic life, while keeping a wary and horrified distance, but it was late in the morning before the hunters returned to their kill accompanied by wives carrying lots of plastic buckets. Grimly fascinated, I watched the greatcoats of blubber folded out, yards and yards of grey intestine uncoiled, and blood making black lakes on the shingle. One woman, elderly and creakingly stout, waded among the viscera in gumboots. Her purple cotton frock rattled in the sharp breeze and every time she stooped to hack at the meat with an axe wielded in scarlet hands her spectacles slipped to the end of her nose. Others – sons, daughters, in-laws – divided the meat into piles on plastic sheets. The scene echoed hundreds of generations of the Arctic hunting culture, when the dangerously tusked beasts with rolling red eyes were harpooned from fragile kayaks then hauled on to safe ice by teams of sled dogs harnessed in tandem,

But nothing of that sort happened here in Barrow in 1977. When the butchering was finished the hunters took their meat home in a pick-up truck rented from Avis.

13

IN PLACE OF SURVIVAL

Their business of living taken away,
Eskimos are snared in a consumer
lifestyle without cash

The procession of giant icebergs fills the end of every street. The great glacier slides into the fjord where it is fractured by the rise and fall of the tide, segments of solid ice capsizing or toppling against each other until, at spring tides, pressure from behind pushes them over the bar into deep water. Every day an average 140 million tons of icebergs sails into Disko Bay in a variety of marvellously sculpted shapes that bring to mind the Matterhorn, flat-iron buildings, Disneyland, and meringues as big as islands. Some, drilled through by whirlpooling torrents of melt-water, have canted over on launching so there are tunnels wide enough to thread with a plane. When the wind brings them back to the village and the bay outside the harbour at Jakobshavn is choked with pyramids of ice more than two hundred feet high, it rates with the Grand Canyon and Niagara Falls as one of the great natural wonders of the world.

At two in the morning the aching stillness of these brooding, sunlit monsters is broken by the sound of engines, and the perfect reflections on the mirror-calm lanes of water are crinkled and corrugated by dozens of dories and red-hulled cutters as fishermen retrieve their set-lines. Every hook seems to have a fish and one halibut after another is shaken off into the boat. When the village is still getting out of bed they head for harbour, weaving between the bergs and

Drifting icebergs looming at the end of every street make the view of Disko Bay from the village of Jakobshavn one of the natural wonders of the world.

occasionally slowing right down to barge through brash ice floating like white gravel on the breathless sea. Formerly the shock wave of large icebergs being calved in the fjord could bounce off pack-ice lying out to sea and form a sudden wave six or seven feet high that funnelled into the harbour; now protective piers have been built and the heavily laden fishing boats snake between them before tying up

at the large, barn-red fish factory humming and hissing like the innards of a steamship.

Boxes of Disko Bay prawns, bright pink from something they eat and reckoned to be the tastiest in the world because they grow so slowly in the cold water, are craned out of the cutters and pushed into the factory. The big slithery halibut, as grey and wet as puddles on a pavement, are winched out of the small boats in baskets, then, after filleting, are dumped in a bin where people can take as many as they want for bait or dogfood. All over the hilly village you see tall racks of halibut, complete with head, tail and backbone, turning a golden brandy-snap brown in the sun and looking almost as appetising. Summer halibut fishing is so lucrative that a man and a boy working hard during a four-week vacation can pay off a glassfibre boat and new outboard motor and still end up with a profit.

Apart from mining, which is capital intensive and does not employ many people, fishing is Greenland's staple industry. Since the Second World War cod catches have been minimal due to a fall in water temperature, and now shrimp catches are beginning to fall, perhaps a sign that cod are returning and eating them up. The fastest growing segment of Greenlandic fisheries is the halibut fishing; at the height of the summer it is a critically important source of extra income for many Greenlanders. But today there was a problem. During this spell of calm and sunny weather so many fish-factory workers had decided to have a holiday – many actually going fishing on their own account – that there was nobody to fillet and process the halibut. Soon bins of fish were lined up around the outside of the factory, spoiling in the sun, and still the laden skiffs came weaving in from among the icebergs.

The fish-factory manager, a young Dane called Palle Roe, called a meeting of some fishermen to outline the situation and suggest that if some of them would work a few shifts in the factory he would pay double time.

The men declined – "We're fisherman, not factory workers. Handling the fish is your problem, not ours." The factory, along with others similarly affected all over Greenland, was shut down. Tons of prime fish were tipped among the icebergs and everybody sat around in the sun while the best few fishing weeks of the year ran through their fingers like melt-water through the glacier, and nobody earned any money. In Jacobshavn the commissioner in charge of all trade activities was Andreas Jorgensen, a man who had made his career in the Arctic and had a sad sympathy for the counter-pressures affecting the native people. He knew only too well that Greenland could sell all the fish she catches but even this comes nowhere near to filling her own quotas allocated by international agreement, so much of her fishing potential is farmed out to trawlers from Norway, France and Germany. He knew that Greenland was expecting up to thirty-five per cent year-round unemployment when the population bulge now in school graduated into the labour market, and that Danish taxpayers subsidised Greenland to the tune of 1,000 million Kroner (£100 million) a year (20,000 Kr for every man, woman and child in the place). "Yet," he said placidly, gazing at a group of erstwhile workers lazily baiting hooks on top of a warm rock, their forms

Greenlanders seem to be born waterproof: fishing is the basis of the economy but abundance of fish appears to be cyclical, linked to water temperature.

making dark silhouettes against the icebergs glowing behind them like walls of light, "when you see these people you can understand why they don't want to work in a factory."

It is a different picture in winter, when fishermen chip out holes in the ice that forms between the icebergs and travel by dog team in conditions dark or twilight much of the time, often foggy, dreadfully cold, and always extremely dangerous because moving icebergs constantly break up the highways of ice. Men don't do it for fun any more, and they bring in only a fraction of what they get by boat in summer. Now everybody wants a soft job in a factory where it is warm, well paid and companionable, but even by switching off the automatic shrimp peelers and having the job done by hand to create work, the amount of fish and shrimps coming in is so depleted that the work force is halved and the rest have to go on the dole.

One of the part-time fishermen in Jacobshavn was Peter Olsvig, a forty-eight-year-old Eskimo and village councillor who worked in

Jakobshavn village councillor, lay teacher, part-time fisherman Peter Olsvig, pictured here with his grand-daughter in national costume, charged 100Kr for a cup of coffee in his house: have Eskimos evolved with different mental switches?

the school teaching traditional skills like hunting, kayak handling and dog-team driving. Originally a lay teacher, he had moved into Jacobshavn from an isolated settlement in 1957, and seven years ago had taken advantage of a four per cent government mortgage system, and an eighty per cent grant towards materials, to have his own house built. Painted browny red, with a kayak on a frame outside, a rack of halibut drying, and half a dozen dogs chained out on the rocks nearby, the house was neat, warm, and had a wonderful view over the icebergs of Disko Bay. When I inquired if I might ride along with him to pick up his halibut lines next morning, in his eighteen-foot glassfibre motor boat called *Saltfish*, he agreed warmly and suggested I call at his house at three o'clock for a cup of coffee.

The coffee and biscuits were laid on a low, tiled table beneath a three-dimensional plastic picture of the Last Supper, and a woven wall hanging depicting an Istanbul mosque. It was the fifteenth birthday of one of Peter's seven children, who was dressed in the beautiful embroidered Greenlandic national costume with tall seal-skin boots, and I had brought her a box of chocolates which she accepted without a flicker of expression. Peter lamented the coming of engines because they had chased seals from Disko Bay and he could no longer use his kayak for hunting them. He showed me his deep-freeze full of whale, seal, halibut, smelt and murres. I photographed him with his daughter and grand-daughter, and promised to send prints. It was a friendly and relaxed visit, and as I prepared to leave we arranged to meet at his boat around five in the morning. Then the blow fell.

When would it be convenient, he asked, to talk about price? The cost of my coming in his boat for one day would be 1000 Kr (£100).

Not so much shocked by the principle as stunned by the amount, I had to cancel the arrangement. It had been in my mind to offer the cost of fuel, which I though was handsome in view of the fact that he was making the trip in any case. I explained as simply and as carefully as I could that as a town councillor and a spokesman for his community he might be helping the outside world gain a broader understanding of Greenland's problems if he helped me. The fact that he was not swayed by this pompous reasoning is unimportant. What is significant was that making a public relations gesture on behalf of the community he represented was so clearly foreign to him. "There's one other thing," he said, tapping the open palm of one hand with the forefinger of the other, "what about the coffee?"

I paid him 100 Kr (£10) for the coffee I had drunk in his house, half what he demanded, and we parted. I had been slapped in the belly with a wet fish often enough before, and this time perhaps I had asked for it, but the bitterness and sense of fury were hard to conceal. Later, with one of Greenland's twenty-seven million annual Carlsbergs in my hand, I calmed down and rationalised my attitude. It had been that of every other White in the Arctic confronted by an Eskimo who does not behave as expected, particularly with regard to work.

Whites forget that just as Eskimos have different sweat glands and different digestive juices, their brains have evolved with different switches. In his old life an Eskimo hunted when he was hungry, and if this required him to squat motionless beside a seal's breathing hole on the ice for twenty or thirty straight hours then he did so. But when it was not necessary to hunt, fish or travel, he relaxed. Now this business of living has been taken away from him and the Eskimo no longer has to struggle: nothing has taken the place of the will to survive which drove him.

When conducting you round a settlement resident Whites often disparage the inability of Eskimos to sustain any kind of work, forgetting that although the Eskimo has adapted to eating cornflakes for breakfast he has not gone as far as going to bed when TV closes down and getting up when the alarm rings. When activities related to White time-keeping are discounted – store-opening hours, school times, aircraft arrivals, TV programmes – visible activity in a settlement is not great but seems to continue at the same even pace day and night. In the Arctic summer men are as likely to set out on a hunting trip, or to strip down a snow machine, at two in the morning as at any other time. Whites, meanwhile, having finished work at five o'clock, eaten dinner at seven and gone to bed at eleven, sleep restlessly and complain bitterly when Eskimo employees fail to show for work at eight sharp next morning. It is difficult to determine whether a man who goes hunting for food is "working" especially if he also brings in a few fox furs which he trades for credit at the store. Survival is no longer in question and there is no pressure driving him to hunt for food or earn money when there is no immediate need of it. So, like the fish-factory workers of Greenland, he switches off.

Also hard to live with is the assumption, universal among Eskimos, that they should be paid for everything they do, even if it is carrying out what Whites would regard as personal or social obligations. Traditionally Eskimos subjugated every personal desire for the benefit of immediate family, even to the point of selective feeding in times of famine so the strongest and most able should survive. Today, except in search and rescue operations (for which snow machine fuel is provided by the government) the concept of community service is virtually unknown. Although it may be symptomatic of confusion rather than selfishness, it is especially puzzling, not to say enraging and disappointing, to Whites who are affected by it – as at Jacobshavn when the fish factory closed. In places like Iceland and the Faroe Islands such action is unheard of: people drop everything when the fish are running and work day and night until the job is done. No such magic exists in the Arctic.

The custom that Whites pay, no matter what, was born when the first anthropologists handed out an iron nail for every Eskimo head that submitted to a measuring tape. An Irish-born midwife in Inuvik who devoted years of her working life to the place, and had personally delivered into the world nearly every person under the age of sixteen, wanted to accompany a local family to their rat-hunting and whaling camps but nobody would take her unless she paid – not merely a contribution to cover her own share of the costs but a disproportionate amount that would have kept her in Paris for a couple of weeks. Any government man who accompanies a group of hunters on a trip finds himself paying for all gas because his mere presence, even if he goes as a friend, makes it a government expedition.

In Coral Harbour, in the central Canadian Arctic, local people show community spirit to the extent that they hold bingo evenings to raise funds (matched by government "cultural activities" grant) to finance a Christmas party. But everybody who contributes to the party, even the nurse who "volunteers" to cook the turkey in a government stove using government electricity, is paid, as are the ladies who lay the tables in the recreation hall and the men who give their time arranging chairs.

Landing there in the Hudson's Bay Twin Otter immediately after it had snowed for a week, then blown until the village was all but buried in snow, we saw every child in the place using the steeply pitched roof of the rec hall as a seat-of-the-pants bobsleigh run. The numbers were swelled by eighteen White teenagers from Brampton School, in Ontario, who had come for five days on an exchange visit; later in the spring the Coral Harbour Eskimo children would visit Brampton. According to the arranged programme, next morning the visitors would go on a trip by *komatik* and watch an igloo being built. But nothing happened. In disconsolate groups the White kids walked back and forth through the snow wondering what to do with themselves. The trouble was that the two men who had offered to build the igloo and drive the snow machine, and who had children of their own going south to Brampton, had suddenly discovered they were not getting paid, so the deal was off.

The Eskimo is a victim of two conflicting images, neither by any means wholly true, but each at least partly so.

Among Whites in the South, well removed from the Arctic and relying on media for information, the Eskimo is the hunter fine and true, deserving of praise, envy, sympathy – and cash to help him continue his noble role in a world that daily treads harder on his toes. But Whites *in* the Arctic are there for only one purpose, to work, and they overlook the fact that Eskimos may not be similarly motivated and are in the Arctic living the whole terms of their lives. Despite the fact that Eskimos have asked for nothing but been given everything, they are generally written off by these people – particularly by those doing manual and skilled jobs (as opposed to teachers and administrators) – as welfare bums with their hands always extended for hand-outs. These images of the Eskimo – hunter or welfare bum? – are further distorted by the fact that many Eskimos may be unemployed in White terms, but not in their own terms.

The extent of genuine unemployment, apathy towards work, and cash hand-outs in the form of welfare or unemployment benefit, is hard to gauge precisely in the Arctic because all these things appear in many guises. In Canada, for example, unemployment benefit is paid only when a person has been in a job previously for eight weeks, so special short-term employment programmes were arranged by the Government of NWT to satisfy bureaucratic necessity to reduce welfare payments. Eskimos can be paid up to one hundred dollars a week for attending adult education classes. In Igloolik a heavy machinery maintenance course was attended by eight men; although there was really room for only one mechanic in the place, four were found work and the others returned to the ranks of the unemployed or went hunting. In general, it is not easy to distinguish where welfare begins and ends.

Eskimos do not have a tradition of attempting to accumulate money, like Whites. What's the good of money on a cold day out on the land? Until little more than a decade ago an Eskimo traded for what he needed, exchanging furs for store goods, or letting you have a carving for a carton of cigarettes. Money was just paper, and there was no concept of saving. To a degree this feeling lingers. Once a man has a snow machine and a rifle, and the few things his family needs, he is content. When hunting turns bad he might seek help in the form of supplementary welfare to keep himself going, but when the hunting is good and he doesn't have any use for money, he doesn't try to get it. He might take on some seasonal work, erecting new houses or working in mineral exploration, but if he neglects to outfit himself with new traps for the coming season he can always get a grubstake from the game officer. In most parts of the Arctic hunting does little more than fill the pot a few nights a week and provide an activity that helps a man feel that he is still a real Eskimo, and although the land will support a trapline it will not outfit one. But this matters little because the Eskimo does not have to worry about a place to live, and finding the cost to run it, because he can take advantage of the biggest hidden welfare item of all – the fully equipped house provided by the government.

In the Canadian Arctic the big new houses that arrive by barge have up to five bedrooms, hot and cold running water, flushing lavatories with pump-out tanks (that may or may not be accessible in winter), washing machines and refrigerators, and would grace any Southern suburb. Running costs are part of the rent, which is set at a quarter of the occupants' combined earnings; minimum rent, for a family with children living on welfare, is about $28 a month. Some families have rent arrears extending back for ten years. The Northwest Territories Housing Corporation has 3,428 houses for which it collects an average $240 a *year*, while operating costs alone (fuel, electricity, water, sewage and maintenance) of each house north of the tree-line is $4,577. To cover these costs fully, let alone the substantial capital costs, a family in one house would have to earn $18,308 a year. Much of the rent which is collected is merely subtracted from welfare cheques, so it cannot be regarded as real income for the government. The Eskimos know the government won't throw them out in the cold, so it is not surprising that there is no individual home ownership among Eskimos: when some houses were *given* to Eskimos by the government they were returned when the first heating bills came in.

A third of all Greenlanders live in apartments, the older ones enormous blocks like those built for refugees in Hong Kong (with a similar space ratio per person), the newer ones smaller and more pleasant. Rent is only forty per cent of the real cost but it must be paid; those who fall behind can ask for help from the village council but can expect to be moved into inferior houses without water or sewage. Danes have encouraged a spirit of independent home ownership with very cheap mortgages and heavily subsidised building materials. For people still living outside the main villages there is the *selvbyguhus*, a do-it-yourself home of 420 square feet on two floors which costs 80,000 Kr (£8,000) delivered, complete with tools, instructions, insulation, fire extinguisher, windows and chimney pot. In north and west Alaska housing is poorly built, fails to meet even minimal standards and is very expensive – a house that costs $40,000 in Seattle costs $90,000 erected in Barrow. The authorities have done little to improve housing conditions. More self-reliant in the modern world because of their trading experiences, Alaskan Eskimos have for many years been gradually changing from sod houses made of traditional materials to jerry-built lumber shacks, but these are being improved or replaced with new housing programmes and funds from the land claims settlement.

The average Eskimo in the Canadian Arctic is healthier, better fed, and better housed than the average poor person in southern Canada, and if he feels like not paying the rent he doesn't. In Greenland there is more discipline and in Alaska the housing has until now been comparatively poor, but in general Eskimos have few material worries. Nobody starves or gets TB any more, and you don't have to get cold in the Arctic these days. The Eskimo would seem to have gained everything and lost nothing except the initiative. But this is enough to lose, for nobody likes being "kept".

A cash economy is the best that Whites can offer, but Eskimos are being denied the opportunity to earn cash while being bombarded with invitations to spend it. The cash economy with no economic base kindles desire without providing opportunities for assuaging it. "What surprises me," said an economic development officer in Frobisher, "is how the Eskimos stand it – you would expect a suicide a week." In the cities and small towns of North America and Europe business activity is the overwhelming characteristic of life, like snow in the Arctic it colours everything we do. The small business, be it butcher, baker, or Ford dealer, is the machinery of the cash-and-carry workshop. The Arctic, by comparison, is an empty shell. One of the first things you notice about any Arctic settlement is the almost total lack of small-scale commercial enterprise. When small businesses do operate they are nearly always owned by Whites. In Jacobshavn, for example, the 2,850 Greenlanders share between them thirty-one businesses (mainly fishing boats) while the 450 Danes in the place (of whom two-thirds work for the government) share thirty-three. It was my overwhelming impression that those Eskimos who do go into business in any of the Arctic countries, running taxis, operating snow-clearing machinery bought cheaply from the DEW-line, or keeping small shops, invariably have one White parent and were raised in the profit-hunting tradition. For the majority of Eskimos, however, it is less a problem of being at the bottom of the economic ladder and more a question of why, in the Arctic, no such ladder exists.

Welfare and artificial work programmes are not the last resort but the only hope. In Greenland unemployment in 1977 stood at eleven per cent, but statistical averaging conceals the fact that half the total work force received unemployment benefits for at least part of the year. On the North Slope unemployment is officially around the same eleven per cent, but is three or four times higher outside Barrow. In both places nearly all work is concerned with servicing communities and is financed by local or national government. As a stopgap measure welfare is rapidly becoming a permanent feature in the Arctic economy: in the Canadian Arctic unemployment benefit has doubled in two years and supplementary benefit has more than tripled. What else is there?

In Greenlandic fishing villages like Jacobshavn at least there is potential enough in fishing and shrimping to encourage a man to establish a small enterprise of his own. As a crew member he can earn enough to put up ten per cent of the cost of a decent new vessel bought with the aid of a government low-interest loan, and this makes other opportunities such as motor repair and ship-wrighting available. In most of Alaska and Canada no such opportunity exists. In a small number of settlements oil companies recruit non-skilled labourers for seasonal work. When a programme was begun in 1971 to train northern residents to operate and maintain gas pipelines and plants, with housing provided for families during training in Alberta and guaranteed jobs if no pipeline was built, 115 of 224 trainees dropped out due mainly to loneliness and homesickness; of four hundred applicants for the jobs only twenty-five were suitably educated. But industrial activity of this kind is also a stopgap measure, and does little to solve the great problem in the Arctic – the lack of a *local* base for commercial enterprise.

What the Arctic conspicuously lacks is small-scale enterprise that helps make communities self-sufficient and gives people reason to feel proud. The Arctic imports everything from clothes and furniture to boats, vegetables and bread. But nowhere in the Arctic is there the kind of communal workshop facility that might enable one man to spend a few months a year building sufficient furniture to supply his neighbours. Or if not furniture, hunting caps, nylon parkas, machine-knitted socks, gloves, watch straps, belts, sleeping bags, or even boats. Bay stores sell birchwood canoes with flat transoms for kickers at a price of $2,100. If he was shown how, one man could make his own mould and build two or three glassfibre canoes a year in his living room then sell them in the community, or tow them along the coast to another village. When the Repulse Bay Co-op tried it with a government grant the work was done in an unheated shed which allowed frost to affect the resin and – so I was told – it was only when a DC3 was chartered to deliver the boats to another community that it was discovered they would not fit through the loading door. Instead of benefitting from this experience the project closed down.

In Canada the government has a history of such botched enterprises, like the whale-meat cannery started in the early 1960s at Rankin Inlet which had to suspend operations because whales were found to contain excessive levels of naturally occurring mercury. The fact that Eskimos had been eating mammals containing excessive mercury for centuries could not be accommodated within the framework of the law so the cannery turned to producing dog meat but by then Eskimos were driving snow machines. Today the factory employs forty where ten would do the job in half the time and sells canned char for $2·50 a pound. Yet delicious smoked char is worth a great deal more and could be done in a small way by individual fishermen – "It might take three days to train them," said one economic development officer, "but it would take three years to motivate them."

Today the NWT Department of Economic Development runs

234 The Hot Arctic

about twenty-five projects, such as the parka-making project in the Mackenzie Delta employing about fifty people, the parkas selling for $135 wholesale and $300 retail on their novelty value, while the $200 parkas made in the South are warmer and better sewn.
sewn.

Government enterprises tend to fail or require subsidies because they employ too many people (hidden welfare), the strings attached to investing the taxpayer's dollar are too restrictive, or, at the first sign of a profit, the department unloads some of the costs of its own overheads which penalise the enterprise to the point that it never gets up financial steam. Lots of enterprises in the Arctic are feasible but not viable only because of the government's terms. Economic development officers can spend as much as they want to get things going as long as they return dollar for dollar. Missing from their equation is the fact that a dollar spent here might save two dollars in health and welfare costs there. The government is geared to help organisations, not individuals, and when it does get into the act the whole machinery of it overwhelms those involved. Also, companies have to succeed in Southern terms and expectations cannot be relaxed just because they are Arctic businesses.

When education was brought to the Arctic it was assumed that this would be enough to get people going, because educated people would automatically *do* something. But it has turned out that when it comes to business Eskimos are not self-starters, and government people are failing to provide the creative leadership that could promote small-scale "appropriate ventures" which would meet the expectations of the people. Fifty dollars worth of subsidy that kept a man and his family content and interested for a week is better spent than a hundred dollars worth of hand-outs that keep him idle and extinguishes any flames of optimism. It is not a question of money, but the right approach.

There is no gentle planting of ideas, nor does the government know how to channel local impetus into ventures that could become self-sustaining. The Arctic may not be a colony as far as the government of Canada is concerned, but in producing semi-educated unemployables it has the same problems as developing countries like Papua and Malaysia. Canadians work all over the world helping such people develop appropriate technologies to be self-sufficient within the context of their resources, but there is no consultation with Canadians working among Eskimos who have identical problems. Neither educated Eskimos nor specialist Whites working in the field are sent to places like Afghanistan or Guatemala to seek out small-scale industrial enterprises that might be adapted for the

Eskimos. In any direction except large-scale mining and oil explora-tion there is a total lack of imagination on the part of White adminis-trators and this extends equally to Alaska and Greenland.

What is truly sinister as far as the future well-being of the Eskimo is concerned is that ideas, no matter how crazy, are not even discussed. There is no pressure on Eskimos to make themselves more capable in economic terms, and Whites tend to dismiss them as non-triers – "Why should they when there are so many hand-outs?" If ideas fail they are not tried a second time having learned from mistakes, but are written off.

Fresh produce in the Arctic is a rare treat. When aircraft bring in boxes of lettuces and oranges the shelves are cleared in minutes. My lettuce in Barrow cost $1·32 and was a sad creature, yet the Univer-sity of Alaska in Fairbanks grows showpiece cabbages weighing fifty pounds out of doors on campus. In Greenland some private homes have conservatories but these are practically unknown in the North American Arctic. In Russia there are acres of greenhouses on the same latitude and in the same sort of semi-forested country as Inuvik. Every community has a large power station with hot exhaust from big Caterpillar diesels going straight up the chimney: why not use it to heat greenhouses, as a hotel owner does with spectacular success near Yellowknife, instead of wasting it? Fish grow so slowly because of the cold and lack of nutrients but exhaust heat from power stations or industrial development such as compressor stations for a pipeline could conceivably be applied to grow such things as trout or Malayan prawns in some of the millions of lakes that dot the tundra.

Eskimo hunters were once transformed into trappers, and there seems no reason why they should not be transformed again – into Arctic ranchers. Everyone in the Arctic and most people in North America and northern Europe, wears parkas for at least part of the year and the best ones are filled with down. Eider ducks nest in the Arctic by the thousand but are not harvested, and freight would be relatively cheap because the down is so light. Reindeer herding, long the mainstay of Lapp people in northern Scandinavia, has never been particularly successful in the North American Arctic but only because of unsuitable regulations or lack of persistence. However, now reindeer are once more becoming economically viable. In northwest Alaska the native regional corporation plans to bring its herd up to 5,000 and butcher 1,500 a year for families who cannot get caribou. Also, a market for powdered reindeer antler has been discovered in Korea where it is in demand as an aphrodisiac. As the antlers are renewed every year and prices of up to seventy dollars a pound can be obtained, the potential is great.

Another animal which may be domesticated profitably is the musk ox. The wonderfully soft *qiviut* or underwool, which protects the musk ox against piercing Arctic winds, has the softness of angora and the toughness of wool without the drawbacks of either. *Qiviut* is combed out of the animals in summer then spun and knitted by village women into scarves, caps and shawls. The wool is so light that a six-foot scarf weighs only two ounces, and one pound can be woven into ten miles of yarn. One good animal can produce enough for thirty-two scarves which wholesale for sixty-four dollars each. The experimental musk ox farm run by the University of Alaska in Fairbanks has built up a herd of 170 domesticated animals from thirty-two captured in the wild in 1964–5. Now the herd has been moved to a farm of 750 fenced acres at Unalakleet, near Nome on the west coast and their wool is enough to employ part-time about 120 village knitters who can supplement their incomes by three or four thousand dollars a winter. Demand for *qiviut* products is insatiable despite their high cost. The craft shop at the university has a three-month waiting list and just a handful of boutiques in Seattle take as much as Alaska can produce. So far the experiment has been heavily subsidised by organisations such as the Kellogg Foundation. The project is self-sufficient but for the high cost of fodder – one ton per animal per year – which has to be air-freighted from Seattle, but biologists are now trying to find solutions to this problem.

This kind of operation might be ideal for the Canadian Arctic, especially as the oases where most musk ox live are so often found to be in the path of industrial activity such as pipelines. But this kind of development implies an intrastructure of airports, roads and transport systems which would make farming easier, and domesticated musk ox are no more disturbed by human activity than ordinary cows or sheep. Even if the feed problem is not beaten, musk ox farms could be established in the vicinity of the new natural gas terminals being planned on Melville Island where large tankers arriving empty once a week will have acres of room on deck for bales of hay brought either once a year or a few at a time.

One kind of small-scale enterprise has developed in the ideal way. In the old way of life carving toggles and hunting tools from ivory, bone or antler was one of the necessary arts of survival. There is some tradition of art for its own sake, but the pieces were either toys or were connected with shamanism (magic), and they had to be small because an Eskimo needed to carry all his possessions. During contact with early whalers Eskimos soon learned to trade souvenir carvings for knives and needles, and in the 1950s these talents were channelled by James Houston, one of the first administrators on

Baffin Island, into a profitable enterprise called Eskimo art. Soapstone carvings and limited-edition prints became fashionable art forms, the "in" things for which buyers queued all night outside galleries showing new collections. Today, Eskimo art is evident at every retail level, from shopping mall boutiques and airport gift shops where small soapstone seals and polar bears vie for room with apple-face dolls and straw trolls, to department stores and the most prestigious art galleries.

Although its form was relatively unknown before 1950, and is "tainted" in the sense that it is done to please Whites rather than themselves, Eskimo art has developed a style and meaning of its own. The prints seem starkly unreal until you recall how people and animals appear, disembodied in a blur of white during an Arctic whiteout. The carvings seem to have been pressed out of stone or ancient whalebone with bare thumbs and are resonant with a sense of primitive intimacy with Nature. This unique rawness is disappearing as the older generation of artists dies out. Young people who have not had the inspiration of a hard life on the land are collecting images from old people before they are gone for ever, but there is little artistic stimulus to be found in their own surroundings – an unbeautiful settlement of wooden houses, a store, an airstrip, carvings done by neighbours and the worst of White junk. The modern Arctic offers few triggers for the imagination and Eskimo art, having become a business worth $3 million a year in the NWT, is in danger of becoming derivative and stale.

Carving is an ideal activity, like knitting *qiviut*, because it requires little in the way of tools, can be done to provide more or less instant cash – it may not be "art" but it serves a useful purpose if a hunter who needs a new scope for his rifle can buy it by carving a knick-knack – and it suits the Eskimo concept of time. Individual artists who persevere and emerge with a distinctive style ultimately receive about twenty-two per cent of the retail price of their work, not bad considering that the cost of packaging and freighting a carving from the Arctic to Ottawa is often more expensive than shipping crystal from Sweden. In some places carving is regarded as unmanly, worse than welfare. Others, like Cape Dorset, have become artistic communities producing prints, carvings and jewellery: the co-op in Cape Dorset, richest in the Arctic, employs forty-five people and has a turnover of $1·6 million a year.

If half the imagination and guile that Whites have put into fostering Eskimo art as a potent small-scale economic and cultural enterprise were channelled into other projects that made use of traditional Eskimo skills, much of the dynamite would be removed from the

Arctic time bomb. Eskimos are a skilful, hardy, adaptable and clever people and the only reason they are not self-starters in the cash-and-carry society is that they do not have to be. Eskimos are opportunists and who would blame them for opting for the easier life? Only one thing motivates a man to get up when the alarm clock rings in the morning and to go to work and that is pressure. But not only is there no pressure on the Eskimo, there is precious little encouragement.

In his old way of life the Eskimo was a personality as formidable and solid as a new iceberg calving into Diskofiord. In recent years, like the icebergs, he has been grounded on the bar, pulverised, and turned over and over. Now he is adrift in the bay and at the mercy of tides and winds. His outline may have changed on the surface but his great strength lies unseen beneath. Whether he drifts seawards and dissipates in the sunshine of the cash-and-carry culture depends only on his ability to start up his own engine and begin to push.

14

ONE CAN OF WORMS

Bureaucratic fair play intended to
help Canadian Eskimos may be
creating a political monster

Alongside the gravel airstrip is the "base" where about two hundred engineers, technicians, weather men, pilots and equipment operators live a bachelor existence in a sprawl of huts and trailers. There are hangars, garages, workshops, radio masts, heaps of fuel drums, a large garbage dump, and a hotel so cramped that there is space for only one of the two occupants of each room to stand at one time. The summer landscape is bare and rounded, like mounds of bread fresh out of the oven, in winter only dusted with white because the dry snow is blown clean away. Four miles away is the Eskimo hamlet, its old way of life so dead that there is hardly a boat to be seen on the foreshore of the large bay it overlooks. Wage-earning opportunities have been available since the first half dozen Eskimos moved here in 1953 to be near White comforts like the store, bar and movie shows, and now these Eskimos are more "acculturated" than most in Canada. Some, like Peter Paniloo, the school janitor, know how to play the White man's game: as a government employee he is entitled to an airline ticket to the South for himself and his family once a year. Instead, he charters a Twin Otter that flies him with his wife and five children out to their hunting camp and collects them a month later, at a cost of $900.

This is Resolute Bay, as far north as you can go in the world by

scheduled airline. Most days a week a Boeing of one of three different
airlines makes the four or five-hour flight up from Montreal, Winnipeg or Edmonton, serving mainly the scientific, oil-exploration
and pipeline-research parties using Resolute as the transport hub of
the Arctic Islands. The place derived its stirringly romantic name
from *HMS Resolute* which took part in two Franklin search expeditions and was abandoned in nearby Barrow Strait in 1854, emerging
from the ice virtually unscathed a year later to be salvaged by an
American whaling captain and bought by the US Congress which
returned her to Britain as a goodwill gesture. When the ship was
finally broken up in 1879 Queen Victoria presented a desk made of
the timbers to President Rutherford B. Hayes. The desk was used in
the White House until 1952 then restored to the Oval Office by
Kennedy and again by President Carter.

   The founding of Resolute was typical of the kind of haphazard
logistics that characterised early days in the Arctic. In 1947 a ship
attempting to establish a joint American–Canadian weather station
at Winter Harbour, 270 miles farther west, was blocked by ice and
decided to sit it out in Resolute Bay. The ship could not leave for
many days because of fog. When it became imperative to sail, or be
trapped for the winter, equipment was thrown ashore and became
the site of the new weather station. The cross-roads of the High
Arctic had been established in a place it was difficult to get out of!
When the airstrip was built a few years later to service the growing
network of weather stations no opportunity was taken to relocate.

   It was here that the federal government of Canada became
entranced with the possibilities of a showpiece Arctic community.
An English architect who lives on a sailing barge in Sweden, Ralph
Erskine, drew up a village that would resemble the imprint of a
caribou hoof. Three-storey buildings would surround the existing
community in a semi-circle. At its apex would be the town centre,
one big building housing a hotel, offices, swimming pool, skating
rink, store, coffee shop, and roofed-in gardens landscaped with trees.
The aim was to sew White and Eskimo communities together to
improve the "quality of life". Base personnel would move into the
new living quarters and bring their wives and kids to the Arctic.
Living alongside Whites, the Eskimos would become even more
closely acculturated.

   The first building contained ten three-bedroom apartments for
government officers planning to use Resolute as a centre for servicing
half a dozen surrounding communities. It cost $1 million, nearly
one-tenth of the budget for the entire project, and was only two
storeys instead of three. Canadians were horrified to find they could

not see out of the low windows without sitting down. Soon after if was finished one end had to be bulldozed away when a heater caught fire. Then Nordair changed its schedule, using Hall Beach instead of Resolute as the trans-shipping point for that part of the Arctic, so government officers were unable to reach the surrounding communities anyway. The building was still empty.

A fancy sewage treatment plant, one of the most advanced in Canada, was built on the shoreline, and another $1 million was spent on the first half of the community's new utilidor. The treatment machinery burned out. Then it was decided in Yellowknife that converting effluent to a product pure enough to drink was a disadvantage because the nutrients it contained would add to the marine productivity of the bay (this took some explaining to the Eskimos!). Meanwhile the Ministry of Transport decided its people should not live outside the base because travelling four miles back and forth in winter conditions would be difficult and dangerous. With millions of dollars spent, only a fraction of the project completed and none of it operational, the Eskimos of Resolute still do not have a community hall. Now the Eskimos have given up attending meetings concerning the future of their community and prefer to watch television in the bar at the base, with the Whites who continue to leave their families down South. For government officer Danny Strelioff, the whole episode has been an embarrassing disaster. "If you drew a graph of our contribution to Resolute," he told me, "the line would go straight up to a dizzy peak and straight down again. From beginning to end the whole thing was a can of worms."

Government in the Canadian Arctic is run with heavy-footed Godfather tactics in which Eskimos have asked for nothing but have continually been plied with offers they could not refuse.

Eskimos are not bitter towards the government that has provided so much. Nor, due to their own lack of worldliness, are they noticeably cynical. In Alaska the Eskimo has been forced to develop a fierce defensive political stance, which will be described in the next chapter, but in Canada, and up to a point in Greenland, the Eskimo is politically passive, as if stunned by goodwill like a child that opens all its Christmas presents then decides to play with the wrapping paper. The moral sabotage being wrought by benevolence coupled with a lack of opportunity is everywhere apparent.

In Canada the administration of territories north of latitude 60 °N (except northern Quebec) is a federal matter. While provincial governments occupy rooms in the ground floor, so to speak, the whole of the nation's top floor and attic is a collective responsibility. If the upper rooms were also "let out" and became independent as provinces much of Ottawa's power would disappear, especially as the attic might yet prove to be full of oil tanks and hidden treasures. The concierge guarding the Arctic door is currently the Department of Indian Affairs and Northern Development (DIAND). This huge and powerful department is schizophrenic by definition, because it is gung-ho for break-neck industrial development of the Arctic while at the same time it is supposed to care for the social well-being and development of those who live there.

A jurisdiction in the form of a territorial council *appointed* by the government has existed since 1875. During the period of numbing apathy that ended in 1951, when the first three members were elected, the council went fifteen years without passing a single ordinance. With the opening of the Arctic after the Second World War the council gained strength and by 1966 all members were elected. Three years later the Territorial Council, and a contingent of civil servants in the charge of Commissioner Stewart Hodgson, moved to a small gold-mining town on the shore of Great Slave Lake, south of the treeline, and at Yellowknife established the Government of the Northwest Territories. Yellowknife administers on behalf of Ottawa the "people" programmes such as education, economic and political development, game management, social welfare, health, and public works – all the nuts and bolts of ordinary life. Yellowknife is responsible not to the people it governs, but directly to DIAND, which has retained control of forest, communications, transport, investment programmes, all land except a few square miles around every settlement, and – significantly – development of non-renewable resources such as minerals and oil. The Commissioner is also a deputy minister of DIAND. In this sense the government of the Canadian Arctic is not democratic but bureaucratic, and Ottawa is cast in the role of a colonial power.

The Territorial Council of fifteen elected members represents a huge chunk of geography but its population of 45,000 (equally divided between Whites, Indians and Eskimos) is that of only a small town, such as Harrogate in England. But the level of political sophistication is generally lower. Just look at the problems. Two council members are John Steen and Bryan Pearson; as councillors in Harrogate they would live ten minutes' drive from each other at most. Bryan Pearson, ex-merchant seaman and store owner in Frobisher, lives two thousand miles (by the great circle route) from John Steen, taxi operator and garage owner in Tuktoyaktuk. To get to a meeting, Pearson's quickest route by scheduled service is like flying to Harrogate from Karachi, or to New York from Peru. Canadians are so accustomed to distances that they do not see its disadvantages. On paper the Council is weighted in favour of Eskimos and Indians, whose members outnumber Whites, but even with the benefit of simultaneous translation it is difficult for native members to keep abreast of the nuances of bureaucratic language and they tend to be left behind; as a result, the Council is strongly dominated by Whites.

Eskimos traditionally lived in small bands, seldom more than one hundred strong, and no form of organised government was necessary. Decisions were not so much arrived at as imposed by the necessity to survive. They travelled to follow the game, moving on the ice when it was hard enough, and back to land when it thawed. Leaders were acknowledged, rather than selected, on the basis of experience and ability to hunt. Whey they collected into settlements this pathfinder style of leadership was not required and the dreamlike simplicity of their lives disappeared. Whites insisted that if Eskimos lived in houses like them, and wore clothes like them, they should also vote like them. It may have been the only alternative at the time but it was nevertheless an alien principle, one of many greeted at first with the customary polite smile and an appearance of interest that ran no deeper than the Eskimo hunter's concern for the hockey league. Now the same people govern themselves – and follow the National Hockey League – avidly.

A political step-ladder was established so communities that proved themselves with a settlement council could opt to become a hamlet council with more responsibilities, then a village council. The role of Whites changed from that of colonial boss in the guise of administrator to political tutor and secretary in the form of "development officer" as councils were led through different stages until Whites worked themselves out of their jobs and became "resource persons" acting as liaison between councils and Yellowknife.

Today some councils meet enthusiastically four or five times a week. Others are uninterested, suffering from overkill like the council at Resolute, or are bored with the detail of maintaining roads and running garbage and water trucks (some of the smart ones have contracted Whites or their local co-ops to do this for them). Those which are finding their political feet most rapidly are becoming cunning in their use of power, like Pond Inlet which suggested that as a mark of celebration on its graduation from settlement to hamlet, the government might remove its empty gas barrels.

A regional council has been established to represent twenty communities in the eastern Arctic around Baffin to take on responsibilities such as social and economic development devolved from Yellowknife. Several regional councils with common geographic or cultural interests would allow regions to develop at different speeds and within the context of their own priorities.

One hangover of the old way of life is evident at any council meeting, where motions are not introduced formally until it is apparent that everybody is agreed. The principle of decision by majority does not sit easily with Eskimos. If agreement is reached the motion is voted on for the record and is invariably unanimous, otherwise discussion passes on to something else. Often Whites become exasperated when a whole council disappears on a hunting trip, but vacations in Ottawa aren't geared to seasonal wildlife migrations.

While Canada cherishes the first buds of a grass-roots political consciousness among her Eskimos and the US tries to keep the burgeoning undergrowth at bay with a machete (see next chapter), the green-fingered Danes have brought Greenlanders to a stage of vigorous but restrained political maturity. Like Canada, Denmark went all out to shoulder the White man's burden at a time when every other colonial power was trying to shed it, with little hope of profit. Since 1951 Greenland has had a solid political foundation in the form of strong municipal councils in each of its sixteen principal communities sending delegates to the provincial council in Godthåb. Distance, as in the NWT, makes its own problems. When provincial councillor Emil Arke, a boatbuilder in Scoresbysund, attends the twice-yearly sessions he must travel to Godthåb by way of Iceland, Copenhagen and Søndre Strømfiord, a trip that can take two or three weeks each way and costs as much as the travel of all other delegates; others have to hitch rides with the USAF.

The municipal councils have always undertaken more responsibilities than their counterparts in Canada, such as social welfare which can be handled on the spot by trained local people who speak the same language and can make decisions within the context of the social milieu; in NWT it is run from Yellowknife. In April 1979 Greenlanders achieved the political status now being sought by Eskimos in Canada. Called *Hjemmestyre*, which translates literally as "home rule", it is in fact nearer to the Canadian terms of provincehood. Greenlanders have control of all internal affairs and Denmark has agreed that lack of money should be no hindrance and is paying 1,000 million Kr (about £100 million) a year with few strings. Greenlanders now run every aspect of home affairs including fisheries policy, the church, police, schools, hospitals, broadcasting, hunting and taxes.

Until home rule, Greenland was run by the Ministry for Greenland, similar to DIAND. Its chief representative in Greenland was the *Landshovdingen* or "governor" who lived in a large but plain

Karl Elias Olsen is typical of the new generation of Greenlandic leaders.
Principal of the Knud Rasmussensip Højskolia (a community college), he was a
Greenlandic delegate to the Inuit Circumpolar Conference in Barrow in 1977.
Here, he waits with Greenland Women's Institute leaders in national costume to
greet Queen Ingrid of Denmark who was visiting Holsteinsborg to open a new
wing of the school.

grey-painted wooden house built on the foreshore at Godthåb in
1831. There were no trappings of colonial power here, although
Governor Hans Lassen did admit to wearing a plumed hat on special
occasions. Despite the five hundred unemployed in the capital he
had no servants. A formal, quiet and thoughtful man who described
his job as being chairman of everything, Governor Lassen spent his
weekends mending the long picket fence that surrounds his
"palace". He told me, "When I walk around the town people like to
come up and shake my hand – though many of them are drunk, I
must admit."

At this point the aims of 1947 have largely been achieved. Greenlanders live twice as long, housing is the best in the Arctic, the school system is verging on success, vocational training schools are opening, Greenlanders have as large a measure of political self-determination as any Dane. The cloud on the horizon is that of unemployment rising out of the serious lack of small-scale industry to serve the home market and provide employment opportunities. The long-term economic future of Greenland lies in development of oil, uranium and iron ore which will require large capital investment and this will lead to the involvement of powerful multinational corporations. It was decided almost at once between Greenland and Denmark that all Greenlanders had fundamental rights to all resources of their country.

In Canada the question of ownership of land and mineral rights, settled so smoothly and sensibly in Greenland, has become a national issue that colours every aspect of debate on anything to do with the Arctic. Instead of a powerful partnership of natives on the spot and the best brains the government can muster, which is evolving between Greenland and Denmark to take on the big corporations, Canada has been side-tracked into a jungle of argument over land rights – a jungle made all the more impenetrable by the fact that the federal government (through its majority holding in oil companies like Panarctic) is itself a developer.

On a national scale the land claims question is at least as much a can of worms as the redevelopment of Resolute.

Traditionally, the concept of land title was meaningless to the Eskimo. If you wanted to run a trap line eight hundred miles in any direction you just laid it out. Like sunshine and air, the land belonged to everyone and anyone; even the intrusion of whalers and traders was never resented on territorial grounds. Until little more than a decade ago the empty spaces at the top of the map were unwanted and valueless, and the question of formal ownership never cropped up. When oil and gas were discovered and governments automatically assumed ownership Eskimos and Indians realised they had no control and became alarmed. It was not so much a question of failing to cash in financially as seeing their precious land leased out to industrial companies, their wildlife disturbed by aircraft and seismic activities, and the whole base of their culture simply taken over.

The native people of Canada's massive land area lying north of her cities realised, through the spadework of radically minded Whites, the significance of the fact that they had never been conquered and had never signed any kind of treaty. Formal treaties had been made only with Indians of the prairies and Ontario. They claimed the land belonged to them through customary tenure, a principle valid in Canadian law, and that the Royal Proclamation of 1763, which expressly recognised Indian hunting territories, had continuing statutory force. Further, the Eskimos argued that their ownership extended over the sea ice adjacent to the mainland and Arctic islands.

At first the federal government laughed at Whites preaching the principles of aboriginal rights but when the precedent was set by the Alaska Native Claims Act, pushed through in 1971 to allow the Alyeska pipeline to go ahead, the government saw a way of getting off the hook. On the grounds that it was inconvenient to have a group of people outside the mainstream of Canadian life the government recognised that the natives had a case. The intention at that time was to settle mainly for cash, as the Alaskan natives had, then the rights could be extinguished and the natives treated like any other Canadian.

The first agreement to be concluded was with ten thousand Cree Indians and a small number of Eskimos in northern Quebec. The James Bay agreement left the natives 1·3 per cent of their traditional hunting land in exchange for $225 million to be paid over several years (about seven thousand dollars per person at current values) and the way was paved for a massive hydroelectric development, the largest civil engineering project in Canada's history. The natives had been told quite firmly that if they did not sign the agreement the development would go ahead anyway.

When an even larger project was proposed, to build the 1,500-mile gas pipeline along the Mackenzie Valley the government agreed in principle to settle outstanding land claims. Unlike the natives of Alaska and James Bay, however, the Mackenzie Valley Indians and the Eskimos of the Mackenzie Delta were not content to settle for cash alone – they wanted the land itself, a share of royalties, cash compensation for past indignities, and political self-determination within the Canadian federation.

For a nation seeing the day-by-day erosion of its unity with six million French-speaking Canadians in Quebec threatening to split, the ramifications were immense. In the spotlight of the Berger Inquiry Indians staked out what they called the Dene Nation – all the NWT south of the tree-line. This opened up an entirely different can of worms, and was described to me by a senior DIAND official as "Canada's little Rhodesia". The Eskimos slapped in their own claim for the land and sea of the Arctic in its entirety.

It had been out of a sense of decency, a feeling that everyone in Canada deserved a fair shake, that the federal government in the early 1970s started funding organisations to represent native interests against its own big guns and those of industrial corporations. With a $30,000 grant, federal blessing and the DIAND minister at its opening conference, Inuit Tapirisat Canada (ITC) was launched "to speak for the first citizens of the Canadian Arctic". Today, this "Eskimo brotherhood" is a loud and potent force in Arctic politics. It runs on about one million dollars granted every year and borrows (interest free) an almost equal amount against the eventual settlement of its land claim. Based in Ottawa, it is the spearhead of five regional Eskimo organisations which also receive grants for operating costs and loans to prepare land claims. One result is that DIAND finds itself in the position of a husband paying his wife's lovers.

ITC fills the role of a super political public relations agency for the Eskimo. Its leaders are young resourceful Eskimos who received a reasonable education during the bad old days of government boarding schools and are backed by an impressive team of White advisers. The Canadian press eats out of its hand because almost anything natives say can be used as a stick to beat the government. Doors in the corridors of power are always open to ITC, partly because the government likes to be seen keeping them open and partly because friends of ITC include many old Arctic hands with first-class contacts. ITC is effective as a pressure group but only because it is allowed to be: it has never had to fight for recognition, nor even for the goodwill which it can turn on and off like a tap. It is powerful because it is skilful at handling the media, but it is hard to imagine it will ever have respect, and real force as a firebrand organisation, as long as it is funded by the government. Ottawa and Yellowknife are proud of their record in avoiding tokenism, or setting up natives in artificial posts to symbolise progress. But lush funding of the opposition smacks of tokenism figuring so large that nobody close up can recognise it.

One of ITC's most significant contributions has been the Inuit Land Use and Occupancy Project, a $500,000 (paid for by the government) anthropological epic. A team of researchers spent two years interviewing hundreds of Eskimo hunters and trappers who plotted on maps everything they had done in their lives – setting traplines, hunting, fishing and camping. Collated in three thick volumes of stunning detail it added up to a total view of where people had been and what land they had used, and an encyclopaedia of everything they knew about the so-called barren land of the Arctic. The study proved that Eskimos have used and occupied virtually all of the land thoroughly and systematically for at least four thousand years, and on this impressive document ITC bases its claim for ownership of 771,000 square miles of land and 866,000 square miles of sea. This area claimed is equal to that of all Canadian provinces except Quebec.

Eskimos do not make the same distinctions between land and sea as Whites do, says ITC. This means they have probably occupied more territory, and for longer, than any single group of people living today. "Indians of North America have occupied more land but have lost most of it. We Inuit, on the other hand, have never surrendered our traditional territory and while we are willing to share it with the rest of Canada we are determined to retain rights to all 1,600,000 square miles."

The first claim for an Eskimo territory called *Nanavut* (our land), embracing all the Northwest Territories north of the tree-line, was presented to the Prime Minister in 1976 but later withdrawn. Devised by White advisers who perhaps saw the Arctic as a laboratory for exercising pet theories, the thick document read with deceptive and contrived simplicity that suggested it had been written by an Eskimo hunter with the education of an Oxford don. Said ITC's executive director Eric Tagoona, who has a grade 12 education: "We realised we had been ripped off by lawyers and consultants – even we couldn't understand it." In its newest proposals ITC is adopting a more rational approach, endeavouring to establish principles rather than details – "The Inuit were never asked what kind of government they wanted; it was, and still is, an imposed government ... Our people have suffered much at the hands of a society which, although well-meaning, has almost destroyed us ... The Inuit are extending their hands upwards, not begging for welfare, or a few jobs, but to grasp their rightful place in society..."

An indication of how far the Federal Government was likely to go on the issue came in May 1978 when a "joint position" was reached with the Committee for Original People's Entitlement (COPE) representing the 2,500 Inuvialuit Eskimos of the western Arctic. Of the region's 115,000 square miles of land the Eskimos would have absolute title (including oil and mineral rights) to 5,000 square miles plus surface rights to another 32,000 square miles; access across this land for exploration would be guaranteed but some of it would be set aside as a national wilderness park and Eskimos would play an advisory role in land and wildlife management throughout the whole region. Cash compensation for giving up title to two-thirds of their land (a higher proportion if traditional sea-ice hunting areas are included) would be $45 million to be paid through the 1980s.

The significance of the agreement had yet to be felt. Other native organisations condemned it as a sell out, but it was by far the best land settlement of any reached so far, and fifteen square miles of land per person is something on which to build a future, even in the Arctic.

That Eskimos were the first Canadians and have moral and legal right on their side, and that they happen to be Canadians who *want* to live in the Arctic, is admitted by the whole of Canada including Ottawa, Yellowknife, the churches, trade unions, and chambers of commerce. Everyone wants the problem settled once and for all, with no blowbacks of the kind that are occurring in Alaska. By funding native organisations, however, Ottawa is setting them at each other's throats, setting all natives against Yellowknife, and introducing racism because the whole concept of benefit and participation in a land claim agreement depends on grades of an individual's skin colour. This provides ammunition for "red-neck" White people to claim that while Anglican bishops and clergy are being expelled from South Africa for opposing apartheid, those in Canada appear to be sponsoring it by advocating racist domains within the NWT.

Sam Raddi, blind leader of the western Arctic Eskimos and chairman of COPE which has won from the Canadian government recognition of surface ownership of traditional hunting lands.

The funding of ITC has also created a climate of contention that sets ITC against the government automatically (except in the matter of collecting its annual grants) always in a negative and seldom in a constructive way. I suspect this has happened due to the influence of young, radical, super-educated Whites acting as advisers or "resource persons". It has taken such a strong hold that in some cases young Eskimos who left government employ to work for ITC no longer dare speak socially with Whites who were once friends and colleagues. As if, having been set up as pets and told "You are the leaders now," they act like frustrated and spoiled children.

ITC is worried that regional councils will go beyond "strictly municipal administrative matters" and get involved in political issues, undermining ITC's efforts to settle the land claim. While ITC resists any kind of industrial activity until the land claim is settled most councils support resource developments, at least conditionally, because they don't want to wait long to benefit from employment and business opportunities. This raises the question of who are the true representatives of the Eskimos, those elected in all communities, or those elected at an annual meeting (at a cost of $110,000) in just one community? ITC barely recognises the councils, discounting them as "instruments of colonialism".

Admittedly there is an element of dissatisfaction and confusion fostered within the system by White civil servants, like one adult educator I met in Frobisher who told me the purpose of his job was "to criticise the government and protect the people against it". It might have been more admirable had he said his job was to help the Eskimos see themselves in perspective, or that he believed that to make a man free you first had to make him capable. Another factor is the "professional deformation" described by Dr Charles Hobart, professor of sociology at the University of Alberta, which leads higher status civil servants to view natives prejudicially, as patients in need of supervision, welfare and rehabilitation, and by this attitude instils in them a set of opposite values – failure, incompetence and dependence.

Whites in Ottawa seem dazzled by hot Nunavut nationalism which scarcely exists in the communities, yet the same people are blind to (or ignorant of) strong political forces emerging in the community councils and the first regional council. The challenge of the Arctic is not developing the country but developing its people, and the way they are going about it in the Canadian Arctic is creating a monster which will do as much for the Eskimo in the political sense as the new town plan and sewage plant in Resolute Bay.

15

A CASE OF COLD SWEATS

*How the slum of the Arctic became
the jittery beachhead of new Eskimo
political muscle and self assertion*

Snaking rivers have changed track countless times, each twist and
turn leaving a different band of trees. Swathes of brilliant gold
alternate with curving waves of dark green to create a landscape of
intricate geometric ripples merging like the patterns made by rain-
drops on a pond. These swirls of forest colouring, surreal brush-
strokes on the great canvas of a sub-Arctic wilderness, might have
been the inspiration of Van Gogh himself had he been fortunate
enough to look out over the dipping wing of a Boeing 737 one day in
Fall as it climbed out of Fairbanks and turned north.

Immediately after take-off the pilot came on the line to check that
no passenger remained unaware of yet one more natural spectacle of
this great State of Alaska. Moments later, in tones that suggested
both had been engineered on the same drawing board, he pointed
out the mud-grey convolutions of the mighty Yukon River and the
silver trace of the Alyeska pipeline. In this majestic and gloriously
hued landscape the sterile glint of the slender pipeline had a peculiar
fascination: as if you were staring at a hypodermic syringe. The
Brooks Range was prettily dusted with snow, but beyond its divide
the splendour faded. Treeless, windswept, cut by thousands of dry
water courses threading out to a low, flat plain of soggy tundra, this
was the North Slope, domain of the Inupiat Eskimo, and the

scenery-struck pilot could not find a word to say. As he dropped the plane low over this monotonous, bitterly raw territory and turned sharply over a leaden sea speckled with desiccated ice-floes, the feeling I had was a tingling wariness, as if riding into old-time Indian country. To tell the truth I was scared.

In a few days of violence (which the deputy commander of the US Naval Arctic Research Laboratory at Barrow later attributed to first sight of the full moon after the summer) a NARL man had been killed in a truck accident, a White had stabbed an Eskimo, an Eskimo girl had stabbed and killed her boyfriend, somebody had put a bullet through the weather office window, and the bodies had just been discovered of a young Californian couple shot to pieces in their tent on the beach. Earlier, Gordon Harrison, president of Canmar, the company drilling for oil in the Beaufort Sea, had warned me to watch my step because kids in Barrow had thrown stones at him and called him *gussuk*, "white nigger". Canmar's Twin Otter had been blasted with a shotgun as it took off. From the Fairbanks newspapers I knew Barrow's police chief was being indicted for misappropriation of funds, two deputies had been indicted for rape and selling pot to minors and four others had resigned after the same incident, and the president of the so-called Inupiat University, and his book-keeper, had been indicted for embezzlement. Whites in Anchorage and Fairbanks, going only by the sensationalised stories they had read in the newspapers, seriously warned me against going anywhere near the place.

On final approach the plane gives you a good view of the tapering shingle spit that juts another twelve miles north. A little way along is the Naval Laboratory, some eighty blue and yellow Quonsets knitted together by thick cables on wooden poles: a picture of stark ugliness you would not expect to find this side of Siberia. Nearby is the large new building housing the trash plant that has never worked, surrounded by garbage. The town itself, on four hundred acres of tussock and gravel, is crowded up to the sea by the airstrip which forms a boundary between the community and miles of empty tundra where nothing can happen except hunting and berry-picking because it has been classified a national petroleum reserve. The community is so pressed for space that it has overflowed around two lakes separated by a shingle causeway only a few feet wide. One lake is the sewage lagoon of the hospital and school, the other is the town water supply. Visitors are advised to drink pop.

All this can be taken in at a glance as the plane taxis up to the wooden shack which serves as a terminal, its cracked panes boarded up with cardboard to keep out the cold, its interior as dark, crowded

and smoke-filled as a gold-rush bar. The town begins just over the
fence, and even when you are hardened to the litter and general
slumminess of Arctic communities Barrow comes as a shock. For
tourists expecting to see nice little Eskimos playing in the snow it hits
like a karate chop.

During the summer season about seven thousand tourists a year
fly to Barrow for the sake of going north of the Arctic Circle and
visiting the most northerly point in the US. Only a quarter of them
stay the night and many, I was told, take one look out of the window
and do not get off the plane. I could see why.

Most of the year Barrow's sins are layered in snow and ice and its
ramshackle appearance is blurred by semi-darkness and blowing
snow. In Fall it looks and smells like a disaster area. Scummy puddles
of household waste water extend across the gravel roads and under
the floors so people have to put down planks to reach their doors. The
houses are connected by a plumber's nightmare of rusty iron pipes
distributing natural gas from wells on the tundra. The pipes are
supported on the jagged edges of fuel drums cut in half and filled with
rocks, and arch over roads on precarious wooden struts: the whole
thing is as dangerous as it looks but so far there has been no major
accident.

Every house is all but overwhelmed by mountains of debris. Old
Army trucks and jeeps, bicycles, motor-bikes, beach-buggies, bulldozers, graders, three-wheel Hondas, cars, pick-ups, up to a dozen
snow machines in varying stages of decay ... but these are just the
vehicles. There are also piles of lumber, heaps of discarded packing
material, insulation cladding lying in soggy lumps like skinned
walruses, tin cans by the thousand, holed glassfibre boats, canoes,
outboard motors and – more carefully preserved – the skin-covered
boats called *umiaks* used for whaling. Scattered about are strips of
whale meat like black mourning ribbons pegged out on wooden rails
to dry in the lowering sun, scraps of rotting blubber, big bunches of
ducks tied at the neck and left lying around, haunches of black
caribou meat, loathsome stag heads with hollow eyes put on the
roof-tops, and wolf or dog skins hanging out to dry. Out front, where
most US home owners would have a mailbox on a post, is the grisly
open-ended fuel drum half filled with human waste. Approach any
house and out of the debris springs a number of fiercely barking,
chained-up, nervy dogs which have to find dry resting places where
they can. The Fall winds seem all the colder for being damp, skies are
grey and seem low enough to touch, there is a lot of drizzle and every
morning the frosts get noticeably fiercer until the lakes of dishwater
remain glazed with half an inch of ice in the middle of the afternoon

and you know that freeze-up and the first sterilising blankets of snow are just around the corner. For myself, shivering in the chill rain as I humped my suitcase between the puddles and heard the roar of the jet taking off again, it seemed a bad time to be visiting the showpiece of Eskimo self-determination and a hell of a good moment to be leaving for Hawaii.

In a country as geographically self-contained as the US it is hard to believe that up to the early 1970s a place like Barrow could exist with only the occasional bush plane coming in and supplies delivered once a year by barge. Administratively the North Slope Eskimos inhabited what was euphemistically called an "unorganised borough". In the century since the first whalers arrived they have ridden a series of boom-bust waves – whaling, trading, fur trapping, working in DEW-line construction, all the while supplementing meagre incomes by hunting, sealing and whaling. Housing was grim, often constructed from shipping crates. Only a few had power, practically none had plumbing. No education beyond Grade Eight was available without going thousands of miles from home; the average education achievement was two and a half years. Barrow had a hospital but in the villages health facilities worth the name

Typical backyard collections of junk in Barrow, Alaska. It is not merely junk on the land that is the problem of the Arctic: the whole place is being developed in the image of junk with junk food, junk reading, junk films and television, junk clothing and – some say – junk ideals.

were non-existent. Compared with the new world being brought to
Greenland and Arctic Canada, North Slope Eskimos were ignored,
depressed, and living in conditions of grinding poverty. Even in 1977
it was something of a shock to find that in the eight communities on
the North Slope – a part of the US as large as Minnesota – only two
had a water supply, two a sewer system, six a power supply, three
television, five a radio station, five a telephone (ie, one telephone, not
necessarily an exchange), two a library, five a post office and seven a
health centre.

Alaska itself had been a poor and remote colony of the US,
inaccessible even by road until the Alaska Highway was built up
through Canada during the Second World War. Then it became a
garrison of strategic importance during the Korean War and the
Cold War and today nearly twenty per cent of the State's 330,000
people are still military personnel and associated civilians. With
nineteen mountains over fourteen thousand feet high, three million
lakes more than twenty acres in extent (together covering an area
greater than Delaware and Maryland) Alaska is more than twice as
big as Texas. On the map, Alaska and its Aleutian chain nearly span
the width of the Lower Forty-eight. With the discovery of immense
oil reserves at Prudhoe Bay in 1968 Alaska entered a new game of
massive statistics. The Alyeska pipeline and the development that
has already taken place is just the beginning. By 1985, according to
some predictions, Alaska will be supplying a quarter of all US
domestic oil and gas requirements, the greater part of it coming from
the tundra and maritime hunting grounds of the Inupiat Eskimos –
the North Slope.

Since oil was discovered at Prudhoe Bay in 1968 the four thousand
Eskimos of the North Slope, with headquarters in Barrow, and a
similar number in northwest Alaska, working from Kotzebue, have
fought and won bitter political battles with some of the world's most
powerful corporations and the West's most powerful government.
Compared with their cousins who are prisoners of other peoples'
consciences in Arctic Canada, these Eskimos have developed the
muscle, vigour and clout of political commandos. Despite past vic-
tories their battle continues on more fronts than before and also from
within, for they now face the disconcerting and alarming fact that
they are no longer simple hunters but capitalists with a great deal of
investment to protect. Further, the uneasy realisation is dawning
that these spoils of victory may be the cause of their ultimate destruction. For these reasons, Barrow in its tense mood resembles a town
under siege.

It all started when somebody shot a duck.

The North Slope people, like all Eskimos, had long suffered the effects of the Migratory Birds Convention Act made in 1916 between Canada, USA and Mexico to protect wildfowl during nesting and moulting seasons. Every spring hundreds of thousands of wildfowl fly north to the Arctic coast to breed, returning in the Fall. The regulations were designed to benefit sport hunters blasting away at them *en passage* and did not take into account the Eskimos who relied on ducks and geese for a significant part of their subsistence. When the hunting season officially opened most birds were gone from the Arctic, and when it ended none had arrived. In 1961 John Nusungingya, who represented Barrow at the Alaska State Legislature, was arrested for shooting a duck out of season. Two days later practically every man in the place – 138 of them – shot an eider duck and presented himself to game wardens for arrest. Charges were eventually dropped and the Eskimos learned a useful first lesson in forceful politics.

At about the same time the US Atomic Energy Commission was planning to create a new deep-water harbour near Kotzebue by exploding a nuclear device. Contamination would spread three hundred miles inland in a swathe one hundred and fifty miles wide, possibly wiping out the great caribou herds and washing radioactivity into the sea where it would affect sea mammals. None of the originators of this appalling scheme of geographic engineering – known as Project Chariot – consulted the natives who lived there, used the land, and depended on caribou and sea mammals for survival. A meeting of Eskimos in Barrow to discuss what could be done led to the founding in 1964 of the Arctic Slope Native Association, the first regional native organisation in Alaska. The nuclear project was killed by the outcry when it became public knowledge, but other native organisations continued to form and were united in a common cause by a newspaper called *Tundra Times*. The common cause was the land grab.

When Alaska became a State in 1959 it was allowed to select 103 million acres for its own use. At that time Alaska's sixty thousand native people owned outright only five hundred acres, had restricted title to fifteen thousand acres, and nine hundred families shared four million acres in reserves. The remaining people occupied and ranged over the public domain which was being parcelled out. By 1966, when the State had secured only three million of its acres, including Prudhoe Bay, the new Alaska Federation of Natives had become strong enough to persuade Interior Secretary Stewart Udall to freeze the land transfer. Every regional native organisation then claimed acreages by virtue of traditional use. The Arctic Slope Native

Association claimed virtually all fifty-eight million acres north of the Brooks Range; in total, all claims added up to more than the whole area of Alaska.

Unlike native organisations in Canada, which have had their teeth drawn by lush funding, North Slope Eskimos fought their own battles with their own money. Cash raised from local bingo evenings and raffles did not buy much but served to unite communities and give the movement real strength, while large amounts required to finance travel, counsel, and lobbyists were raised discreetly from the American Association of Indians, Ford Foundation, and other organisations. Many thought the native claims for land ridiculously ambitious – until the State auctioned the new oil leases to 450,000 acres in Prudhoe Bay, and in the course of one afternoon received $900,220,590.21¢. The story of the battle for recognition of land rights, in which North Slope Eskimos played a major role, is one of complicated and bitter in-fighting in the course of which Alaskan Eskimos matured as a forceful pressure group. Finally it was the oil companies, concerned at delays in the construction of the pipeline to get Prudhoe Bay oil to the south, which put their weight behind the natives. The Alaska Native Claims Settlement Act, passed by Congress in 1971, allowed natives to select and own outright forty million acres. This was little more than ten per cent of the State, though more than was held in trust for all other Indians in the US. As compensation for giving up claim to the remainder there was a cash payment of $962·5 million, to be paid in instalments up to 1992, plus a share of oil royalties.

To capitalise on these resources about 220 village councils would select a little over half the land for local subsistence use and would finance village services. Twelve regional corporations, run by directors elected by the native people who were stockholders, would receive and handle the money and land on behalf of all. About half the money would be dispersed to villages and individuals, the remainder invested in a way that returned the best profit. They would assist and supervise villages, and own the mineral rights to all native land.

For the first three years corporations were pre-occupied with choosing their land. When the first payment of $209 million came in 1974 the regional corporations built hotels, grocery stores, fishing boats, sawmills, bought all kinds of businesses such as construction firms, and four corporations combined to establish a bank. At Kotzebue the Northwest Alaska Native Association (NANA) built a fancy museum and Eskimo cultural centre, and a hotel, to make money from tourists. It also went into business catering for pipeline workers, providing security services at pump stations along the pipeline, herding reindeer and carving jade. The Arctic Slope Regional Corporation (ASRC) built a grand $4·5 million headquarters in the centre of Barrow and put much of its effort into technical, construction, and communications companies serving oil and pipeline development in Prudhoe Bay. It built the $2·5 million Top Of The World Hotel in Barrow and when I finally trudged in with my suitcase it was to find the hotel overbooked, though for a mere twenty dollars a night I would be allowed to sleep in the lobby,

The effect of the Act has been to make capitalists of the Eskimos, buying them out once and for all. The US had purchased Alaska from Russia in 1867 for two cents an acre; now its value was $2·87 an acre, some of it to be paid out of oil royalties: in principle, the price might as well have been counted in beads and hatchets. The entire North Slope was constituted as an enormous municipal borough, a move resisted tooth and nail by the oil industry trying to avoid property taxes, and Eskimos resented this attempt to strangle them at birth. For the Act also brought a change in mood. Eskimos could run their own show, with their own money, but their hard-won freedom had the effect of casting them adrift on a sea of White indifference and exploitation which had a new edge – "Now the Eskimo is the same as any other American let's screw him for all we can get."

First priority of the North Slope Borough was to make good the years of neglect and upgrade its own standard of living with an ambitious capital improvements programme. Raising $140 million in bonds over five years it financed the provision of basic services like water, sewage, schools and health clinics for each of its eight communities. One potential problem was the speed of upgrading: if twenty houses were erected in ten years, instead of two hundred in three or four years, any mistakes or shortcomings could be identified and put right. As it is, most of the houses and other facilities will be complete before design failures become evident. Inevitably, many mistakes have already been made. The Borough's first large project was a $5·5 million school in the small village of Anaktuvuk Pass in the Brooks Range. Contracts were signed in 1974 and the work went largely unsupervised by the Borough. In 1977, with more than three million dollars spent, the only actual facilities were two canvas domes which were designed for the Arctic but did not work. A three-unit apartment intended for teacher housing was being used as classrooms; this building was budgeted to cost $263,000 but actually cost $410,000. Other funds were rapidly eaten up by architectural services and construction management. The whole episode was a discouraging blow to pride, for the Borough was supposed to have been the answer to all the Eskimos' problems.

This incident was merely a taste of what was to come. Like any developing nation, the North Slope people had to decide whether to put everything in limbo while their own people were educated, or to hire other people to do the job. When the Act came into effect only seventy-three natives in the whole of Alaska had any graduate-level training, but the twelve regional corporations alone required at least 250 administrators and executives with some further education, and an equal number trained in clerical jobs. Supply of native people with any sort of qualification was so short that salaries sky-rocketed, attracting many away from government and enticing students out of school before they had completed their education. In 1971 an air crash cost Barrow a whole generation of high-school students, many of whom today would be qualified. Pressures on the Borough were so intense that its own political and economic development could not be delayed so it was decided that outside consultants should fill the gap while simultaneously training Eskimos to do their jobs. Progress at once became so rapid, administration and corporate affairs so complicated, that a new generation will probably never catch up, especially as many are being tempted out of school by high-paid jobs on the grounds that even if they cannot spell Mississippi at least they know what it is.

The small group of men of mainly middle age who were locked into the leadership at an early stage have an average education level of about Grade Eight, and soon reached a level of incompetence that required support by outside consultants. It is unfair to suggest the leaders are not smart or able, but whether they have the breadth of experience with which to judge the quality of expertise they hire is another matter. Many consultants see the place as a goldmine and try to keep the people dependent on them. The leaders recognise this but are in a dilemma, because every year they advance into new areas requiring even greater expertise. Housing is in such short supply that consultants flit back and forth, charging high fees for air time as well as expenses, and have no real involvement in the place except as a source of income.

One of the leaders is Nelson Ahvakana. Aged thirty-nine, educated to Grade Twelve, he is corporate secretary and an elected board member of the Arctic Slope Regional Corporation, president of Barrow Utilities and Electric Co-operative Inc, member of the North Slope Borough Assembly, executive vice-president of Arctic Slope Regional Construction Inc, a commissioned lay preacher, partner in a whaling crew and father of three children – "We're all spread too thinly," he told me, "anybody who can write his name in this place is snowed under with work."

The result is that the Eskimos might play the role of plotting their own course as captains of their ship, but the real navigating officers are sophisticated techno-industrial orientated Whites with a financial stake in preserving the status quo. Who is in charge, the Eskimo with a White assistant or the White consultant working with an Eskimo figurehead? And what financial power do the consultants wield behind the scenes when their employers run in local elections? These questions are difficult to answer, but all developing countries have been ripped off while developing expertise, and the North Slope would appear to be no exception.

The ultimate aim of the Alaska Native Claims Settlement Act was the total assimilation of the native people, to transform them in the shortest possible time from hunters and gatherers with a "special" place in society into capitalists like everyone else. This is creating conflicts between those who continue to use the land for genuine subsistence, and the new class of super Eskimos whose standard of living and level of material sophistication has improved immeasurably with their jobs as corporation executives; the future of the corporations depends on the industrial exploitation of the self-same land now used for hunting caribou.

In the past, Eskimo leaders have cleverly made political hay from the lush pastures of previous exploitation by Whites – the arbitrary declaration of half the North Slope as a petroleum reserve in 1923, the moving of a village to make way for a DEW-line station, the wholesale take-over of their hunting grounds at Prudhoe Bay by the State. Today by far the largest forces of growth and development are the Borough and Regional Corporation themselves. To sustain their existing rapid pace of progress it is they who, in the future, will be doing the people-moving. How long will it be before the massive coal reserves of the North Slope, estimated to be 150 billion tons in seams twenty to sixty feet down, will be scraped out of the tundra for export to Japan? Could the day come when the future of regional corporations becomes so dependent on expansion of oil development that they are forced to support the oil industry that is resisting developments in home rule in rural Alaska? Eben Hopson, mayor of the North Slope, believes that in the fight for local self-determination the influence of the oil industry may lead regional corporations to fight against it. "Even now I wonder if we could have organised the North Slope Borough today against the opposition of my own Arctic Slope Regional Corporation, of which I am a vice president," he told the Berger Inquiry in Canada. "I worry about the direction the politics of oil are taking among our people in the Arctic – now most people are for anything that will keep the boom going ... but Arctic oil development should be treated as a problem rather than as an opportunity for our people."

It is difficult for individual super-Eskimos in positions of responsibility to resist seduction by ruthless and charming corporation presidents. At home in Barrow it might be possible to present a united front but it's a different story when men are lured to the plush halls of business in the Lower Forty-eight. Everyone has hooks into the Eskimo: not only oil companies but mining interests, construction companies, transport operators, airlines, shippers, and many others. Plus, of course, the army of consultants advising Eskimos on everything from environmental protection and speech-writing to film-making, accountancy and drain-laying.

Meanwhile, the National Petroleum Reserve of 37,000 square miles, covering nearly half the Borough, has always been available for subsistence hunting but is now being intensively explored by drilling crews and seismic surveyors. The Arctic Wildlife Refuge at the eastern end of the Borough is coming under increasing pressure to be explored. Offshore oil exploration will begin in 1980 and if potential is realised the Eskimo marine hunting and whaling areas could be turned into something resembling a Lake Maracaibo, with rigs and drillships everywhere in sight, while the tundra becomes another Kuwait. The Alyeska pipeline brought an unwanted attachment in the shape of a high-grade "haul road" which is due to be made public. Even if it is controlled up to a point, Prudhoe Bay and Barrow will become the most northerly accessible points in North America and the target of every adventurer on four wheels. The proposed Nunamiut National Park straddling the Brooks Range is planned to show the relationship of Man to his natural environment, thereby permitting subsistence hunting by Eskimos to continue, but it will be seven and a half times larger than Yellowstone and attract many visitors: the total number of North Slope Eskimos, already outnumbered by Prudhoe Bay oil-patch workers, is only four thousand.

For all these reasons the North Slope Eskimos are in a cold sweat. They are beginning to realise that the land claim has sold them out. Cash flow will dry up when the guaranteed State and Federal payments cease in the mid-1980s. In 1991 individual stockholders in the corporations will be able to sell out to non-natives, and native land will be subject to property taxation. Sold out, ripped off, threatened with cultural annihilation from within and pressed on all sides by a largely unsympathetic White society which believes the land settlement was fair and just, it was small wonder that from Mayor Hopson down everybody in the place seemed to have the jitters.

The weekend of violence before my landing in Barrow had been bad for everyone, creating great tension, but it was nothing like the news that came in the newspapers from the South which painted a picture of Whites and Eskimos on the point of declaring war. That month an article in *Harpers Magazine*, under the headline "An Alaskan Tragedy" gave a biased and unnecessarily offensive account of Barrow, concluding with the statement, "We'll be sorry we were ever kind to the Eskimo". Mayor Hopson, a mild-mannered man with a will as forceful as a harpoon strike, had been accused in Anchorage newspapers of *racism* because, during State Governor Jay Hammond's short visit to Barrow, he did not agree to be interviewed by the accompanying reporters who happened to be White.

The Borough offices in Barrow are located in a beautiful new building that looks something between a Japanese pagoda and an Indian tepee, for its galleried, open-plan interior gives the impression of being held up by poles lashed with ropes: ideal for California perhaps, but less so north of the Arctic Circle because the upper levels get too hot while the ground floor is too cold. It was here, while the wallpaper sang softly with Johnny Cash's "I'll Walk The Line", that I went to talk with Eben Hopson. Before hearing any of my questions he vented – with some passion – his views on journalists. Then stalked from his room in an agitated state with sweat on his brow. If I had been able to ask why the mayoral office cost more than $500,000 a year to run, or how he justified a personal salary of $63,000, anger might have been in order. As it was, my few opening words had been on the uncontroversial though greatly more significant subject of the first Inuit Circumpolar Conference, which the Mayor had recently organised and hosted in Barrow. For him – as for the teenagers I had seen rampaging at Point Hope, and for Akpaleeapik who had chucked the White man's new piss-pot out through the roof of the igloo – it seemed that the world had become too big to handle and his gesture was more eloquent than words.

At that moment he was fighting yet one more rearguard action against interference by Whites. Every April and May the great bowhead whales come spouting and gasping along the foggy leads that open and close as the frozen ocean forces its way around the outflung barrier of Point Barrow. For thousands of years the North Slope Eskimos have hunted them. In former times, probably within Mayor Hopson's memory, the whale hunt was *essential* to survival. Practically every part of the whale had a use. The baleen, cut into strips and braided, made lines for lashing and fishing, nets for whitefish and frames for crab traps; it was also fashioned into containers, walking sticks, sleds, in-soles of shoes, and used as frames for stretching the seal intestines that served as windows. Bones made sled runners, *umiak* keels, rafters, maul heads, adze blades, shuttles, needle cases, ladles, and many other things. Whale meat was the main source of protein, iron, and vitamin B; the whale skin or *muktuk* provided vitamins A and D. The meat was eaten raw, frozen, boiled or fried, as was nearly all the rest of the whale including the heart, liver, stomach, lips, intestines and even clots of blood: two-thirds of its weight – in total anything up to thirty tons – is edible. What was not eaten by humans was fed to dogs. With other forms of hunted meat such as caribou, seal, walrus and fish, whales are still reckoned to provide at least half the food for most North Slope Eskimos.

In this age of the frozen TV dinner the whale is no longer critical to survival but it does play an essential role in an economic sense. More important still, it is whale hunting that is regarded by North Slope Eskimos as the most important of the "old ways", which provides their unique identity as Eskimos, and which they most desire to be passed on to their children.

Every moment of whale-hunting is rooted in tradition: the early part of the season, when whaling crews hack access routes over the pressure ridges and nearly the whole town moves to ice camps on the floe edge, the harpooning of whales by hand from skin boats which make no vibration to alarm the whales when launched from the ice edge, the sharing of meat, when a flag is flown from the roof of the successful captain's house and the crews' womenfolk cook whale meat for the whole community; when news spreads of a successful kill offices and shops empty and even meetings of the Borough Assembly are adjourned. In June every captain who has killed a whale sponsors a celebration called *nalukataq*, when there is feasting and dancing. "There is only one way to describe the importance of whale-hunting to us," said Eugene Brower, a young Eskimo technocrat who is deputy director of public works and captain of a whaling crew. "You can say it's the equivalent of Christmas, Thanksgiving, football, vacations and eating steak – all in one."

It was this activity which the sixteen nations of the International Whaling Commission, at its twenty-ninth annual meeting in June 1977, voted unanimously (USA abstaining) to stop. The whole move was political, part of a much wider campaign to bring muscle to bear on nations like Japan and Russia hunting other types of whale. It was reckoned hypocritical to press for a world-wide ban on commercial whale hunting if a small group of US citizens were permitted to continue hunting for recreation and subsistence. But the move did have ammunition in the form of a survey by the US National Marine Fisheries Service which showed that during the 1977 season twenty-six whales had been landed at Barrow but another seventy-seven had been "struck and lost". And it was this survey which had stung eighty North Slope whaling captains into action and brought them to a meeting at the Borough offices to decide what action to take. It had much of the feeling of the 1961 duck shoot about it – a deep sense of beleaguered outrage, an earnest level of attention, a feeling of intense commitment to get something done.

The captains spoke of how they had been misinformed about the purpose of the survey when speaking to researchers, most of whom seem to have gathered their information on the beach by talking to whalers' wives. The word "lost" itself was contentious because a lost whale was not necessarily a dead whale; often whales were caught with several harpoons from previous encounters still in them. The IWC had admitted that the bowhead stock could support an annual kill of about fifty whales a year; the hunters had landed twenty-six

Eugene Brower, of Barrow, with his wife Charlotte who is the village magistrate, and their children. The couple are archetypes of the new-generation Eskimo. Born and reared on the land, now earning $68,000 a year between them, they hunt and fish because they must – "Without the whale we might as well live on welfare – in California."

and at the outside would not have killed the same number, so by its own rules, the captains said, the IWC had nothing to complain about.

The Eskimos were scathing about the lack of information – "An abuse given the colour of science" – on which IWC was prepared to base its action. "We have to use sail boats to get close to the whale," said one hunter, "so how can a researcher expect to get an accurate picture if he is surveying by aircraft that is overhead only thirty seconds? A young whale can dive for as long as it takes that aircraft to fly all the way to Fairbanks!" Obviously, people like these could not be pushed around.

The most vivid speaker was Charlie Edwardsen, a local hero for his work in the land claims fight. Now thirty-four, lank-haired and wide-shouldered, speaking in staccato bursts to disguise a slight stammer and displaying a comic propensity for unwitting malapropisms ("People of the temperamental nations regard the Arctic as a wasteland") he addressed the meeting in fiery terms that left you in no doubt as to the intensity of feeling among the North Slope Eskimos: "I have never been so insulted in all my life as when I was told somebody's interests elsewhere were more important than my own community's livelihood," he said. "In order for us to execute the whale, and for whale and Inupik to continue this special relationship, we're going to have to argue, to get into a fight that is demeaning ... And in doing this we have two hundred and twenty million people to educate: that is, the populations of the sixteen countries who voted against the Eskimos ... There is a greater right than the exploitation of the whale, the right of a people to live their own way and to enforce psychological tyranny by depriving them of it is probably the greatest depredation any people can undergo ... Our total community psychiatry is at stake, and it is not for sale! Without the whale there is no Eskimo!"

The upshot of a series of meetings resulted in the formation of the Alaskan Eskimo Whaling Commission. Its first move was to agree to limit the kill of bowhead whales during the 1978 season to three, so a proper whale count could be done. This self-discipline and sense of purpose, remarkable in the circumstances, is more than anything else a measure of the maturity and self-discipline that the North Slope Eskimos have achieved, although in the event four whales were taken. In 1979 the quota was eighteen.

Now some of this resolve may spread to Eskimos in other countries. Eighteen delegates from Greenland met similar numbers from Canada and the North Slope at the Inuit Circumpolar Conference in June, 1977. In addition there were many observers, including

220 from the US. For the first time ever, one of the oldest-established peoples of the world met together as one, communicating in their own language (almost wholly successfully, the main drawback being that many North Slope Eskimos knew only English). The conference embraced every aspect of Arctic affairs, predictably calling for such things as safe technology in the development of resources, unrestricted access to east–west travel, and local control of wildlife. The significance of this conference (and others planned for the future) in uniting all Inuit in a powerful pan Eskimo movement of the kind Eben Hopson visualises has yet to be tested by time. Meanwhile it served to demonstrate vividly the different paths along which Eskimos have been led into the modern world:

By Danes, who solved their Eskimo problem by marrying them and creating a new race called Greenlanders, now achieving political self-determination under the guiding hands of kindly White uncles ...

By Canadians, who have shelved their Eskimo problem by putting them in a kind of sanatorium where every need is met and Eskimos have gained everything except the strength to fight their way out ...

By Americans, who have done nothing for Eskimos except boot them into the deep end and now stand on their heads each time they come up to breathe.

Speaking for myself, it was as hard not to be impressed by the vigour of Barrow as it was to remain unmoved by the sight and smell of the place. The guys in rubber aprons and long gloves baling out the shit tanks by hand grinned piratically when I passed. Everywhere there were signs of new construction and improvement. Nobody called me a *gussuk* or threw stones, and Eskimos were easier to talk to here than in Canada or Greenland; their leaders were prickly rather than hostile, but they had much to be sensitive about. The man who murdered two Whites camping on the beach turned out to be a psychopath: it was the kind of sad accident that could happen anywhere. When I left Barrow for the last time the plane was full of White consultants flying to their homes in Anchorage and Seattle for the weekend. We took off in the first snow flurries of the winter, dipping a wing over tundra ponds glazed with mid-afternoon ice while the flight attendants took orders for martinis and bloody marys. The man beside me had a thin moustache and a thick briefcase, and he curled his nostrils as he stripped rubber overboots from his glossy street shoes. When our drinks came he caught my eye and dipped his glass in mocking salute. "Here's to the Eskimos," he said. "God help them – and God keep them rich."

16

THE LAST FRONTIER

The role of illusion in the "White pollution" that is the most sinister threat to the Eskimo future

Yipping and yowling, their plumed tails curled as high as smoke signals, the six huskies bounded joyfully along the shoreline as the yellow speedboat creamed around the tiny island in a spray-glittering arc and then headed in. Berthe took the wheel and cut the 25-horsepower Evinrude while Abia sat on the bow with his feet dangling and fended off as the glassfibre hull kissed the low-tide rocks. Propped in one of the upholstered seats, deeply sunburned after camping up the fjord, and screwing his nose against the 11pm sunshine, one-year-old Mikki giggled as the big dogs all but leapt aboard, the push of their paws sending the 15-foot boat drifting away. Quickly Berthe chucked a rope and Abia pulled them in again.

The island was a grassy knoll, no larger than a suburban lot, where Abia marooned his dog team during the summer months to save them the unpleasantness of being chained up between the houses in the west Greenland village of Egedesminde, just north of the Arctic Circle. Twice a week Abia collected de-filleted halibut from the fish factory, where his mother worked, and sped five or six miles across the bay, dodging floating ice that could rip like a knife through the thin hull, to feed his dogs. As he humped the big sack of fish skeletons on his back and staggered between the rock pools they leapt against him half fiercely and half playfully, and 29-year-old

Abia Abelsen, 29, an Eskimo, and his half-Danish wife Berthe, 21, and little Mikki – the midnight sun is good weather for young people.

Abia, chortling happily, was nearly buried beneath a surging scrum of golden fur.

For half an hour the family sat on a warm rock sheltered from the crisp breeze and watched the dogs tearing at the fish bones and gulping them down – heads, backbones, skin – without chewing. At 3am Abia was going murre shooting with his brother, because the sun was so nice. He hadn't slept a night through for a week, but he napped in the boat, as Mikki did in his carry-cot, when he felt tired. Language teacher and house master at a residential boys' school, Abia had the weather-beaten, dark-eyed look of the true Eskimo while Berthe, whose father was Danish, had more European features. Their little boy would be a true Greenlander, a blue-eyed Eskimo.

Before the sea froze over Abia would collect his dog team and lay up his boat, spending free time in winter and spring fishing by nets set under the ice. Each dog, and each member of the family, consumed one fish a day and it was always hard work keeping them supplied, but the young couple had found what for them was a satisfactory level in life, and were content. In their small apartment with its hanging baskets of pot plants, Philips stereo, Snoopy money box, fondu pot, and a vase of little pink flowers air-freighted from Denmark, they lived like any contemporary Danish couple.

But in their way of life – running a dog team, living from fish caught in the traditional way with their own hands, hunting sea-birds for the pot, camping on the land in summer – they were Greenlandic Eskimos. "We think life in Greenland is good enough," Abia said, snuggling his back against a rock and sipping soup from a Thermos. "Greenlanders want to do things their own way but we know we're not educated enough. Midnight sun is good weather for young people and they don't want to work, but they don't have responsibilities either, so you can't blame them."

Low necks of land separate lagoons and long arms of muddy sea from the intricate pattern of lakes, and from the air the landscape of Tuktoyaktuk seems two-thirds water. For most of the year this is not significant because land, lakes and sea are sealed in one great sheet of solid ice, while in summer it is only the layer of spiky tussock grass that prevents the ice in the silty soil from melting and being stirred into porridgy silt by the waves. Except for gravel spits, the whole place is afloat on ice. The green hill on which the radio mast stands, and others dotting the horizon like small, round-topped volcanoes, are slow-time eruptions of solid ice, called pingos. One of the largest, in the heart of the hamlet, was hollowed out to make a community curling rink but was used instead as a deep-freeze and the tunnel of ice, roofed with razor-edged flakes of hoar frost, was stacked with caribou carcasses, fish, wildfowl, whale and seal meat.

"You can live really well here, there's no reason to go hungry," says 54-year-old Eskimo Jimmy Jacobson. "I've got a hundred geese in the deep-freeze but my kids don't like native food more than once a week, it's too rich for them, and we have to buy six-dollar steaks down at the store." With five sons and five daughters, Jimmy Jacobson finds it all too easy to spend one hundred dollars a day on food – "It's always available down at the store, that's why we're always broke."

Tuktoyaktuk, on the Beaufort Sea, is the base of operations for Imperial Oil's programme of drilling for oil from artificial islands, and for Canmar's offshore drilling. Day and night helicopters blat overhead, wheeling in and out of the fenced-in enclosures of the company base camps as if rushing new crops of casualties to M*A*S*H. Jimmy Jacobson's house is surrounded by the bits of whalebone and soapstone which he carves to supplement his summer income as a harbour monitor checking for pollution caused by industrial operations. The house is small and spartan. Jimmy and his wife Bella were offered a larger one but preferred to remain by the sea. The lino is bare and worn, a banner depicting the Kennedy brothers hangs on one wall, a print of a black mustang on another. There is a new colour television set.

Until recently Jimmy Jacobson was a successful trapper. Born the son of a passing White Russian who changed his name, and given away to some Eskimos at the age of five months, he has only a Grade I education but lots of horse sense – "Enough to see how the White man's education has buggered up our kids: they're caught in the middle, not good enough for White men but not tough enough to live on the land. We Eskimos aren't lazy – just screwed up."

One daughter works for the hamlet council but the other three of his children who have finished school do casual work for the oil companies during the season, "blow their money" in Inuvik, and are out of work in winter. "If it wasn't for the oil money we'd be poorer.

"We Eskimos aren't lazy, just screwed up. Our kids aren't tough enough to live on the land, but are not good enough for the white man . . ." Jimmy Jacobson and his wife Bella, who have ten children and live in Tuktoyaktuk where Jimmy is a carver in winter and anti-pollution harbour monitor in summer, express the dilemma of their people.

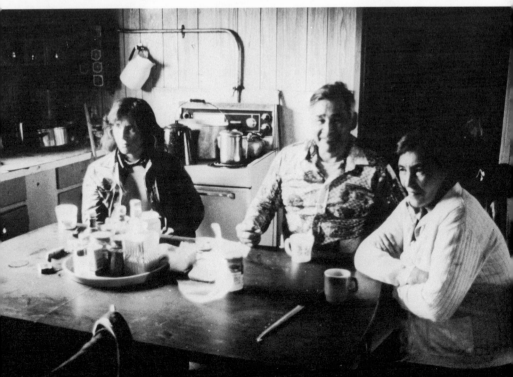

At least we've got Skidoos, guns and kickers. But to find game we have to go a very long way – eighty-five miles for those geese – and to run a trap-line you have to go two or three hundred miles. But the kids get used to the big money and don't know how to live off the shore. The land's too tough for them. Life's easier for everyone now. But happier? – I dunno."

At the head of the table Eugene expertly carved the roast caribou he had shot a few days before and shushed the children into half silence. Nailed on the door behind him, curving to a fine tip like a long claw, was an eight-foot strip of black baleen from the first bowhead whale Eugene had harpooned as captain of his own crew two years before. Outside were pegged the strips of seal meat that would provision his crew during the next spring hunt. Eugene's wife Charlotte, jolly and chatty behind specs as round as flying saucers, took baby Shannon-Marie on her knee and cut the caribou meat into small pieces, obviously a recipe for beauty because she had just won the baby contest at the summer's "Eskimo olympics". The older girls, April and Mary-Jo, smothered their portions with steak sauce from a bottle but Crystal had toothache and clutched a Snoopy pillow while gazing unhappily at the elaborate colour television. Charlotte had cooked the caribou in a micro-wave oven. There was a $10,000 Blazer cross-country vehicle outside, plus snow machine, boat and outboard engine. One of the two shotguns with three rifles in a glass-fronted cabinet against the wall belonged to Charlotte.

"Eugene told me if I shot a goose he'd buy me a shotgun for my birthday," she said with a twinkling glare of challenge across the table at her husband. "I wanted that goose so bad I chased it across the tundra for two and a half miles!"

Thick-set, strong, wearing heavy black-framed spectacles, 29-year-old Eugene Brower is an archetypal new-generation Alaskan Eskimo. He lived in a camp on the land until he was seven, then came to Barrow to be sent to school. He did not stay long in high school and in the expansion of job opportunities that came with the formation of the North Slope Borough landed the job of deputy director of public works. Charlotte, aged twenty-seven, is the Barrow magistrate. They own their house, and between them earn $5,680 a month, of which they net just over half. Their cost of living depends on how successful Eugene is at hunting.

"I hunt because I must, not because I want to," he claims. This winter the quota system had allowed him six caribou, one for each member of the family, but he had a low opinion of game managers – "Look, when I see caribou so close that they run along the airstrip it's pretty hard not to shoot them. When I need a caribou to feed my kids I go and get it – it's my right, and theirs."

Eugene also fishes for whitefish and salmon, shoots ducks and hunts beluga whale, walrus and seal. But his great joy is hunting the bowhead whale. While Charlotte takes the kids "out" for a holiday – last year to San Diego – Eugene and his ten-man whaling crew, three of them his brothers, hack a path over pressure ridges to the floe edge where they establish camp and wait for the lumbering bowheads to come through. Eugene had been in his father's crew from the age of nine, and knows all the arts and crafts of the job, such as the importance of launching the light, skin-covered *umiak* only when the whale is exhaling, when it is unable to hear anything above the roar of air jetting from its blowhole in clouds of spray.

"At the camp I don't have to worry about vitamins or iron," he says. "I just live on *muktuk*, caribou and seal meat – and come home healthy." Outfitting and feeding his crew and providing all equipment costs about six thousand dollars a season, but it's worth it for the excitement when his pink, green and white flag goes up on a nearby pressure ridge to signal a catch and the great beast, typically thirty or forty tons in weight, is winched on the ice by block and tackle to be butchered and shared. "It's whaling that makes us what we are," says Eugene. "Without it, we may as well go and live on welfare in California."

"That's what people in the South don't understand," Charlotte said. "Save the whale means kill the Eskimo."

The tourists paid $199 each for the thrill of flying north of the Arctic Circle and spending a few hours in "the land of the midnight sun". The fact that the aircraft looped only a few miles north of the Arctic Circle before turning back and landing at Frobisher Bay, which strictly speaking experiences only a midnight twilight, did not seem to spoil the fun for sixteen plane-loads of 113 people who made the trip from Montreal and Toronto during the height of the summer. Nor did it seem much of a drawback that the whole place looked dead because it happened to be the middle of the night. The handicraft shops opened up, as did the Co-op in the airport terminal, selling an average three thousand dollars worth of carvings and knick-knacks to each plane-load. Buses drove the passengers round the sights – a patch of drizzle-soaked tundra where they mushed about in street shoes and cardigans looking at the moss and feeling gallantly frozen. Then they climbed aboard again for the three-hour return flight with a special "Arctic" supper of char and champagne.

Most people seemed to enjoy it, if only out of a sense of masochism for having paid so much to see so little. For them it was perhaps an "experience" that might have provided some small insight into real life at the top of the map: their guided tour through the sleepy streets, seeing the ugly government high-rise, the garbage dump where Sir Martin Frobisher is thought to have landed in 1576, and Shitbag Hill, might at least have dispelled the commonly held image of happy little Eskimos crawling in and out of snow houses. As the Post Office was closed, the visitors' postcards were put in a basket for posting later on and it was too much of a temptation not to take an unprincipled glance at what they had written:

"Love from the North Pole"

"Seen lots of polar bears"

"Fantastic ride in dog sled"

"Had seal meat for supper – ugh!"

Not only were there no polar bears in Frobisher, and no dog teams, but there was no snow. Even when allowances are made for tongue-in-cheek sense of humour, it was clear the tourists were living a dream and had refused to believe what they had seen with their own eyes. For them, the visit to the Arctic had been in the image of the scenes of traditional Eskimo life depicted on glossy postcards purchased in the airport terminal.

The Arctic may be called "the last frontier" for any one of many reasons – politically, it faces the USSR across the polar ice; geographically, ships are only now finding a way to smash through the concrete-hard lid of ice that seals it up for most of the year; technologically, it faces staggering drilling and transportation problems; economically, it promises great untapped resources; spiritually, a person willing to challenge the environmental abuses of cold and darkness may still find space to live his own way. For Eskimos it is a last frontier in a cultural sense because the land itself is their single anchor, the one thing enabling them to retain their individuality as Eskimos in the breaking storm of consumerism. In each of these ways except the last, as the Arctic is moulded into the image of small-town White society, the frontier is being "won".

In one respect, however, the fences around the Arctic are nowhere near to being broken down. It has nothing to do with geography, technology or culture. And it does not exist in the North, but in the minds of the people in southern cities who, through votes and pressure groups, control events in the Arctic. I am referring to the frontier of understanding.

It is incredible in this modern age of so-called enlightenment and instant communication that the general picture of real life in the Arctic is so distorted by what White society *wants* to believe. The most sinister threat to the Eskimo people is not black pollution, by oil spreading over the sea from a subsea blowout, but White pollution – the imposition of stereotyped ideas on a very small number of people whose defences are down, by a very large and aggressive number of White people who *think* they are doing the right thing and who reason from a base of nearly total ignorance. While a serious oil blowout is a remote possibility, the White pollution is already happening.

Illusion has always played a role in the process of expansion of the known world; in the long run it was the mental map of a region that was more significant than the geographic one, like the image of the New World being worth little except as a stepping stone to Cathay, which persisted for two centuries. It was also thought that a land without trees was unfit for humans and for about two hundred years the short-grass prairies west of the Missouri were known as the Great American Desert. In the North, Cartier had sailed the cold and foggy Labrador coast in 1535 and, seeing only patches of ice, empty bays and stunted trees, had called it "the land God gave to Cain". More than four hundred years later it was still regarded as a cold-ridden wilderness of no use to man or beast, despite the fact that people and animals lived there successfully. Now, especially in Canada, that image has been supplanted by another image that is equally inappropriate and damaging.

From their experiences with the North American Indians, White people have regarded the Arctic and the Mackenzie Valley as their last chance to do everything right, thus hoping to assuage the guilt of past injustices to native people. At the same time, oil and gas resources in the Canadian Arctic – more a fervent hope than an illusion, perhaps – have been disappointing, with nothing found in super-abundance. Had the oil companies found several new Prudhoe Bays the attitudes of most Canadians might well be different. As it is, the borderline economics of oil and gas development merely serves to enrich their contention that the best thing they can do for the Eskimos and Indians is to put a stop to any kind of industrial development. For the current image of the northern native, Eskimo or Indian, is that of the noble savage – one man against the wilderness, living as he was meant to live far from artificial encumbrances such as commuting, mortgage payments, keeping up with the Joneses and all the pressures of a consumerist, competitive, suburban society.

It is an idealised image, easy to believe if you don't know the facts, easy to sell in newspapers, television, church sermons, and politics. But it is a long way from reality, and it is disturbing to think that it is the prevailing image in the minds of those with money and muscle, and that this image will determine the future of the Arctic, and of its people. History is repeating itself: again we are creating a pattern which defines what we want from a country, then we try to develop the country of our wants.

The fact that the vision of beauty in the North is in the eyes of the South was evident throughout the Berger Inquiry, when the blinkered publicity machine "sold" the native as a person whose lifestyle was admirable and enviable. The colour pictures in Berger's own report, and those shown on television, suggested the kind of lifestyle every Canadian most desired when camping on vacation: a simple life in a cabin with smoke curling from the chimney, striding out with a gun under the arm to knock off a caribou for supper, canoe pulled up on the shingle with a stack of fish ready to dry, float plane alighting on a sun-drenched lake, nets coming up full of fish, blue skies and fantastic sunsets. It all added up to a nice kind of health farm where you could send your conscience for a work-over and have it returned morally toned up.

Little or nothing was said about the extensive changes that have already occurred, and the social decay that has happened without any kind of industrial activity within a thousand miles. Whites in the South were not concerned about the yawning abyss that awaited native children graduating from school in the same way that they were concerned, say, about musk rats. They were unaware that happy little Nanook of the North was already living in the image of Kojak, sucking lollies, reading comics, wearing a hockey shirt and plastic boots. Nor did they question the ability of the land to sustain a larger and better-equipped population, or wonder what cruel forces of hardship, worry or hopelessness might have etched such deep lines in the picturesque faces of elderly natives posing innocently in the pure Arctic sunshine.

It was assumed that all problems of the native people were due to industry and all new development would be bad. Berger was swayed by the fact that numerous native people suffer "personal frustration, despair, and a sense of worthlessness in the face of the growing White community" and that this would grow "disastrously" in the event of a pipeline being built along the Mackenzie Valley. But a sense of worthlessness can be replaced by only one thing – a sense of capability. To make a man free in the modern world he must first be made capable. While the pipeline itself may not have produced the opportunities for which the new generation craves, it could have been used as a lever to achieve other imaginative and positive economic and political ends.

The whole pipeline debate was seen as the last chance for the native, when it should have been heralded as the first chance. Berger made only passing reference in his report to the lack of an intermediate economic base and the dearth of research on means of improving productivity in the North. "We do not have adequate inventories of the various species available, not even for the Mackenzie River. Nor for that matter do we know much about the intensity of renewable resource use. We do not know enough about food chains and ecological relationships to be able to predict what effect an increased harvest of one species might have on other species. We have not considered whether or not new systems of marketing and price support might strengthen the native economy ..."

Crucial to the future of the Arctic, such points should have been the starting point of any judgement on the value of industrial development, not an afterthought. Berger cited the example of the Lummi Indians in the State of Washington, who rejected proposals for the building of a magnesium-oxide plant in their bay, which would have provided wage-earning opportunities, and turned themselves into highly skilled farmers of oysters, clams, sea trout, salmon and seafood products. The success of the aquaculture project meant they could maintain their close ties with the sea in the twentieth century.

One reason a project of this kind is difficult to get started in the North, as the musk ox farm in Alaska has proved, is the lack of a basic transport infrastructure for freighting raw materials and products at reasonable cost. The Lummis were faced with a choice: a factory or their own project. In the North, a project like a pipeline occupies little space while providing the links by which natives would have the option to plug in small-scale commercial projects tailored to suit their own needs.

If Berger had judged with his head instead of his heart, and if input to his Inquiry from natives and their White advisers had been positive instead of destructively negative, he could have used one to win the other while laying down priorities and limitations that might well have had the effect of gaining a ten-year moratorium but might have kindled and stimulated sparks of optimism and imaginative economic planning. Instead, the people have been put in the freezer for ten years. Berger wanted to strengthen native society, *then* develop the pipeline, which is right in principle. But his decision to wait and talk, rather than plan and do, removed the natives' single strong card and sentenced them to a continuing dream-time. Most Whites in Canada believe the Eskimos and Mackenzie Indians have been granted a favour, and it is likely that when oil and gas are discovered in the western Arctic in useful quantities, and when the energy crisis comes, as it must, the pipeline will be put in quickly, over-riding every other consideration. The natives will have lost both ways.

At the age of three months Ellen Binder came from Lapland to Alaska with her parents who had been hired to drive a reindeer herd to the Mackenzie Delta. Until she was twenty-three she lived a nomadic camp life, hunting and following the reindeer. Officially she is an Eskimo, and has been married to one for thirty years. Mother of eight children and a village councillor in Inuvik, Ellen is a warm character whose strong heart was nearly broken by Berger's decision. "To live on the land in the old way you had to make a lot of sacrifices that I wouldn't wish on my children," she told me. "There is no exhilaration in hunting when you are hungry. If life was so glorious for the Eskimos out there in the camps, genocide would not have begun at home.

"Nostalgia for the land is mainly among those who have never experienced it. Sometimes, when the bills come in, I wonder if I would rather wake up in a tent at minus forty degrees and find all the pots frozen up, but it's only a fancy. Two of my children, the twins, were born premature – if we lived in the bush they wouldn't be alive.

"Now what am I supposed to tell them about their futures? That they have to leave home and go South in order to live? Every time they want to come home for a visit the air fare will cost them as much as flying the Atlantic!

"And think of it this way – we've been sentenced to a trapper's life by the same people down South who are trying to put an end to trapping (the Humane Society) and the fur hunting (Greenpeace). So what chance have we got? I tell you, the winters can be *very* long up here when you don't have money and are forced to live on social assistance. There's nothing else in sight for my children – nothing."

While the Greenland Eskimos have a basic resource base in their fishing, and the Alaskan Eskimos have cash, those in Canada have one unique resource – space. Few people in the South have anything like a true perspective of Arctic distances. In trying to answer how the Space-Age Eskimo can prosper from the technological frontier it is essential to realise it is not just a question of technology versus ecology: there is lots of room where the old way of life may continue out of sight and hearing of the new. Ecologically, there is even a case to be made *for* development. The land surface can be modified so that it will improve, growing lusher grass. It seems ironic that the hungry land must be denied nourishment in the name of "environmental protection".

Only in the exploration phase of oil and gas operations is the landscape consumed. This is temporary, unless something is found. When discoveries are made the actual areas of terrain involved are small. The Arctic is so large it ought to be easy to isolate industrial areas: Prudhoe Bay is only twenty miles by ten, and even within this area the intensity of development is relatively light. The main visible activity is road building and drilling: oil extraction itself is silent and automated. Alex Hemstock of Imperial Oil estimated that in Canada north of 60°N development of oil and gas reserves will require a total of 1,350 square miles (a square measuring a little over thirty-six miles each way). Allowing for aircraft noise and long-distance visibility, as well as some wishful thinking, and adding in a couple of pipeline corridors then multiplying this area *tenfold* makes an area a little larger than Holland but smaller than Switzerland, in an Arctic region at least three times bigger than Western Europe. It would add up to less than one per cent of the NWT and Yukon, and could be dropped in Great Bear Lake with only a little overlap.

There is nothing beautiful about the oil business except its profits. I should hate to have it in my own back yard, and I wouldn't wish it on an Eskimo. But that is not to say it couldn't be fifty miles away, giving people the chance to work for good money if they so desire, to hunt in a controlled way over rigorously protected game reserves extending in the opposite direction, and to latch into some of its spin-off services provided by the company as a condition of its operating permit. These could be anything that benefitted the local community, such as subsidised freight that could make a small-scale Arctic business competitive with those down South, transport of raw materials such as fodder for musk ox ranches, waste heat that could be used in greenhouses to supply a settlement with fresh produce or to run a fish-farming operation in a lake. This is the kind of opportunity which Berger – and Ellen Binder's children, Jimmy Jacobson's children, and thousands of others like them – have missed.

Canada believes it is at the bar of world opinion that her treatment of Eskimos will be judged. Policies and administrative actions must not only be good, but must appear to be good, with nothing about them that smacks of coercion, either physical or psychological. In the first place, Canada should have the courage to do what is right, not what possibly ill-informed international onlookers think might be right, and secondly, Canada is already applying coercion of the most subtle kind by providing Eskimos with so little to do for themselves that they don't even have to organise their own spokesmen. But it is a difficult case to prove at the bar of world opinion – that Eskimos in Canada are being gentled to death, murdered by benevolence.

Whites also have the idea that they are required to feel guilty for modernising the Eskimo so quickly. At the time, lives couldn't be saved quickly enough and the fact that the Eskimo personality is suffering some jet lag seems a small price to pay. Imagine what it must have meant, when every aspect of your well-being depended on hunting and skinning animals and fish, to be given a sharp steel knife to do the job instead of a piece of stone! The homes, hospitals and other material comforts brought by Whites were the logical extension of the same process. Canadians and Danes have little to be ashamed of in their motives for helping the Eskimos: it is what happens now that is critical.

In Alaska the Eskimos were victims of a typical American solution to any problem, which was to pour money on it until the problem disappeared. Compared with their cousins in Canada and Greenland, the Alaskan Eskimos are the new Arabs of the Arctic, with all the political muscle, cultural dilution, and character stress that the label implies.

The image of Alaska where space is lord, a part of America's geography of hope where there is still room to move around, is also taking a beating. Until the past few years Alaska was always the unfilled space in the map where an American could set out with a pack on his back and find the "frontier experience" that was part of his heritage. The land settlement, State land grab, and the oil boom have changed all that. There are lines on the map. Many people thought even the defining of blanks on the map as wilderness was offensive, and for them Alaska is already lost. But America could not stretch for ever: the end of the frontier era had to come. No longer can a man carve a niche out of the wilderness for himself, because now there are too many lines on the map and too many people with a stake in what they mean. From now on the free-ranging frontier spirit of America will have to turn in on itself, finding different kinds of satisfactions.

This does not mean that wilderness no longer exists or that natural beauty has been spoiled: it means only that Americans will have to change their mode of appreciation. Europeans have for long had to live within the limits of their geography (since the American War of Independence, in fact) and have learned to enjoy natural beauty preserved in parks or contrived, like the English countryside which is almost entirely man-made.

It is in this context that the fight to retain Alaska as a spiritual resource should be judged. The Alaska Native Claims Settlement Act of 1971 gave the natives forty million acres of land, and as an epic consolation to environmentalists authorised the Secretary of the Interior to select up to eighty-three million acres of "national

Can Alaska be both oil barrel and national park to the nation? This sea arm near Valdez, southern terminal of the Alyeska pipeline, is alive with sea otters and is totally unspoilt, accessible only by those who have their own boats. For some, merely defining wild country as wilderness is desecration enough

interest" lands for protection and preservation as national parks, forests, wildlife refuges, and wild and scenic rivers. At the time there were already forty-eight million acres of national parks and wildlife refuges, so the total would be more than one-third of the whole State and twice as large as Colorado.

This was not enough for environmentalists. Arizona Democrat Morris Udall and eighty co-sponsoring conservation organisations introduced a Bill demanding an additional forty-three million acres. The Alaska Republicans countered with a Bill that to the existing parks would add only twenty-five million acres (of which ten million would be national forest that could be developed) plus fifty-eight million acres to be put in a holding pattern and managed jointly by State and Federal governments. Udall presented the issue as one of wilderness v. industry but it ran deeper than that, for Alaskans saw it as a last-ditch attempt by Washington to keep control of large areas as the State emerges into self-sufficiency. Despite long queues at gas stations when the Senate vote was finally taken in May 1979, the conservationists managed to push through protection for 126 million acres, the most sweeping legislation of its type in US history. A 22·5 million petroleum reserve was set aside on the North Slope. Oil companies would still be able to look for oil in 95 per cent of the State. And the 400,000 Alaskans would have an area twice as big as California in which to do their own thing.

Alaska is still a roistering, jump-on-a-plane-and-go kind of place that is basically out of tune with the rest of the nation which realises land must be protected. The frontier mystique, which anywhere else in the US can only be lived at weekends, is part of the way of life. But the exquisite irony is that in this tremendous wilderness in an undeveloped area one-fifth as large as the rest of the USA, people consider themselves fortunate to have a lot fifty by one hundred feet to call their own. In the great battle for Alaska individuals have found the land beyond reach. Discounting the new native lands, less than half of one per cent of the State is privately owned, and so much of the rest is parcelled up as parks, forests or petroleum reserves that people who have built small cabins in the bush are finding themselves being rooted out and sent back to town.

But the Alaska lifestyle is in any case as much an image as a distinct set of attitudes. Two in five residents of Fairbanks cut and gather their own firewood. The same proportion helped to build their own homes, one in every two people fishes, hunts, or gathers his own food. But the free-ranging Alaska lifestyle is not cheap. It is not easy to be self-reliant in Alaska, you need a chain saw to cut the wood and a snow machine or pick-up to go out and get it. The oil development will permit more people to buy the Alaska lifestyle and this will crowd the poorer, truly self-reliant who already have it. Like Jim Kowalsky, director of Friends of the Earth in Fairbanks, who lives in a geodesic dome made of tar felt and wood tiles, double-glazed with polythene, ten minutes' hike from the end of the road. Water is carried in on his back in a five-gallon jerrican filled in the university's mens' room, and he carries a car battery out for recharging every two months so he can listen to music. It is easy to sneer at people leading the frontier life and wanting to halt the oil development while themselves still as utterly dependent on oil as any urban dweller. But he and his young wife had just done a fifty-mile hike through the mountains with their eleven-weeks-old son. "Rural people must have landscape: without it they're dead," he said. "It is hard for them to understand because, to them, the landscape has always been there and it is inconceivable that it could be denied to them."

While the furious land grab of Alaska continues, the biggest threat to the State is not pipelines but roads like the Alyeska haul road which slipped through without being examined properly by Congress. "The environmentalists went to sleep on it," says Jim Kowalsky. "It was just assumed from the beginning that a public road was necessary – in the American mind building roads is synonymous with progress and already the State is drawing lines all over the map showing how the rest of Alaska will be opened up." If the North Slope Eskimos' traditional whaling is finally stopped the Alyeska haul road will be welcomed because natives will have to look South for all cultural input. Meanwhile natives are powerful enough to say they don't want to be connected to White society by roads. This may be a short-sighted policy, however, because by failing to agree to the planning of transportation corridors they may be isolating their own development lands. The effect of a network of roads through the heartland of Alaska and into the Arctic could be devastating. The Alaska Highway itself, 1,532 miles long, attracts a third of Alaska's visitors for its own sake because just to drive it is an adventure: a road to the Arctic will be even more of a challenge, the mobile adventurers will set out for the Arctic by the thousand.

Eskimos are people who *want* to live in a frozen and environmentally hostile and difficult part of the world that nobody else wants except for purposes of plunder. They are probably the most self-reliant and stoic people in the world, yet there is no native people for whom so much has been done in such short time. Now that survival is no longer a question for them, they are only just beginning to live. All they want is a chance to combine the best of the old with the best of the new so they can enter the swim of the modern world on their own terms, as Eskimos. It doesn't seem much to expect on behalf of a people so small in number that in the national population the percentage is hardly visible – Eskimos comprise 0·8 per cent of Denmark, 0·07 per cent of Canada and only 0·0036 per cent of USA. One wonders what chance they've got in the world when publicity machines like the Canadian Broadcasting Corporation, covering an event like the publication of the Berger Report, hails it as "the only war the Indians have won" and every picture on television – even those of blue skies, clear visibility, and people with not a hair out of place in the calm air – is soundtracked with the low moan of an imagined Arctic wind.

The last frontier begins here.

Index

Eskimos – *cont.*
attitude changes, 227–8
attitudes to money and saving, 230
attitudes to Whites, 73–4
"Back to the land" encouraged by government, 218
boredom of teenagers, 202–3
common language, 185
preservation, 200
continuity of culture, 186
coping with cold, 29–30
cultural changes in Greenland, 208–9
cultural importance of Arctic, 274
decline in living conditions, 190
destruction of family life, 213
different objectives from Whites, 229
economic importance of caribou, 149
education provision, 191, 193, 195–6
effect of whalers' crews on lifestyle, 188
employment problems, 196, 234
ethnic origins, 184
expectation of payment for everything, 228–9
homesickness, 201
idealised in White images, 275
imposition by Whites, 275
in Greenland, 207
lack of encouragement, 238
land claims against pipelaying, 116–19
land ownership, 246
land use study, 248–9
see also Berger Inquiry
life expectancy in 1956, 191
longterm technological advancement, 280
medical problems, 211
migrations from Asia, 184
from Siberia, 6–7
physiological differences from Whites, 30, 209
political organisation, 248
learning to exert pressure, 257
political passivity, 241
population, 185
growth, 211
rapid development in lifestyle, 16, 62, 193, 195
receive pensions and allowances, 190
representation on Territorial Council, 243
reserved characters, 59–60
sociological research, 64–5
Southern clothing adopted, 59
standards of living from fur trading, 189
territory claim, 249
threat of over-hunting by, 153–4
traditional clothing, 26
traditional culture, 185–6
traditional decision-making pattern, 243

traditional familiarity with ice and snow types, 161
traditional seasonal way of life, 37
use of White consultants, 260–1
written communications, 200
Eureka Sound, 4
Explorers, 19
see also Franklin expedition

Fairbanks, effect of pipeline construction, 115–16
Feet, protection from cold, 26–7
Fire hazards, 52
in oil camps, 79
Fish farming, 235
Fishing, 221–3
by nets under the ice, 269
during winter, 225
fluctuations in catches, 223
Fog, 36
Food
growing glasshouse crops, 235
requirements, 28
see also Diet
Fox trapping, 154
Franklin expedition, graves at Beechey Island, 137
Frobisher, development, 53–4
Frostbite, 31
Fur trapping, 188–9
economics, 217

Gas
blowouts, 99, 100
carriage in icebreaking tankers, 170–1
exports to pay for pipeline, 171
pockets affecting oil drilling, 99
Polar Gas pipeline project, 120
resistance to pipeline, 113
routes of pipelines, 113–14
shortages, 87
Gas fields, 85
Glaciated mountains, 12
Glass in buildings, 50, 52
Government staff, 66–7
Greenland, 12, 14–15, 205–7
apartment buildings, 231
coldest part of Arctic, 33
crowded communities, 43
early colonisation by Whites, 207
economic prospects, 246
Eskimo writings, 200
Eskimos' cultural change, 208–9
fishing, 221–3
lifestyle, 270
political maturity, 244
problems for telephone and radio, 53

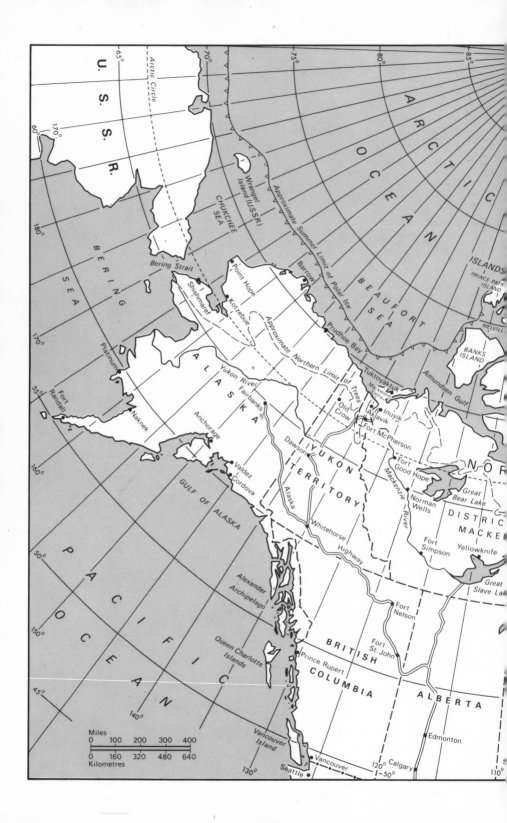